ALSO BY BRANDON SNEED

Head in the Game:
The Mental Engineering of the World's Greatest Athletes

SOONER

SOONER

THE MAKING OF A FOOTBALL COACH—
Lincoln Riley's Rise from West Texas
to the University of Oklahoma

BRANDON SNEED

HENRY HOLT AND COMPANY

NEW YORK

Henry Holt and Company
Publishers since 1866
120 Broadway
New York, New York 10271
www.henryholt.com

Library of Congress Cataloging-in-Publication Data

Names: Sneed, Brandon, author.
Title: Sooner : the making of a football coach—Lincoln Riley's rise from
West Texas to the University of Oklahoma / Brandon Sneed.
Description: First edition. | New York, New York : Henry Holt and Company,
[2020] | Includes index.
Identifiers: LCCN 2020010382 (print) | LCCN 2020010383 (ebook) |
ISBN 9781250622167 (hardcover) | ISBN 9781250622150 (ebook)
Subjects: LCSH: Riley, Lincoln, 1983– | Football
Coaches—Oklahoma—Biography. | Football players—Texas—Biography.
Classification: LCC GV939.R55 S64 2020 (print) | LCC GV939.R55 (ebook) |
DDC 796.332092 [B]—dc23
LC record available at https://lccn.loc.gov/2020010382
LC ebook record available at https://lccn.loc.gov/2020010383

Our books may be purchased in bulk for promotional, educational, or business use.
Please contact your local bookseller or the Macmillan Corporate and
Premium Sales Department at (800) 221-7945, extension 5442, or by e-mail
at MacmillanSpecialMarkets@macmillan.com.

First Edition 2020

Designed by Steven Seighman

Printed in the United States of America

1   3   5   7   9   10   8   6   4   2

To Rick Stewart,
my advisor, mentor, and friend

And to all leaders who show
young people what they can do

Contents

SOONER

Prologue

CONCEPTS

HE EXITS MEMORIAL STADIUM through Gate 12, the brick walls of the arena towering behind him, and makes his way toward the Everest Training Center across the street. Hip-hop music throbs from speakers, its bass so strong you feel it in your chest. *I Milly Rock on any block / I Milly Rock on any block*. Along the white walls, stretches of crimson contain white lettering that remind all who enter of national titles won and other honors achieved. The walls and white ceiling and striking green turf envelop him as he joins a crowd of players and coaches and staff, among whom he looks at home. There's a faint but distinct smell of sweat, of young men at work.

Lincoln Riley moves lightly on his feet, bouncing to the music, as the Oklahoma offense gets loose for some light drills. There's a pair of slide sandals inexplicably strewn on the turf in the middle of everything. Lincoln searches for their owner: Baker Mayfield, the team's star Heisman finalist from the season before. The kid's making some quick warm-up throws wearing shorts and a T-shirt, and nothing on his feet but socks.

"Hey," Lincoln says, his Texas accent thick. "Nice shoes. Try not to get stepped on."

Then Lincoln moves along, leaving the star quarterback, the Heisman contender, the future of this team's season, to continue playing football in socks.

Lincoln moves like an athlete in his crimson Dri-FIT team shirt, black shorts, and gray running shoes, and he works up a light sweat as he makes his way around the field. From quarterbacks to running backs to receivers, he fist-bumps here, shoulder-checks there, bobs his head and shoulders, bobs in rhythm with the beat—more or less—all with a grin on his face. It's a Monday night in August 2017, and the season starts soon.

He's thirty-three years old, and he's the head coach of the Oklahoma Sooners, one of the best college football programs in the country. Growing up, he never thought he would end up here. He grew up six hours west, in a tiny town called Muleshoe in West Texas, close to New Mexico, about as far west as West Texas goes. He was as close to the aliens in Roswell as he was to any football powers.

Practice begins.

Baker tosses footballs to running backs working on routes. He's accurate and their hands are good. He doesn't get stepped on. Lincoln lets it slide for now. He'll have plenty more serious problems with Baker soon enough.

Lincoln organizes receivers for release drills, lining them up against each other to practice the violent art of breaking free. They snatch their defender by the forearm, the elbow, the whatever, fling them out of the way, and sprint past.

Lincoln lines up across from the biggest receiver there. ("I've never been one to just stand on the sidelines," he says. "I like being in the mix.")

"All right, ready now," he says. He takes the defensive position.

The receiver stands some six and a half feet tall and his biceps are thick. This is a big young man, more built than most receivers so tall.

"Ready," Lincoln says. He lowers his head and looks up at the receiver, his chin jutting out as he speaks, and a charge of competition fills the air. "And. Go."

The receiver launches forward, snatches Lincoln's right wrist and yanks, pulling Lincoln aside. The receiver flies free. Lincoln, going with the momentum from the pull, turns in a half-circle. He claps and roars at the kid for a job well done. Then he lines up again, against another receiver, and tells the others to do the same. And they all go again. Soon a dozen football players are whooping and hollering, their noise echoing around the building, feeding off their coach and the energy he gives them, their grunts and roars blending with the music.

Lincoln shakes his arm and rolls his shoulder. "Dang," he says. "You really start to get that tinglin' feeling after a while." He's downplaying it, but when the receivers yank his arm and pull free, for an instant before turning to clap and cheer, Lincoln winces. His shoulder hurts.

A couple hours later, Lincoln settles into a soft and beautiful brown leather couch in his office across the street, where he tells the story of what happened to that shoulder, and what it means to hurt yourself and then heal.

Before he was a coach, he was a player with big dreams that he failed to achieve, and despite fantastic success as a coach, he still feels pain from that failure. He feels it, physically, in his body, to this day. That may sound like a curse, but it has also been a gift as he has allowed it to teach him, to make him the coach the young men in his charge need. His story is as much about becoming a man as it is about becoming a coach.

Many who know Lincoln say he was born with a gift, with a different sort of brain, with a unique ability bordering on genius. But then, watching a hometown star achieve great things has a way of distorting the past: some in town who knew him well claim that he was also his high school class valedictorian or salutatorian, which he wasn't. Lincoln, for his part, pushes aside any such talk. He says he's just lucky. He's lucky he got to work with good coaches, he's lucky he got to coach good players, he's lucky in a lot of other ways. He doesn't care for when people try talking him up as a genius. He appreciates the sentiment—he knows they mean well—but he can't help but disagree. "I came up in good environments to learn," he says.

When Lincoln downplays his accomplishments like this, it can come off as almost disingenuous, because when you trace the course of his life, this obvious pattern emerges: where he goes, teams don't just get better, they are transformed. And yet, when he talks about not being a genius, about being lucky, you believe that he believes it, too. He really seems to think that he's only gotten here because of other people. And, of course, it's true. None of us are who we are on our own.

Lincoln, however, seems hyperaware of how other people have affected him—or at least he would much rather talk about other people than himself. He worries about people thinking that he thinks he's "got everything all figured out." He made the mistake of acting that way when he was younger. He also made the mistake of believing that he *did* have to have everything all figured out, and he saw how that hurt him. Now, part of the joy he gets from what he does is feeling that there's always something else to learn.

Right now, he's trying to figure out how to balance the new demands on his time while also maintaining healthy relationships with his players. He'll text players, call them, stop them in the halls or on sidewalks around campus and just . . . catch up. And it's the nature of the relationship, the things they talk about and how they talk about them. "There's a lot to it," he says. "You feel like you're half football coach, half academic counselor, half Dr. Phil. Yeah, there's a lot of that. But it helps them. It's necessary to play at a high level to get them all mentally into place. And balancing all that to find what they do well. It's almost like having a new puzzle each year and you just gotta make all the pieces fit."

He sometimes finds himself concerned about not getting to know them well enough. "You spend so much time with them, depend on each other so much—how can you not care about them?" he says. "I don't feel it in terms of success or winning or not—I don't have to convince myself to feel that. I just can't imagine doing my job if not. I really can't."

Lincoln starts to say something else, but he thinks about it first, as though knowing it might sound too over-the-top. But then he says it anyway: "I just care about these guys almost as much as my own daughters. I just don't know how else to say it . . . My motivation to get to know them goes way beyond just, *Oh, if I get to know them better they'll play better or I can reach them more.* I understand that's one of the benefits of it, but I would do it even if it wasn't a benefit. I enjoy doing it. It's one of the best parts of this game."

When the season begins in a few weeks, Lincoln will have just turned thirty-four. He's the youngest major college football head coach in the country.

His new office is enormous. Eighteen hundred square feet. And it is extraordinary. You know new car smell? This has new office smell. It's not all that different, just with more leather. Leather couches and chairs form a meeting area in the center. A desk sits to the right when you walk in, another couch is to the left, and huge windows are straight ahead, letting sunlight pour in. Two flat-screen TVs adorn walls, massive, one on each end. The room is like a miniature cathedral, just with more dark wood and crimson. His wife, Caitlin, takes their young daughters, Sloan and Stella, with her when she brings Lincoln his lunch most days. Sloan runs to the windows every time and says, "How high up we are!"

This office wasn't made for him. It was made for Bob Stoops, Oklahoma's coach for the previous eighteen years. A case in the corner displays a slew of Stoops's rings and watches, prizes from championships and bowl games won. Stoops retired suddenly in June and said Lincoln should replace him. He had put the case of watches and rings in here as a diversion months ago. He knew he was going to retire, but he wanted to keep the impression that everything was normal until the time came to let Lincoln take over.

It can be overwhelming. "You gotta get away from it sometimes," says Ruffin McNeill, his assistant head coach and longtime friend. "Go somewhere and have a great time and forget you're a coach for a little while. It's going to be waiting on you when you get back."

Sometimes, Lincoln takes his wife and daughters to a lake three hours south, near Dallas. Other times, to Vermejo Park in New Mexico, where they hike and explore and fish. He's long turned to the water for solace, for escape, starting with when he was a boy. He loves this life, he loves this job, he loves what he does, but sometimes he just has to get away.

This life can strain a man in unnatural ways. Sometimes it can threaten to stretch him into a person beyond who he wants to be, the demands of such a prominent and powerful position fraying the more pure and innocent parts of himself that made him into the kind of man who could get here. That's another thing a coach must always be figuring out: how to maintain what he's doing without losing who he is in the process. There's a part of him, a part he might be a little blind to sometimes, that can want too much, feel too hungry.

A gold chain around Lincoln's neck glints in the low office light. "It's my wedding ring," he says. "I hate wearing rings. I hate wearing things on my hands."

This aversion to rings is not unusual where he comes from. "We're from West Texas," Caitlin says. "And a lot of farm workers—like my dad and his dad, neither one like wearing one. For safety." A breaking of tradition, in the name of not getting hurt.

Lincoln chuckles, remembering where he was in life when he got the necklace. "I don't know if it's pure gold or not," he says. "We probably couldn't afford pure gold at the time we got married."

It has certainly been a journey from there to here.

He's here because, as Ruffin says, "Not only is he smart, he's also wise." An affable African American man nearing sixty, Ruffin comes off a bit like a jolly much-older brother. He explains, "Coaching is a lot about grasping concepts, and Lincoln sees the concepts very well."

By "concepts" Ruffin means offensive and defensive formations, the way players are aligned on either side of the ball. Certain concepts make certain things more and less possible. Some favor runs, or prevent runs, while others open up the passing game or enhance your defense against it. Football is the art of using your concepts to explore and then exploit the weaknesses of your opponents.

"The best coaches," Ruffin goes on, "make the quickest adjustments. If something's hurting here, they have answers. He does that well. He's good at having the answer."

If something's hurting, having the answer.

In his office, on his couch, Lincoln tells a story about something hurting and the answer he found to it. The answer wasn't what he wanted it to be.

The answer also made all of this possible. It taught him new levels of what makes not only a successful coach, but a successful man. It taught him commitment and grit and how to beat long odds. It brought him relationships and growth and heartache, and with the heartache, wisdom. It moved through humble pockets of gridiron Americana along the way, carving through small Texas towns and football meccas and ghettos alike. It showed him his gifts and how to make the most of them. And it introduced him to people without whom he could have never made it here.

For better and worse, none of us are who we are on our own.

He learned how to grow from a boy into a man, and then into a better man. He learned how to be shaped and reshaped by the people and places he encountered throughout his life. He learned the pain that sometimes comes with the shaping, the hammering of chisel into stone. He learned to live with pain when it hurt the most, and how to play with the pain, and even harder, how to heal. He learned to find what was hurting him and to find answers for it. He learned the difference between growing pains and killing pain. He learned about growth. And joy. And love.

He learned a lesson an old high school coach used to talk about a lot: *Don't do things that are gonna hurt you.*

Which brings us to the shoulder.

He rolls it some as he talks.

In a way, everything comes back to that shoulder and how he hurt it.

"So stupid," he says, shaking his head.

The shoulder's been hurting for nearly twenty years. It hurts more today because the receivers' drill pulled on the old injury, but he can always feel it. When he talks about what it took for him to get here, that means talking about that shoulder and how he hurt it and the astonishing effect hurting that shoulder had on his entire life. He's learned to look at it as a gift of its own. It helped him become the coach he is now. It gave him deeper empathy for the struggles his players face. He's been where they are now. He's been one of them, only to lose the ability to carry on as such. In some ways, he still feels like one of them. We can grow from the things that hurt us, but we never forget who we were when we first got hurt. So he's always reaching out, always wondering how he can better help them.

He rolls his shoulder again. Tender is the gift that came from pain. Doesn't always feel like a gift, really. But that's another kind of concept that goes beyond the field. Pain and the answer to the pain, and the meaning of healing, and how to deal when he healed in a way that prevented him from living the life he was planning to live before he hurt himself, in a way that took something from him that he wasn't ready to give up. Such a thing can destroy a person, or it can steer him toward a life he never thought possible. There's no way to know how things will turn out, of course. The only thing that's certain is that after a man breaks, as he learns how to heal and puts himself back together, he will become someone different. He'll have new strength filling in where the cracks were. New wisdom. And new hunger.

1

Muleshoe

Once upon a time, Lincoln Riley was a quarterback, and he was good.

He grew up in Muleshoe, a tiny West Texas town in Bailey County about three hours north of Odessa. Population: five thousand. You can find it about an hour north of Lubbock in the middle of nowhere, tucked in a region of West Texas known as the South Plains. The town started after a Civil War veteran and aspiring rancher named Henry Black laid claim to some forty thousand acres out here in 1877. While settling the land he came upon a muleshoe on the ground, and thus Muleshoe Ranch was named.

The land was beautiful. Will Rogers passed through here in his youth, before he became a famous actor, writer, and cowboy. He was a simple ranch hand, eighteen years old, driving cattle through West Texas. The beauty of Muleshoe's land moved him deeply enough to write about it thirty years later. "That plains was the prettiest country I ever saw in my life," he wrote. "As flat as a beauty contest winner's stomach, and prairie lakes scattered all over it. And mirages! You could see anything in the world—just ahead of you."

A couple decades after Henry Black built his ranch, the town formed around a railroad station built nearby. By the 1970s, it was booming. Some two hundred small businesses called Muleshoe home. There were also two hospitals, two banks, a library, a newspaper, and a radio station. Main Street was full of life.

In the 1980s, however, everything that had made Texas prosper fell apart. Oil rigs once worth $13 million were going for $150,000. And Muleshoe was not immune. By the turn of the twenty-first century, Main Street's buildings were mostly abandoned and had been for years. The area was quiet. Dull. To an outsider, the town simply wasn't much to speak of. There were a couple of parks and "Lake Muleshoe," a small pond dug out beside a park behind the local nursing home. That was about it. There wasn't even a Walmart.

But the spirit of the place remained.

Muleshoe Ranch itself still stands. A fifth generation of the area's descendants run the place. There's a statue in the center of town of a mule named Old Pete, a testament to the townsfolk's work ethic. The economy is evolving, too. Oil rigs are still out there, but so are windmills, rising from the plains and whirling like gleaming white pinwheels, their wings larger than tractor trailers and sounding like jet engines.

The people who call Muleshoe home are warm and friendly and eager to make you feel good about yourself. "It's great people," Lincoln says. "Very strong sense of community. And I don't think I'm much different from a lot of people from that part of the country . . . Taught the values of treating people the right way, and think of others as far more important than yourself. And so I was raised that way, both by my parents, and by my whole community."

When Lincoln was growing up, the boys on the Muleshoe High football team talked a lot about how much butt they were kicking on the football field, even though they were actually terrible at football. Seems the boys put more effort into their partying than anything else: Bailey County was a dry county, so some kids bootlegged booze from Clovis, New Mexico, a bigger town about thirty miles west. (Others just took it from their parents.) Their parties got famously out of control. There were fights. There were girls dancing on tables in various states of undress, and there were drunken adolescent boys cheering them on. And that's just what people heard about.

But that was the culture here. The people who made America into the United States were different, unlike anyone else walking the planet, full of piss and vinegar and fire in their guts that burst forth from their minds like a million miniature big bangs. And then there were the men who made Texas. They came here and took the land and claimed it as their own, and the animals that roamed the land, the cattle and the buffalo and the horses. They killed the people who already lived here. They were savage. They had unique spirit to them, spirit that seemed born of fire, and that spirit still lingers around West Texas to this day. There's less savagery—we've at least evolved beyond that—but wild cowboys' ghosts still seem to stir people up in small towns called Nazareth, Sudan, Eden, Earth. And Muleshoe.

More immediately, it could also be the open prairies that surround the town as far as the eye can see. They might as well be an ocean. Could be how the highways to bigger cities many miles away are surrounded by an awesome nothingness. Could be the way the sky feels bigger here, somehow, and the cinematic way it burns beautifully every night and then gives way to a display of stars that will engulf you if you look long enough. Some here call the sky their "true spirituality."

Life in Muleshoe can feel like life on an island. Liberating, unless you feel marooned. A place the mind can rest, but only for so long, and then it begins to race, feeling starved. When there is little to be found to satiate that hunger, the natural next step is to find an escape. There were two primary means of escape for the children of Muleshoe: partying, and delusion. It's hard not to feel for them. For adults settled there who call it home, Muleshoe can feel okay, but it's hard to imagine being a teenager bursting with all the energy of adolescence and surrounded by a great desert sea.

Making matters both worse and better, the Muleshoe football team was bad, but beloved. Sports were the center of Muleshoe's social universe. Muleshoe High hosted pregame meals where people could pay to eat with the team. And Muleshoe was one of those towns that largely shut down for every game. Everyone was in the stands at humble Benny Douglas Stadium, a grand name for a simple small-town high school football field tucked in a small valley behind the school, in the middle of town. Bleachers sat on each side of the field at the 50-yard line, a simple scoreboard beyond the east end zone. Imagine a lower-stakes version of Odessa from *Friday Night Lights*, only with no expectation of success. Muleshoe coaches lasted two years on average. Talented players kept leaving town for better football schools on other rural islands out in the desert. Nobody knew what to do and nobody expected anything to get better. Small wonder the kids made partying their favorite sport. It was the only thing they could truly master. Nobody believed things could get better because nobody could see how.

Then, in 1996, everything began to change.

Lincoln was in seventh grade that year, just turned thirteen. He had that West Texas fire in his spirit, and a dangerous competitive streak that would get him in trouble more than once as he grew older. But he wasn't a party animal. "I'm an old soul," he says. "And that kind of thing just never really tugged at me."

He was the son of Mike and Marilyn Riley, Muleshoe natives who'd ventured out of town for college at the University of Texas seven hours south in Austin, then promptly returned home. She was an interior designer and he was a businessman. The Rileys went to church regularly, and they raised their boys on discipline and kindness. "My folks are two very hardworking people," Lincoln says. "They gave me room to grow, but they were also very strict in a lot of ways. They really stressed just kinda basic core values of, I can make a mistake, but if I lied about it, that was way worse. You know, being humble, treating other people right—they were big on that. And they were great examples, too, because they lived their lives that way, and still do. So they were no-nonsense with academics, and they pushed me, but they raised me the right way."

Mike Riley seems a self-motivated man with an independent streak. He ran his own business, Central Compress, warehousing cotton in Sudan, about fifteen miles south of Muleshoe. The South Plains grows a lot of cotton, and Mike helped sell it for those who grew it. Farmers would harvest their cotton and send it to cotton gins to be pressed and baled, and then Mike would store those bales in his warehouses and ship out orders to merchants. It's a simple business but not always an easy one, especially as an independent outfit competing with the farmers' co-ops that fill the area. The goal of those who run co-op compresses is generally to maximize volume. The goal of an independent compress like Mike's is generally to maximize income. To do so, he maximized his outfit's efficiency and profit margins, such as by building warehouses using many wooden beams instead of all steel. He also packed his bales in such a way that they were not always easy to get to, maximizing the usable space in every warehouse, so sometimes forklifts ran into the beams while loading and unloading cotton, and the beams cracked or broke. But wooden beams cost much less, and if they got damaged or broken they could just be repaired or replaced. This sometimes meant more work, but it was also more efficient and cost-effective, so it was worthwhile. A water tower rose from the grounds there, the name Central Compress stenciled in huge letters on its side.

Lincoln grew up working with his father, hauling some of the five-hundred-pound plastic-wrapped bales of cotton, and driving forklifts and trucks around the place by the time he was thirteen years old. The warehouses, with their metal siding and utter lack of insulation, get hot as a sauna during the summers and cold as a freezer in the winters.

The Rileys weren't especially wealthy, but they did well enough to live in a neighborhood called Richland Hills, which locals nicknamed Rich Man Hills.

They had a home on the corner of West Twentieth Street and West Avenue F, just down the road from a field full of white caliche rocks and mule deer and occasional rattlesnakes. Sometimes Lincoln and his friends played there. By the time he was eleven years old, playing football with friends in backyards and rocky fields, he just saw the game differently from the other kids. The plays he drew up weren't standard backyard football plays. His friend Jeff King remembered, "They were as complex as you could be at eleven years old . . . Running backs crossing paths in the backfield, and a toss over a ducking running back to the back guy, who caught the ball. It was all an illusion."

Lincoln's father and grandfather had both been quarterbacks before him. Claude Riley, Mike's father, was the quarterback for Muleshoe in 1938. The Mules had gone undefeated and won the state championship. Mike's teams fared less well. "We weren't any good," he likes to tell people, matter-of-factly. He quit his senior year. "Didn't see eye to eye with the coach."

Still, Mike stayed involved in the school's athletic programs, especially as Lincoln and his brother Garrett—younger by six years—got more involved in sports. Mike served on the school board and was part of the booster club that painted a big mule at midfield every Wednesday night during football season. Thursdays were for middle school and junior varsity, Friday nights and their lights for the varsity.

That's what tugged at Lincoln. Football. He played baseball briefly as a kid, and he played basketball and ran track as he got older, but football was the game he loved. From an early age he had a natural feel for being unnaturally good at the game.

Muleshoe's coaches noticed Lincoln early on. "He was that kid," says Ralph Mason, the coach of the junior high school team. "When he came in and started to play, even in seventh grade, you looked at him, and said, 'Hey, there's our leader right there. That's the guy we want to lead this group of kids.' And he had that, combined with good athleticism. But I think probably his greatest attribute was his leadership and his drive, more so than maybe his skills, at that point . . . It's just one of those things that some people have and some people don't."

On a Sunday morning when Lincoln was in junior high, as he sat in a Sunday school class at church, his teacher taught a lesson about how Christians should encourage people the same as Jesus had. Looking at Lincoln, she asked, "How would you feel if there was no pep rally before the football game? Or if the band didn't show up? Or if the student body didn't come? Or there were no cheerleaders?"

"That would be okay," Lincoln replied. "I just love football."

He loved the way plays unfolded. "Football just made sense to me," he says. "Just the Xs and Os of why you do things."

He loved working hard to get better. Mason remembers helping Lincoln throw a tighter spiral in seventh grade. "He was determined—that was gonna get taken care of," Mason says. "And in the meantime, he was just gonna work at it, where a lot of kids give up and go to something else."

And Lincoln loved the fire and intensity that were as much a part of the game as anything else, especially in West Texas. When he was in ninth grade, Muleshoe High's freshman team was coached by a man who was, in the words of varsity coach David Wood, "just crazy." "Not crazy like loopy crazy," Wood says. "He just . . . he would head-butt kids who had helmets on."

At the first practice, Lincoln and his teammates were in the locker room, dressed and ready to go, when the crazy coach came in, turned off the lights, and started yelling. He yelled about passion and toughness. He yelled about how much passion and toughness you *really* need to be *great* in this game and to be *great* in life. And at some point in all the yelling, the coach squared up to Lincoln, who already had his helmet on, and head-butted him. The blow split open the coach's forehead and made him bleed. All through practice, blood streaked his face and stained his thick mustache.

In some ways, now, that feels like the vestige of another time, the coach who strives to inspire his players by splitting open his own forehead by head-butting one of them in the helmet. It is a type of violence that feels addictive and primal, as much psychological as it is physical. It's a coach, a grown man, a leader, head-butting you, a child, to the point of drawing his own blood. Horrifying, yes, but to some, also thrilling for the rush that such violence provides.

"He just scared us all to death," Lincoln recalled.

He still remembers the crazy coach's thundering voice, his mustache turning red.

And, he said, "It was awesome."

By his sophomore year, Lincoln had not only made Muleshoe High's varsity team, he was competing for the starting quarterback spot. He threw like a pro, with textbook form, over the top, passes leaving his fingers in tight, beautiful spirals.

Still, none of that would have mattered much without the right coach, especially the way Muleshoe High's football teams had been for so long. Lucky for Lincoln, a few years earlier Muleshoe had hired David Wood, who was just right for him. To understand Coach Wood is to understand the effect he had on Lincoln as both a player and a person through high school. He wasn't just a good coach, although he was that, too—Lincoln watched him change everything about Muleshoe High's culture. Watching this man, Lincoln saw what it meant to have a unique vision and then work hard and be dedicated to seeing it through to the end.

In 1999, Lincoln's sophomore season, Wood was thirty-three years old. He was tall, thick-chested, and broad-shouldered, and he had endured many tribulations through his early years in Muleshoe. The high school had hired him in 1996 to be its new athletic director and football coach, and he'd ridden into the place like a new sheriff ready to clean up the town. Especially the football team.

The job was a risk. Muleshoe was the worst 3A high school football program in the state of Texas. They'd won zero games in 1995 and they were expected to win zero games in 1996. But Wood had wanted a head coaching job for a long time, this was the best opportunity he could find, and he had a plan: "I'm not here to win games," he said. "I'm here to change lives. The wins and losses will take care of themselves."

It was a big task. Wood's father was supportive when they discussed the job—*Nowhere to go but up*, they'd agreed—but secretly, Jim Wood worried the job would be a dead end for his son. And even he didn't know the full picture.

After Wood was hired, Muleshoe High superintendent Bill

Moore took him for a drive. They parked at the Sonic in the middle of town and Moore pointed to an empty lot across the street. Some two dozen teenagers were gathered there, congregating around pickup trucks and drinking right out in the open, in the middle of the day.

"Man," Wood said, "those guys—I guess they don't want to be part of any program. I'd sure like to have them."

Moore replied, "No—they *are* the program. Those are your athletes. That's why we hired you."

Wood had twenty-two players, total, on his football team that first season. Most of them were "renegades," he says. "Just outlaws."

Muleshoe reminded Wood of his adopted hometown of Quanah, another rural island about three hours east. "Quanah was very much the same way as when I took over Muleshoe," he says. Wood himself, like Lincoln, had never been big on partying. "I don't know why I wasn't, but I was never an outlaw," he says. He never drank in high school. He was a sophomore in college when he drank his first beer. "I saw it a lot," he says, "but I just didn't understand. *Why are you doing that? We're playing football.*"

His senior year, he was Quanah's starting quarterback, and his father was the coach. Jim Wood had been an All-American defensive end for Oklahoma State in the 1950s and got into coaching not long after that. Spent a few years as the head coach for New Mexico State, then a few more years coaching the Calgary Stampeders in the Canadian Football League when David was a kid. He moved to Texas for David's freshman year so that he could become a scout for the New York Giants. Soon after that he decided to become a high school football coach.

"He was a big disciplinarian," David says.

Jim's discipline boiled down to a simple rule: *Don't do stuff that's gonna hurt you.*

At Muleshoe, David Wood laid down the law: no facial hair and no cussing, for starters. "But that wasn't under the big rules," Wood says.

Here were the big rules: no smoking, no drinking, no breaking the law, no associating with those who do, no getting suspended from school.

No doing stuff that's gonna hurt you.

And while he was at it, he put a stop to all the bragging his players liked to do. They'd talk and talk about good plays they'd made as if those plays had won them the Super Bowl, like prospectors celebrating fool's gold. *Talk is cheap*, Wood would tell them. *You guys don't really know how to win. You know how to talk the game. The way you talk, you feel like you won a state championship every year. But the way you work is not even close to it. And you gotta do the walk before you can do the talk.*

Wood enforced his rules with diligence. There was a grill across from Muleshoe High School where kids would hang out during lunch so that they could smoke inside. Wood regularly visited during lunch hour. The owner protested to Wood, angry, saying that he had to quit coming in like that because it was hurting business. (Wood declined.)

Those who broke the rules faced severe consequences. Culprits ran ten laps—two and a half miles—every day, followed by four sets of "hard yards," four-hundred-yard sprints, crawls, and other exercises up and down the football field. Most, at some point, threw up. They did this at every practice until they were back in good standing, which could be achieved upon service of their ultimate consequence: suspension.

The suspensions shocked everyone. Coaches didn't suspend players in high school for things like partying. Wood knew this as well as anyone. Before Muleshoe, he'd been an assistant coach at various West Texas high schools for eleven years, most recently at 5A Canyon Randall High an hour and a half northeast, near Amarillo. He says, "A lot of coaches come in and say, 'Don't get caught. Don't do it, or, if you do do it, don't get caught.' Or, they'd get caught, and nothing was done to them."

Even if coaches did give out discipline, it never seemed to accomplish much. They'd make players run and that sort of thing, "But it didn't really make a difference in the kid," Wood says. "It didn't make an impression on them. They would run a hundred laps if they could still play the game, and they still got away with it in their minds."

Wood felt the kids weren't learning anything. "We were successful," Wood says, "but I didn't see a change in their lives, really, some of those kids. And I wanted to make a change in their lives . . . I don't want to teach them a lesson after the fact. Let's teach them the lesson right now. Don't make mistakes twice."

Wood saw the same challenge faced by all young men, especially those playing football. *Don't do stuff that's gonna hurt you.* This was easier said than done. Too often they don't know something hurts them until they feel it hurt them. The trick was to learn without hurting too much first.

So when Wood came to Muleshoe, he taught them the best way he knew how: "Take something away from kids that meant something." He wanted to teach them the difference between pain that wounds and pain that heals. "Let's make the mistake one time," Wood says. "And they'll learn from an early age. Then they won't get in trouble after they get out of school."

He started with the quarterback. The kid kept going out drinking, Wood kept finding out, so the kid was suspended two full weeks to start the season.

"The quarterback, the very first year I got there, missed the first two games of the season," Wood says. "Plus, he ran twenty laps for twenty days straight during the summer just to be on the team. Then he was going to miss the first two games."

Wood didn't stop there. That first year, he felt as if he was suspending someone new nearly every day. "Every football game except for one, the first year I was there, I had suspensions, because of some stupid thing like drinking or something."

People were enraged. His players started calling him Dad. It was not a compliment.

"They really didn't know how to take me," he says.

Wood walked out his front door many mornings to find beer bottles thrown into his yard and FOR SALE signs others had staked into the grass during the night. Some parents tried to get him fired.

So he doubled down—but not how you might think. He didn't up the ante with the psychological violence embraced by most football men of the time. He didn't treat his players like some kind of gang to be broken, like an enemy to be defeated. He didn't meet their rage with more of his own, so as to outrage them into submission.

Make no mistake, he maintained their discipline: laps were run, hard yards done, guts puked up, suspensions sure as hell served.

But Wood walked his talk. He gave them what he wanted them to have. He was calm. He was not the crazy freshman coach, commanding respect through dramatic physical and emotional violence. Rather, he led with a calm and powerful strength. He reminded his players what they were capable of. He didn't demand results but sought to inspire them. He saw their needs and he met them. He saw how the fire of their spirit was turning inward and burning them alive, and he worked to help them use it the proper way, because used the proper way, fire in the spirit makes someone great. He led by example. He didn't allow his assistant coaches to talk to referees. He wanted them to feel grace under pressure and so grace under pressure he gave them first. He saw their pain and found answers for it.

He loved them.

And the Mules went 1–9 that first year instead of 0–10 as predicted.

His second season, they went 5–5.

His third season: 10–2, and they won their first playoff game since 1983.

The insult—"Dad"—began to feel more like a term of endearment.

Suddenly Muleshoe football's future actually looked bright.

Lincoln made the varsity team Wood's fourth year there, when he was a sophomore. Wood saw that Lincoln had some fire in him, too, but he also knew how to use it. Lincoln was already good enough to compete for the starting spot, and Wood felt that he could be a player who changes everything. "Lincoln helped me get established and stay here," Wood once told a reporter. "As long as I could have kids like Lincoln, I knew I could compete."

And Lincoln Riley felt the same way about Coach Wood. As long as he had a coach like him, he could compete. Wood's ideas about discipline and love were changing the culture of the team, but they weren't the only reason the team was becoming successful. "[Muleshoe High] at the time was pretty innovative and wide open," Lincoln says. "And now by today's standards it probably wouldn't be, but at that time . . . [we] did a lot of different things offensively that kinda piqued my interest."

This was as important for Lincoln as anything Wood was doing off the field. Lincoln needed a smart coach. Although he downplayed this, Lincoln's hungry, racing mind made him brilliant. In middle school, his teachers had signed him up for a math competition, the Number Sense Contest, that was sponsored by the University Interscholastic League and was one of the oldest, biggest academic contests in all of Texas. Lincoln held no particular passion for that sort of competition, but he went anyway. "He went and won the thing," his friend Kyle Atwood said. "He didn't have any desire to do that."

In high school, Lincoln baffled and amazed his teachers—he would take no notes and do little homework, and yet ace all of his tests. To ensure he wasn't cheating, some teachers made him take tests right in front of them. Debbie Conner, Lincoln's high school math teacher and a longtime family friend, remembers Lincoln suggesting new ways to do formulas as she taught them, as though he were rewriting them in his head.

"School was not his primary motivation," his mother, Marilyn Riley, said. "But he had a really good memory, was really good at math, and he was very competitive. He wanted to win in the class-room like he won on the field."

Lincoln had a flair for the dramatic, too. Alice Liles, his English teacher, still remembers an essay he wrote about the novel *The Education of Little Tree*. "One of the phrases that the little boy, the main character, would use in the story, is that Grandpa would say so-and-so, and he'd say, 'which is right,'" Liles says. "And at the right place, it made the point. And Lincoln answered the question, and he identified the literary points he was supposed to talk about, and made some last comment—and then he said, '*which is right.*' And it just—it flowed."

Wood says, "He wasn't one of these scholars who stayed home studying. He didn't have to. He read it one time and he had it. He learned it. He wasn't a bookworm or anything like that. He just didn't have to be."

Girls liked him, too. He was handsome, with his brown hair and bright blue eyes. "All the girls always wanted to date the Riley boys," Liles says.

Wood fully expected Lincoln to grow up to become a NASA engineer, a bona fide rocket scientist, or something equally impressive-sounding. "He was a computer on legs," he said.

Ralph Mason, who in addition to being the junior high school coach was also the varsity's offensive coordinator, taught high school biology classes. "He could've been anything he wanted to be," Mason says. "A doctor, lawyer, anything he wanted to be."

Alice Liles says, "He could cure cancer if he tried."

Debbie Conner said the same thing nearly verbatim.

Lincoln's take on all this? He chuckles, as though bashful, and says, "Exaggeratin' a little bit."

Exaggerated or not, Lincoln clearly had a gift for learning, and he loved football deeply, in a way that might be its own kind of gift. Football grabbed his mind and his heart like nothing else. "For some reason, I couldn't remember basketball plays in high school," he says. "I just struggled with them. It's weird, because there's only ten guys on the court. I knew them, but I didn't—I would really have to kinda really focus on them. Where the football stuff just didn't seem that hard."

It took Lincoln no more time to learn Wood's playbook than it had taken him to learn how to throw a better spiral. Wood ran a traditional Wing-T offense, and focused on running the ball, as everyone did at the time, but he would get creative. He liked trick plays, such as having the quarterback pitch to the running back who would, in turn, throw downfield. Wood also used a variety of option plays, which Lincoln ran particularly well. On long downs, Wood sometimes called a stunt play called "circus," in which, under center, Lincoln yelled "shift," the tailback went to the line of scrimmage as a receiver, and Lincoln was left alone in the backfield with an array of receivers to throw to.

"You only had to tell him one time, or he only had to see it one time in practice," Wood says. "And he knew what everyone else was supposed to do . . . Watching film, he didn't have to go over and over it. He'd see a defense as we were watching film—not only did he see it, he could see where they were going on the snap, whether it was a disguised secondary coverage, and he sees it one time, how they roll—oh, it looks like a Cover 4, the strong safety moves down, the other safety moves over, and the corner's back. It's a Cover 3. And he says, 'Oh, that's gonna be a Cover 3.' Next time down, that's a Cover 3, and sure enough, he rolled up, and boom. He's just smart."

It wasn't just that Lincoln understood such things that impressed Wood, but the quickness with which he did. "We could teach that to other quarterbacks," Wood says, "but it would take them all week long, and then they're wasting time not learning their progressions, or not learning the new plays you put on that week, or whatever."

And Lincoln knew how to improvise along the way, too. "He'd come off on the sideline after a series," Wood says, "and say, *Hey, they're really bringing that outside linebacker a lot, we could do something here.* And he was just one of those kind of guys—a coach out on the field."

At the quarterback position, Lincoln was competing with a senior and a junior, one of whom would most likely get the starting job, but Wood could not rule him out entirely—not only was Lincoln mentally sharp, but he was physically impressive as well. Lincoln was already tall, standing some six feet tall. He could throw. He was athletic, having also played basketball and run track. And he was the type of player Wood needed, someone the coach didn't have to worry about getting caught up with the outlaws in town. Lincoln didn't go to the grill during lunch hour to smoke. He'd hang out at Sonic. He was a regular at church, and though he was no zealot, Lincoln also wasn't afraid to lead the occasional team prayer. In the locker room, he was a fun teammate—even if some of the fun they had was a bit strange. "Lincoln and his buddies took the longest showers after practices and games in the history of mankind," Ralph Mason recalls. "The water bill at Muleshoe probably went through the roof during the time they were there."

Mason says they'd spend a half hour in the shower. "I'd go in there and say, *Guys, I gotta go home*," he says. "And they'd just laugh and keep talking. That's where a lot of their conversations occurred, was in the showers. It sounds kinda weird. But they weren't doing anything kinky or anything. But I swear it was the longest showers I ever seen."

"They'd stay in there until the water ran cold," Wood says. "They'd run the hot water out."

And they would get into "shower racing," too: "They would get on the floor, and slide around that shower, and race each other," Mason says.

"They'd lather up," Wood says. "And they'd scoot along, they'd push their feet against the wall, on their rears, and shoot across to the other side. They got soap all over their body. Scoot back."

Mason adds, "It was the craziest thing I ever saw."

And on the field, Lincoln was a natural leader. Even by seventh grade, Lincoln had stood out. "He was that figure that everybody was attracted to," Mason says. "Every one of them looked to him for the answers, whatever it may be. Lincoln was that guy. That's what a good leader is. That's what a good quarterback needs to be: somebody to trust in."

By his sophomore year, it seemed all of Muleshoe was convinced Lincoln would one day be great. "Every small town's got its heroes," Wood says. "And he was one of ours."

Lincoln's future was bright on the field in Muleshoe's Benny Douglas Stadium. On that field, under the big West Texas sky, Lincoln could see the whole world coming into view ahead of him. He saw himself becoming Muleshoe's starting quarterback and leading them to glory. He saw himself going on to play in college—maybe at the University of Texas, his parents' alma mater and his favorite team. He saw himself winning big games, and playing in the Rose Bowl, one of college football's largest and most impressive stadiums, a dreamlike arena. Maybe he'd even go on to win a national championship. And after that, he would go pro. He would be drafted by an NFL team, and he would keep playing, and he would keep winning, and one day he'd win the Super Bowl. He could see it. He could see his life taking shape ahead of him. Every day out there in that unrelenting Texas summer heat, the anticipation of the Friday night lights, and all that lay beyond them, appeased his starving mind.

But then, as summer gave way to fall and practice led toward the season, as Lincoln had a real opportunity to outperform his competition to win the starting job, he screwed up. He got too hungry. He did something that hurt him.

"It wasn't smart," he says. "But I was pissed."

2

Hurt

LINCOLN AND THE MULES were in Amarillo, a city of some two hundred thousand people about an hour and a half northeast of Muleshoe. It's an oasis among the West Texas rural islands. Playing football in West Texas, especially in a small town like Muleshoe, you learn to fall in love with long road trips. "Out here in West Texas," David Wood says, "it's not uncommon for a team to travel three hours for half of their games. Or five hours. Or whatever." And there's not much on those rides except open prairies and room for the mind to roam.

They were playing Palo Duro High School at Dick Bivins Stadium. The field was beautiful for high school football, much nicer than Muleshoe's, a bowl-shaped arena with grassy green hills sloping up on all sides around the field.

It was a preseason scrimmage. Lincoln was at quarterback, and he was feeling good. He was growing stronger, reaching new levels of physical ability. His passes were sharp and accurate. He could run. He had that brain of his. David Wood and Ralph Mason had many imaginative concepts in their run-based offense, which Lincoln executed with precision and authority. And when it came time to throw the ball, he threw one accurate pass after another. His professional, over-the-top throwing motion seemed in excellent form.

Sometimes, however, no matter how perfect the pass, a receiver could drop it, and when receivers dropped perfect passes, it made Lincoln angry. As he grew stronger and more capable as a quarterback, his hot West Texas competitive streak grew hotter, too. He played with some fire to him, and he had yet to master it. That's how he threw the last perfect pass of his life that day in Amarillo.

Toward the end of the scrimmage, as the Mules approached the end zone one more time, Coach Wood put in a receiver who mostly rode the bench, and called a play for him. A little slant route. He and Mason wanted to get him his first touchdown.

Lincoln called for the snap, dropped back, and threw a pass that hit the receiver right in the chest. He didn't catch it. The ball bounced into the air. A Palo Duro linebacker intercepted it and ran the other way. And he had a clear shot at the end zone.

Incensed, Lincoln chased the linebacker, streaking down the field in a furious attempt to stop him. He caught him and took him down. "I smacked him . . . I went all out," Lincoln recalls. "And I hit him good."

But then, as he tried to roll over and return to his feet, something felt wrong. "Trying to turn my body, to get up, I couldn't feel my right arm," he says. "It felt like my arm was cut off."

He'd gone all out and hit the kid good, and it had felt good, damn good.

It wasn't smart, but he was pissed, and now he was hurt.

He had hit the linebacker shoulder first.

Throwing-shoulder first.

And now his shoulder was dislocated.

When the doctors reset his shoulder, they said he needed surgery to fully repair the damage, but he put that off until after the season.

Losing him as a quarterback that season was bad enough. "That was a big blow to us," Wood says. But Lincoln had more to offer. He was also a talented defensive player, and, being of unusually large stature for a Muleshoe football player, started at defensive end. He played with his right arm in a leather brace that strapped his arm to his chest and his side like a shoulder straitjacket. He played almost every down and he played as well as could be expected, flying around the field, finishing tackles, breaking up passes, and making all manner of other plays.

It was reckless, but that was the way of the world for a teenage football player in West Texas. It was the way life was for any boy, the way they were taught you become a man. You don't endure your pain or heal from your pain, but rather seek to defeat your pain. You act stronger than what hurts you, even if that risks hurting you more in the future. You mistake stubbornness for strength. And so you suffer. And you call it *will* and *fortitude* and *guts*. It's not smart, but you're pissed. You're pissed at your pain for all that it is taking from you, because being pissed feels better than being hurt. In your anger you develop a hunger to accomplish things so great that they make your pain pale in comparison. And anger fuels this. So you soak in the anger and forge on in spite of your pain—to spite your pain. This makes you feel strong. Anger can be one hell of a drug. Anger will compel you to suffer for the glory of being more stubborn than your pain, and it will do so specifically by blinding you to the ways you are hurting yourself for the rest of your life. Marcus Aurelius, the Roman emperor and philosopher, once wrote, "How much more grievous are the consequences of anger than the causes of it." Lincoln would learn that lesson soon enough.

The Mules went 8–4 in 1999 and won a playoff game for the second straight year, then Lincoln had his surgery in Lubbock. "We went to a guy who was one of the team doctors for [Texas] Tech," Lincoln says. "Knowing that quarterback was probably my future."

But when the time came to throw again, Lincoln discovered that he was no longer the quarterback he used to be. "That surgery changed it all," Lincoln says. Before the surgery, he could throw like a pro. "Over the top," he says. "Had a real strong arm."

Now, he could barely get his arm above his shoulder. "I had to . . . redevelop a whole new motion," he says. "Almost like a golfer changing your whole swing."

His new motion was almost sidearm. "More shot-putting it," Wood remembers.

"It was never the same," Lincoln says.

He refused to allow this to stop him, however. His junior year, busted shoulder be damned, Lincoln was competing for that starting spot again.

He could still run, and what he might have lacked in speed and evasiveness, he would make up for with sheer force. "He wasn't gonna blow by anybody," his friend and teammate Kyle Atwood told a reporter once, "but he was going to run over somebody."

He couldn't throw the way he used to, but he could still throw. "He could get it out there," Wood says. "He couldn't get it behind his ear and throw it like normal guys do. But he made it work for us."

That's what you do, too. You want to do something? Forget how much you've been hurt. You make it work. Lincoln had been hurt, and his shoulder and his ability to throw would never be the same, but the hurt had done nothing to dampen his hunger to perform, to compete, to win.

"He was strong," Wood says.

And he still had that brain of his, too.

Lincoln was named a team captain, which meant more on Wood's team than it might have on others. Wood had stopped simply allowing coaches and players to elect their captain. "Early in my career, early years of Muleshoe, they were choosing teammates that weren't really good leaders," he says. "We knew they weren't very good on Saturday night. I mean, the leaders you want . . . Some of the captains they came up with were just outlaws. So I came up with a system."

That system consisted of an eight-question survey that all the players filled out. "With every question, they could choose three people that fit that category," Wood says. "And after they all put that down, they still chose their teammates that way. I wasn't taking that out of their hands, but these questions were questions that were interested in morals, team leader—someone that you would trust to go talk to coaches. Those kind of questions . . . So it made the players think, and we got a lot better captains . . . And therefore, if you're a captain, it meant more."

Lincoln was Wood's ideal captain. "When he talks, people listen," Wood says. "He didn't say a lot, but when he talked, it meant something. When he did something, it meant something. When he stood up in the locker room at halftime, he didn't yell or scream, but when he stood up at halftime, everyone got quiet. It was just one of those kinda things. People knew he wasn't just coming up with something just to say something. He studied. He knew what to say."

And he knew how to say it, not only understanding what his teammates would benefit from hearing, but also sensitive to how the message was delivered. Same as he had a natural feel for how to play the game, he also had a feel for how to communicate with his teammates—for how his behavior affected their feelings. He was the type of leader who could affect the mood of an entire locker room. "You don't run across those kind of guys too often," Wood says.

On the field, Lincoln regularly came up with new and creative ways to trick the defense, a master of little deceptions. Wood says, "He'd always come to the sideline and tell us, *Hey, this is what they're doing, the middle linebacker's moving over a little bit, let's call this, but I'm actually gonna go this way with it.* Stuff like that. Little things, all the time . . . Basically, he'd come to the sideline and tell us what the defense was doing . . . so the coaches could better call the plays. And a lot of kids do that, but a lot of kids just see something coming from the left. They can't specifically say, they're rotating down, the safety's coming over, you know? But he already saw what they were doing on film, and he could relay that to us pretty easily."

Lincoln split time under center with a senior who was a better runner, but Lincoln was Muleshoe's quarterback, and the Mules produced their best season yet under Coach Wood. Some of Lincoln's receivers were also his good friends, such as tight end Jeff King and wide receiver Kyle Atwood, and he ran option plays beautifully with star running back Danny Ramirez. They didn't just win games; they dominated. In the second game of the season, after being tied 8–8 at halftime with Slaton, the Mules won by a final score of 49–20, and Lincoln put on a show with his teammates. In the third quarter alone, the Mules scored twenty-two points off three touchdowns—one a long kick return, another a long run by Danny, and the third a sixty-five-yard touchdown pass from Lincoln to Danny. By the end of the game, Muleshoe's offense had put up 511 total yards, 360 of them on the ground. Danny ran for 209 yards and caught for 65 more, to total 274 yards for the game.

That built useful momentum heading into the following week's game against Friona. The Chieftains were Muleshoe's archrival. For those boys and their fans, Muleshoe-Friona was Oklahoma-Texas. "It was kind of a year-round deal," Lincoln told a reporter once. "It was something I remember we constantly talked about as players, and I think we understood that game was just a little bit different, and you couldn't really prepare like it was just another game, because it wasn't. If you convinced yourself of that, then you were going to be a little ill-prepared for the intensity and all that of the game. It was heated. It was competitive, and it was definitely the most fun to play in."

Muleshoe had lost to Friona the year before, which was common. Historically, Friona owned Muleshoe. The Mules had won maybe three games against Friona in twenty years. And their games had a way of becoming especially dramatic, such as two years prior when the game began in a torrential downpour that became so overwhelming that officials postponed the second half until the next day. People called it the Mud Bowl.

Now, this year, Muleshoe played well. Its defense held Friona and its powerful offense to 127 rushing yards. On offense, Danny Ramirez gained 114 yards on seven carries that game. Lincoln was responsible for every Muleshoe touchdown, passing for two and running for one.

The final score: Muleshoe 23, Friona 13.

"It was the biggest win in Muleshoe in the past twenty years," Wood says. "It was the first time we'd beaten Friona in like ten years or something. And it was a big deal."

The victory over Friona put them at 3–0 for the season and set the tone for the rest of the year. By the end of the regular season, they were 10–0. Their young backfield matured, avoiding turnovers while producing big-yardage plays that fostered punishing drives. Lincoln became the team's dominant quarterback, starting most games, taking most of the snaps, managing the offense well, throwing many good passes, and breaking off his fair share of big runs, too. On defense, he moved from defensive end to safety, and he was the Mules' punter, too, a job for which he also garnered acclaim after consistently pinning teams deep with superb kicks.

Muleshoe clinched the district title with two weeks left in the season, and their fans followed them everywhere. "It seems the whole town has been at every playoff game for us," Wood told a reporter.

They won the first round of the playoffs 37–0, then kept winning. In the Class 3A Division II regional championship game against Midland Greenwood, Muleshoe won 43–13. Lincoln passed for a hundred yards that game and rushed for seventy-six more.

That put them in the state semifinals for the first time in school history.

It was the best season a Muleshoe team had seen since 1938, when the Mules went undefeated—led by Lincoln's grandfather, Claude Riley, at quarterback. Members of the 1938 team gathered in Muleshoe to reminisce and to cheer on the 2000 team, and then everyone headed east, to Dallas.

The Mules would need all the help they could get.

The semifinal game was played on the Dallas Cowboys' hallowed turf at Texas Stadium. Muleshoe faced the Forney Jackrabbits, who may have had a 10–4 record but were far more imposing on the field than 14–0 Muleshoe. They had a practically unstoppable running back named DaBryan Blanton, who had racked up 1,595 yards and twenty-four touchdowns on 180 carries—nearly nine yards per carry—in just nine games. He missed five games with injuries, three of which Forney lost. Of the nine games Blanton did play, Forney lost only one—and by a single point—and outscored its opponents 190–7.

Forney's defense was equally impressive, allowing just 161 yards per game and shutting out six teams that season. "Near impenetrable," one reporter called them.

Hours before game time, as coaches and families took pictures on the Cowboys' star at midfield, Lincoln was going through throwing drills with a teammate. When it was time to take the field for the game, as the Mules trotted onto the turf in their black jerseys with white numbers and trim, most of them couldn't help but gawk at the massive stadium in which they were about to play. This was a legendary place for any high school football player, let alone the boys from Muleshoe.

Lincoln, however, did not gawk. "Everyone was oohing and aahing and he was just all business," Wood said. "He was poised and focused. If you looked deep into his eye, you could tell he was playing the game before it even started."

Texas Stadium may well have been the Mecca of American football. And yet, while most of the other players were swept up in the glory of the arena, Lincoln was focused on why they'd entered it.

The Mules kicked off to start the game, and Lincoln took the field as a free safety. He played like a coach on the field, pointing and calling out tips to his teammates. When the ball was in play, he was an athlete, flying around the field, with broad shoulders but a frame that appeared skinny next to some of the bigger Forney players. The Mules made the Jackrabbits go three and out on their first possession, and after the punt was down at the Muleshoe 12-yard line, Lincoln took the field again, this time at quarterback.

He carried himself like a professional, jogging slowly to meet the team in the huddle, his hands loose by his hips. The team huddled around him as he called the first play and clapped his hands with calm authority. Taking position under center, he surveyed the field, checked behind him, called for the snap—and a flag flew as a ref's whistle sounded.

First play of the biggest game of his high school life, and one of Lincoln's teammates screwed it up with a false start.

Lincoln calmly handed the ball to a referee, put his hands on his hips, dropped to a knee as his teammates gathered in a huddle again, and called the next play.

After two running plays that gained them just a few yards, the Mules faced third and eleven from deep in their own territory, a miserable start to such a big game. With some receivers lined up wide now, one to the left and another to the right, Lincoln took the snap and dropped back. Forney linemen immediately broke through. Lincoln rolled left and a defender closed in hard and fast. Lincoln fired. And his sidearm, shot-putting form did the job. The ball zipped over the defender and past another one reaching out and hit a receiver in the numbers on the 25-yard line. It was a beautiful and clutch fifteen-yard pass.

Lincoln and the Mules rolled for a few plays from there. One play he pitched to Danny and immediately turned and threw a block. He patted his teammates on the back, encouraging but not overdoing it. On another third down, on a play-action pass, he again rolled to the left, and again found a receiver down the field. He looked smooth, gliding as he took a hop-step to square his shoulders and throw, and when he threw it followed the squaring of the shoulders with great fluidity, all in one beautiful motion. He knew what he was doing. The ball sailed just over the arms of a defender and traveled eighteen yards through the air before being caught by a receiver who took it to the 50-yard line. Lincoln walked up to the receiver nodding with quiet joy and shook his hand as though acknowledging a business deal well made.

Then he got back to work.

Two plays later, on the third third down of this long opening drive, Lincoln lined up in shotgun, took the snap, looked downfield, where he had a receiver open deep, and threw. It was an aggressive play beautifully executed—except for one thing. Lincoln under-threw it. His sidearm shot-put motion didn't get enough on the ball, and what might have been a touchdown was instead inter-cepted by a Forney safety.

A few plays later, Forney's DaBryan Blanton broke free on a big run. Lincoln was way back in his free safety position and moved to grab Blanton, but Blanton put the moves on him and turned him around. Blanton tore through Lincoln's lunging hands and blew past him, and made his way to the end zone for a forty-one-yard touchdown run.

It was a dominant performance and a demoralizing sequence of events for Muleshoe. And the rest of the game proceeded in like fashion. The Mules played hard and Lincoln led them well, but every break went Forney's way. The Jackrabbits were simply the better team. Lincoln was hit hard several times, and he threw two more interceptions and gave up a fumble that was taken back for a touchdown.

And as Muleshoe's struggles compounded into the second half, the fire in Lincoln's spirit burned ever hotter. A few plays after he'd thrown his third interception, Lincoln was lined up at free safety with Forney on the Mules' 12-yard line. The Jackrabbits' quarterback took the snap, dropped back, and fired a sharp pass to a receiver running an inside slant. Touchdown. As that receiver caught the ball, he was beyond Lincoln's grasp. The play was over, but Lincoln still leveled another receiver standing nearby. It was an aggressive and unnecessary play, one that seemed driven by frustration at how the game has been going—by anger, by the dark side of ambition left feeling deprived, feeling hungry. And it was dangerous.

The score was 38–3 by the end of the third quarter, but Lincoln played as if the outcome were still in doubt. He still had more to give and so he gave it. On defense, he chased guys down, fought through blockers, dived to make some tripping tackles.

In the fourth quarter, Muleshoe pulled off a long drive full of option plays, with a couple quick passes thrown in, then finally got into the end zone off a triple-option play in which Lincoln pitched to Danny Ramirez before taking a hard hit. But that was about all Lincoln could do that game. The next drive, Lincoln kept fighting, making a hard tackle, and he did it leading with that right shoulder again, competitive fire burning caution alive. Soon he was subbed out, and the game ended with a final score of Forney 41, Muleshoe 18.

To his coaches, however, the team's loss and Lincoln's struggles defined him far less than how they saw him react to them. Yes, he laid out that one Forney receiver, but that was forgotten in the aftermath, with more emphasis given to how Lincoln handled his teammates. "He was calm," Wood says.

"That was pretty much him," Ralph Mason says. "That's an important quality of a leader. You can't show signs of panic or distress in those kinds of situations. The rest of the team's gonna follow you."

When All-District honors were announced shortly thereafter, Lincoln was named honorable mention at quarterback, second-team at defensive back—and first-team as a punter. Danny Ramirez, who finished the season with sixteen hundred rushing yards and two thousand all-purpose yards, was named district offensive MVP. Another Muleshoe running back made first-team All-District and a receiver made second-team. Soon after that, Ramirez was also named second-team All-State and Lincoln was named honorable mention All-State.

By all accounts, it had been a magical season. "To finish the season at 14–1, and to play in Texas Stadium, was beyond our ability to imagine," David Wood wrote in an open letter published by the *Muleshoe Journal*. He went on to praise the players for the way they never took individual credit for their accomplishments. "Every interview was a joy to read, hear or watch," he wrote, "because each of you always insisted it was the team, and never 'I.' As the spotlight began to focus on you more, the heat must have been intense at times, and yet you continued to be yourselves."

Lincoln had shown real leadership qualities, and in many ways he was mature beyond his years, but he was still very much a teenager. "I was not unlike most guys in high school," he says. "From time to time, I found myself in trouble."

His senior year, Lincoln went full outlaw for a night.

Nobody's sure exactly when this happened. It could have been sometime in the summer of 2001, before Lincoln's senior season began.

One night, Lincoln drove to Friona with three friends. They went to the water tower in the middle of town, climbed the ladder, and painted the score of the previous year's game on its side: *23–13*.

Someone spotted them and called the cops, and soon people were calling around Muleshoe asking questions. When Mike and Marilyn Riley asked Lincoln if he knew anything about it, "I lied about it," he says.

But the lie only lasted so long. "I eventually came clean," he says. "They were more disappointed I didn't tell the truth than what we did."

Lincoln took a valuable lesson from that: mistakes were okay, but you had to be honest about them from the start. "I wasn't always perfect with it," he says, "but I always felt it, too . . . I tried to be. And when I wasn't, it hurt me."

Mike picked up the phone and called David Wood, who was at his vacation cabin in Colorado.

"Lincoln's got something he wants to say to you," Mike said.

Then Lincoln took the phone and told his coach what he had done.

"We'll take care of it when I get home," Wood said.

Lincoln was grounded. His driving privileges were revoked for a while, he had to write an apology letter, he had to apologize to the Friona coach in person, and he had to pay some restitution. "There was some real fallout," he says.

And when practices resumed, Lincoln says, "Coach ran us until I couldn't see straight."

Privately, however, Wood couldn't help but laugh about it. "I, uh, remember climbing up our water tower growing up and writing something on it," he says. "So I couldn't get too mad." He laughs. "Kids will be kids. It wasn't something nasty or bad. If he'd put some cuss words up there, or something derogatory, it would've been different, but . . . people chuckle about that."

Friona responded with a challenge of their own. The town didn't immediately paint over the graffiti, instead leaving it on full display as motivation for its football team, as well as a challenge to Muleshoe, to try beating them again. Lincoln and his teammates had pulled off quite the stunt, but painting the town water tower was nothing compared to the challenge of actually defeating the Chieftains on the field. They had to be able to back it up.

When Muleshoe played Friona later that fall, Lincoln threw for 236 yards and two touchdowns and rushed for 97 yards on top of that, including a forty-five-yard touchdown run. All that, in less than three full quarters. The game got called on account of lightning with more than three minutes left in the third, Mother Nature herself once again seemingly moved to chaos by the rivalry. Lincoln had put forth a dominant performance, and the final score was Muleshoe 42, Friona 24.

Lincoln played like that throughout his senior season. In a 33–12 win against Tulia a week later, he rushed for 227 yards and two touchdowns to lead a Muleshoe rushing attack that gained 454 yards on the ground. By the end of the season, Lincoln was named first-team All-District on both offense and defense, along with a defensive player of the week honor. His friend Kyle Atwood, a wide receiver, was a first-team All–South Plains selection, along with running back A. J. Flores. Lincoln was named honorable mention at quarterback, finishing with some fifteen hundred passing yards and fifteen touchdowns. He also made All–South Plains as a punter.

The team didn't go as far in the postseason, losing its second-round playoff game to the Crane Golden Cranes. Crane had a nightmarishly good defense, and they pounded Muleshoe en route to a 22–0 shutout. The game felt so one-sided that by the fourth quarter Ralph Mason just wanted to get his basketball players off the field so they wouldn't get hurt before hoops season started.

Even still, respect grew for Lincoln among his peers and throughout the community. He was always in the stands for the junior high games, watching his kid brother Garrett play. Garrett was also a quarterback, and Lincoln could often be seen working with Garrett, spending as much time coaching his brother as he could. "Every junior high kid in a small town, they idolized some-body," Wood says. "Lincoln was the guy they idolized."

It wasn't just the junior high kids, either. Lincoln became a leader not just for his team, but for the high school at large. "Every pep rally we had," David Wood says, "the cheerleaders would choose players to say something at the pep rally, and I remember him standing up in front of the school as a player."

Same as when he spoke to the team in the locker room, Lincoln had commanding presence when he spoke in public. "He stood out when he talked," says David Wood's wife, Jody. "He was just good with words. And his temperament—he wasn't a real macho type of person. He was humble. And kind of shy. He'd give a little smile. He's just somebody who, when he started talking, you would lis-ten. You would go, *Wow, this guy's pretty sharp. And got a lot of spirit, for a quiet guy.*"

He'd become, in a word, the town hero. "Everyone's got a hero in a small town," Wood says. "And Lincoln sure fit that bill. They gotta have somebody, and Lincoln was that guy."

Some smaller schools, such as West Texas A&M, recruited Lincoln to play football for them, as well as some schools in the Ivy League. "The main one was Dartmouth," he said. "That was the one I prob-ably got the closest with. I had several conversations with them . . . They're obviously incredible, but at the end of the day, that just wasn't me."

Lincoln was most interested in Texas Tech. On the surface, this made no sense, even though Texas Tech was right down the road in Lubbock. Lincoln's parents had gone to the University of Texas, and Lincoln himself had grown up a Texas Longhorns fan to his bones—and Texas was Texas Tech's biggest rival. Texas Tech hadn't even recruited Lincoln. Despite all of this, he wanted to go there, and there was one reason why: Texas Tech's new football coach, Mike Leach, and the new offense he'd installed there. Leach called it the Air Raid, and his quarterbacks were throwing the ball fifty, sixty times a game. It was antithetical to everything football coaches were supposed to believe in—everyone knew you built a good football offense around the run game. People thought Leach was nuts. But to Lincoln, the Air Raid seemed complex and exciting, and he craved becoming part of it. "I grew up seventy miles from Lubbock," Lincoln says. "So it was big news what they were doing offensively, and it was unique, and I knew it was something I wanted to learn about. I was intrigued by it. I didn't know a ton about the game, but it intrigued me, watching them."

Lincoln developed a simple plan: he would enroll at Texas Tech, join the team as a walk-on, and, in time, earn the job as the Red Raiders' starting quarterback.

Upon sharing this plan with his coaches at Muleshoe, he was met with resistance, to say the least. They offered him their perspective: Lincoln had played for a tiny high school, and he had played well for them but hadn't put up mind-blowing statistics, largely because of his mangled shoulder. On top of all that, Mike Leach had no clue who he was. "He wasn't some blue-chip prospect," David Wood says.

Wood told Lincoln he was proud of his high aspirations, but he had to be realistic. "You're not going to walk into that place and wow everybody," Wood said. "If you really want to play college football . . . I don't know if Texas Tech is the place for you . . . Maybe look to go somewhere else."

Lincoln wouldn't listen. Wood says, "He was just like, *No. This is what I wanna do.* He had that plan. There was no talking him out of it. He knew what he wanted to do."

Lincoln knew the challenge he faced, but if he didn't go for it, he could more or less predict his future: play small-time college football, have some fun, then become a high school coach in a small town like Muleshoe. That would have been a fine life. A fine future. He could see it clearly, like a math formula written on a chalkboard for him to copy into a notebook.

But he always was rewriting those formulas in his head, finding a better way to do things. That's what he wanted to do with his future. Something about Leach's offense called to him. He knew he could learn it. He knew he could execute it. He knew he could work hard. And that was all he needed to know. He had a dream to chase. Never mind the fine line between dream and delusion.

As for his shoulder—yes, it was a problem, but it didn't have to stop him.

He had a solution: he would have access to Texas Tech's facilities and trainers, and he would make the most out of them. He would work hard, and get stronger, and do everything required to fix his shoulder. He would undo the damage he had done to himself chasing the linebacker, and heal.

He went to Lubbock.

3

Lubbock

A SPORTS BROADCASTER IN the 1990s once said that there was "nothing but Tech football and a tortilla factory in Lubbock," and while factually that can be disputed, that is also how Lubbock can feel. Some have said that the city of Lubbock feels as though it is located on the far side of the moon, and to visit there is to know that to be true. Tucked away in West Texas, Lubbock lies two hours south of Amarillo and two hours north of the Odessa-Midland region of *Friday Night Lights* fame, neither of which is any larger than Lubbock. To get to a real city, you need to drive five hours east to Dallas–Fort Worth, or Austin six hours south.

But compared to Muleshoe and the other rural West Texas islands like it, driving into Lubbock can feel like finding land.

Known as "Hub City," Lubbock is the focal point of the South Plains, and Texas Tech University is the focal point of the focal point. The area of Lubbock that surrounds the campus feels very much like a college town, with shopping and trendy restaurants and a hip new hotel and conference center, not to mention a street full of bars. When Lincoln enrolled at Tech in the fall of 2002, the area was run-down and impoverished, an area that most people, especially students, tried to avoid. More recently, some developers pulled off one of the most expensive redevelopment projects in the country. It's nicer there now.

About a mile away, the Depot District offers more grown-up nightlife, along with some nice restaurants and theaters and other artistic venues. The Buddy Holly Center sits on Crickets Avenue— the man the Beatles credit with inspiring them and changing music forever had gone to Lubbock High, right up the road.

There's more to Lubbock, too. It's a bigger city than it looks, laid out like the ranch houses so popular here: flat but sprawling, as it covers some 126 square miles. Several miles from campus, a boom- ing medical district sits near a mall and a swath of other shopping. A city this size could be a nightmare for traffic, but city planners did well at keeping infrastructure ahead of population growth. The roads in the city are laid out wisely, in ways that maximize traffic flow—there are several six-lane roads right in the middle of downtown—and then there's a freeway looping around the city with plenty of exits for you to slip off right where you need to be. It's not hard to get where you're trying to go.

You still get those spiritual West Texas skies here, too. The sun- sets are breathtaking, especially from the patio of a bar on the edge of town, a patio that sits twenty stories high and overlooks every- thing, starting with Jones AT&T Stadium. The Red Raider fandom is a rowdy one. A ten-foot statue of Will Rogers atop his horse, Soap- suds, sits on campus, and the statue has been strategically placed so that the horse's backside faces the direction of another rival school, Texas A&M. After Texas Tech defeated the Aggies in 2001, the fans tore down their own goalposts and threw them in the visitor's section. And then there's the tortilla tradition—fans hurl tortillas onto the field at kickoff every game. The practice was outlawed years ago, and security checks for tortilla contraband as fans enter the stadium. The team can even be penalized if tortillas actually reach the field of play.

Football season weekends see Tech faithful congregate from all over, many driving or flying in from Dallas–Fort Worth to gather at the stadium. Designed with an aesthetic that echoes the Spanish Renaissance, the arena rises from the university district like an open-air West Texas cathedral. Come football season, when the Red Raiders are playing at home, that structure becomes the center of the universe.

Following his plan, Lincoln made the team as a walk-on. Head coach Mike Leach liked Lincoln from the start. "He really laid it out on the line to be a walk-on and go do something like that," Leach says. "It requires a great deal of faith and confidence to do that in the first place. And even somewhat unrealistic faith and confidence. Without that, you don't have any chance."

Lincoln was eager to jump right into things when he went to his first position meeting. He and eight other quarterbacks—Leach liked to have options—got settled in.

Lincoln sat down excited to learn from the coach who was revolutionizing football. Then Leach entered the room, withdrew a can of dip tobacco from his pocket, and stuffed a huge wad in his lip.

Seeing someone load up a fat dip wasn't new to Lincoln. "I'm from Muleshoe, Texas—I've seen guys put in big dips before," Lincoln said. "But he put in the biggest dip any human being has ever put in. Ever. I mean, I was just blown away. He had so much—he had it all over his face, number one. He had so much in his mouth he couldn't really talk. Like, he couldn't get the words out."

And not only that, but Lincoln says Leach used this meeting

to talk about nothing but dip. "It's day one," Lincoln said, "and I just walked on, and have to learn this offense that's revolutionizing football—and he starts talking about how dip is made, and how they cut it, and the different types of tobacco, and how you pack the can, and if you drink lemon juice or lime juice after, it'll help bring your lip back so that you can keep putting it in."

Leach protests that Lincoln's memory is exaggerated. "I think there's a portion of that that's facetious," Leach says. "I can't talk about any one thing for ninety minutes. I mean, how can you? And we don't have the most polished quarterbacks in the country . . . But I may have talked about dip. That's highly possible. But in between, there was plenty of talk about football."

Wherever the truth lies, Lincoln recalls sitting there baffled, waiting for Leach to turn their attention to his offense. That was the whole reason Lincoln was here. "A lot of the base concepts and way of thinking at Tech—it was a lot different," Lincoln says. "They were throwing it all over the place."

From what Lincoln had seen so far, he loved it, and he couldn't wait for Leach to quit talking dip and start talking football. Leach was a freethinking coach with a rebellious offense the core ethos of which seemed to be freedom itself, which meant, in the buttoned-up militaristic world of football, this was all quite revolutionary.

In this way, Leach would be so good for Lincoln. Being raised on a rural island of a small town can confuse bright kids into behaving in ways that downplay their intelligence—as Lincoln sometimes did—because it can become uncomfortable, thinking so differently from everyone else around you. Live truthfully and embrace your intelligence, and you risk being denigrated as arrogant, even if that's not how you feel. Sometimes, you might even begin to believe you actually are arrogant simply for thinking differently, and, in an effort to avoid loneliness, begin to put yourself down in order to gain acceptance.

By comparison, however, Mike Leach was so unique and so intense and so brash that anything Lincoln could have said or done seemed downright normal by comparison.

That's what Lincoln began learning from Leach from day one: "Thinking outside the box, you know?" he says. "Not being afraid to implement something outside the box. Some people will think it, but never have the guts to do it, and he did."

Leach was unabashedly, stubbornly himself.

And his Air Raid offense was certainly outside the box. Leach had Tech's starting quarterback, Kliff Kingsbury, throwing fifty or sixty passes a game, and he was using more receivers—rarely fewer than four every play—than anyone else ever had. And maybe most stunning of all, he ran no-huddle offenses for the whole game, not just as the clock wound down. With his offense in nearly constant hurry-up mode, playing every possession as though it were a two-minute drill, Leach was also able to run more plays while also draining defenses physically and mentally. Most college football teams averaged sixty-five to seventy plays a game. Tech ran closer to ninety. "The more shots on goal you get, the better," Leach once told a reporter. "That's how we saw it."

The college football world didn't quite know how to feel about it. Michael Lewis, the author of *The Blind Side* and *Moneyball*, once wrote, "Leach's offense is not just an offense, it is a mood: optimism." The *New York Times* sportswriter Marc Tracy once called the Air Raid offense "as much about audacity as intellect . . . While coaches who run it need to know their Xs and Os, they really need chutzpah."

Chris B. Brown, the author of the *Smart Football* blog and the book *The Essential Smart Football*, wrote, "It's actually a bit hard to remember now, but for most of football history, if you were a 'throwing coach' you were considered more of a trickster than a real coach."

And Leach was more than a mere "trickster"; he was the proverbial bull in the china shop.

While the college football world regarded Leach's offense as a sideshow, Tech's fans had even stronger feelings about it. By the time Lincoln arrived as a freshman, they were two years into the Mike Leach Experiment, and "people did not like Mike Leach football," says Don Williams, a longtime sportswriter for the *Lubbock Avalanche-Journal*. Leach had led the Red Raiders to respectable winning seasons that culminated in bowl games, but they lost those bowl games, and the fans were restless. Leach and his offense couldn't have been more different from who and what he replaced. Before Leach, Tech had a beloved head coach named Spike Dykes, who had coached West Texas high school football teams for years before coming to Tech as defensive coordinator in the 1980s. In 1986, he was elevated to the head coaching job, and he did well for thirteen seasons. The Red Raiders consistently had winning seasons and would pull off semi-regular upsets against their much larger rivals at Texas and Texas A&M. Same as every other school, Tech's offense had been based on the run, and two running backs had won the Doak Walker Award for best running back in the country during his tenure. "They threw the football," says Williams, "but they were a run-first team, and had a lot of success as a run-first team."

But Dykes's winning seasons rarely got much better than 6–5 and 7–4, people wearied of the mediocrity, and Dykes retired.

Leach arrived as Spike Dykes's replacement in 2000, following one season as the University of Oklahoma's offensive coordinator. Despite being in his first head coaching role, Leach quickly developed a good reputation among his peers. Art Briles left a secure coaching job at Stephenville High School to join Leach's staff. Briles had built Stephenville, a Class 4A school, into a powerhouse that had won four state titles in his twelve years there. He was making more than $100,000 a year there—one of the only high school coaches in Texas to do so—and he had a five-year contract when Leach offered him a job coaching the Texas Tech running backs. Briles took the job without thinking too hard about it. He told a reporter, "I felt comfortable making the jump because I knew there were good West Texas people in control of the athletic department . . . I also felt like this was going to be a great situation. It was a little bit of a leap of faith, but I had confidence that Mike would have this program going in the right direction very quickly."

But Leach could be an acquired taste, and not just because of his offense. College football coaches are by and large a buttoned-up lot, seemingly happy to wear khakis and golf shirts and sneakers every day of their lives unless they're feeling a little crazy on vacation. Leach dressed as if he were always on vacation. He'd wear board shorts and baggy shirts and flip-flops. He seemed like a delightfully weird dude. He'd go on stream-of-consciousness rambles about anything from dip to politics to pirates. Michael Lewis once described Leach as entering a locker room "with the quizzical air of a man who has successfully bushwhacked his way through a jungle but isn't quite sure what country he has emerged into." Leach's agent, Gary O'Hagan at IMG, told Lewis, "He's so different from every other football coach it's hard to understand how he's a coach."

He's a coach in large part because of that offense of his, which he'd spent years developing alongside another coach named Hal Mumme. And it's important here to get an idea about who Mike Leach was, to fully appreciate just how outside-the-box his thinking was, and the way that showed Lincoln how to think likewise. The best way to understand that is to look at how Leach became a coach at Texas Tech at all. He was a lesson for Lincoln in many ways, most of all being one of the simplest, most difficult things for a young man to learn: *Just be yourself.*

There were many times in Mike Leach's life that people around him were telling him he was wrong and he just didn't listen, and things somehow worked out in his favor. That started with how he became a coach in the first place. He hadn't played much football even in high school—he rode the bench—but went on to graduate in the top third of his class at Pepperdine's law school, and he became a successful lawyer.

He didn't love it, though. And one day he impulsively quit the profession and announced to his family that he was becoming a college football coach.

His first job paid $3,000 a year, and he bounced around for a little while until Hal Mumme hired him as an assistant coach at a tiny NAIA school, Iowa Wesleyan.

It was Mumme who first introduced Leach to the spread offense.

Mumme had discovered it first while at the University of Texas, El Paso, coaching against LaVell Edwards at Brigham Young. Edwards was the first college football coach to use a "spread offense," spreading receivers across the line of scrimmage, so that he could then "throw the ball all over the place."

Mumme and Leach were both weary of college football's self-serious traditions. They wanted to experiment. They wanted to throw the ball and they wanted to do so as many times as possible in a game. This was about overwhelming a defense, but it was also about fostering a new psychology in players: "With so many people touching the ball," Leach said, "it elevates the enthusiasm of the whole team."

That was the core foundation for what they wanted to do: make football fun.

They loved visiting places like the Alamo, and not to motivate their players with overwrought pontification on the nature of football and war and the strange analogies men like to make between them—they went to such places to gain perspective. Yes, the game of football was violent and warlike and, to them, beautiful for it— but it was a game, and games were meant to be fun, and the way most coaches coached football was a snooze compared to what they saw as possible.

Everywhere they went, people reacted badly at first. Even when they took over teams that were in the range between mediocre and downright awful, the locals complained about their new offense. (Change is hard, even when you're terrible.) And everywhere they went, after they began to win—and they always did—they would become beloved. In three years at Iowa Wesleyan, they took a team that had gone 0–10 their first season and went 25–10, ranked second in the nation in passing two seasons, and ranked first the other. They passed like mad. One game, their quarterback went 61 for 86.

From there, they went to Division II Valdosta State. The local reporters said their wacky newfangled offense wouldn't work at all. Fans who ran into them in public straight-up told them to just run the ball right up the middle. Mumme and Leach ignored them all—naturally—and did their thing. They set all manner of Division II records. Their quarterback won the Division II equivalent of the Heisman. They went 40–17–1 over the next seven seasons.

Part of their success came because they never stopped learning, never stopped challenging even their own ideas about what would work best. They made trip after trip to BYU to learn from LaVell Edwards. They spent hours in local coffee shops and restaurants scribbling plays on napkins. (One restaurant manager got mad because they wrote all over their reusable cloth napkins.) They'd take what Edwards was doing, pull it apart, and piece it back together. They sketched crossing routes and screen plays and put wrinkles on them that would confuse defenses and give their players unprecedented advantage. Eventually, they boiled it all down to a handful of running plays and a few key passing concepts, and they started having their quarterback throw out of the shotgun more. "We knew we were changing the game," Mumme told ESPN's Kevin Van Valkenburg. "We just weren't sure if anybody else was going to change with us."

After seven seasons in Valdosta, Mumme and Leach were hired away to a Division I school, the University of Kentucky, where they went through more of the same. More controversy, more proving everyone wrong, more fun. Kentucky's quarterback, Tim Couch, had thrown for fewer than a thousand yards the year before they got there. In their first season, Couch threw for more than three thousand yards. The Wildcats' offense went from 109th in the country to No. 6. Couch became a Heisman finalist, Kentucky's first in decades, and was drafted No. 1 overall by the Cleveland Browns. For seven seasons under Mumme and Leach, the Wildcats went for it on fourth down forty times a season, nearly double any other team in the conference, and they shocked college football superpowers like Alabama. Attendance surged from about forty thousand fans to nearly sixty thousand per game.

This was also when their offense became known as the Air Raid. Leach worked with Kentucky's marketing team on that. They made up AIR RAID T-shirts and bumper stickers. They blew an air horn in the stadium during games. When they got in trouble for that, they moved the horn to a building across the street from the stadium to skirt noise ordinance laws designed to prevent the stadium from getting too loud on game days.

Mumme and Leach became the ones getting visits from other colleges—even from coaches at big-name schools like Auburn, Florida State, and Georgia, who wanted to know what they were doing. One was a young coach from Notre Dame named Urban Meyer. And there was Oklahoma's first-year head coach, Bob Stoops. In 1999, he hired Leach to install his offense for the Sooners.

And again, in Norman, more of the same. Sooner fans hated it all at first. Oklahoma was a proud program, one of the best in the country when coached by Barry Switzer decades earlier, under whom it had dominated rivals like Nebraska and Texas. They were built on the power-running wishbone formation, one of the hallmark running offense concepts of that time. Even Leach had love for it: "A thing of beauty the way it flowed."

Despite differences between the wishbone and the Air Raid, the two approaches share the same spirit: they used every skill guy on the field. Even though basically every play out of the wishbone was a run, it was designed so that defenses never knew which player was going to get the ball. "It's about constant threats," said Emory Bellard, the coach who had created the wishbone decades earlier. "That's why I like Mike Leach's offense."

Soon the Oklahoma fans did, too.

The Sooners won their first three games in 1999, averaging forty-four points per game through their first month. From there, Oklahoma had a solid but inconsistent year—they lost to archrival Texas 38–28, then blew out No. 13 Texas A&M 51–6, then lost to Colorado, then blew out Missouri and Iowa State, then lost to Texas Tech.

Still, Texas Tech liked what Leach had done with the offense at Oklahoma and wanted him to be the Red Raiders' head coach. Leach knew about Spike Dykes and his legacy in Lubbock—"a local hero," he's called him—and phoned Dykes before taking the job, to ask his blessing. Dykes gave it.

As he settled in at Texas Tech, Leach became close with some older men who became friends and mentors to him, who believed in him even as the rest of the football world still figured out what to make of him. One was Barry Switzer, the legendary former Oklahoma coach who had run the football program there from 1973 to 1988, during which time the Sooners won three national championships. "Barry Switzer kind of took me under his wing," Leach says. The other was Donnie Duncan, who'd been on Switzer's staff as an assistant coach from 1973 to 1978, went on to become Oklahoma's athletic director for a little while, and then ultimately played a critical role in forming the Big 12 Conference. "Donnie was the head of our conference," Leach says. "So once I'm the head coach at Tech, I'm in meetings hour upon hour upon hour upon hour upon hour with Donnie Duncan . . . And Donnie became my friend and mentor, somebody I would call, touch base with, all the time." By 2003, Leach and Duncan were close enough that Leach trusted Duncan's word almost blindly, hiring a defensive ends coach named Charlie Sadler based solely on Duncan's recommendation. "I hired Charlie, just straight out of the word of Donnie Duncan," Leach says. "He steered me right on that . . . I wouldn't have hired Charlie without Donnie. I wouldn't have known about Charlie. And Charlie was just utterly outstanding. Outstanding, smart. Very stable. All of a sudden, some crisis is going on, you know, Charlie's one of those guys, you can sit down and sort your way through it."

Relationships such as these provided a valuable foundation for

Leach as he let his active imagination run wild and went about upending the college football status quo.

Once practices began, Lincoln felt lost. He once recalled, "I had to go out there, and ask . . . 'Guys, what the hell are we doing?'"

He asked older players and coaches a million questions. He wanted to learn not only how to run this offense and what that required, but *why*.

The *why* of it all had to go beyond just making football more fun, because there are lots of ways to have fun that might be entertaining for players and fans alike, but don't necessarily lead to wins. Leach based his offense's philosophy in no small part on a quote from *The Art of War* by Sun Tzu: "If he (the enemy) is superior in strength, evade him. If his forces are united, separate them. Attack him where he is unprepared; appear where you are not expected."

Leach wanted to do the same thing every other coach in football wanted to do: make things difficult for your opponent. He just wanted to do that in a way that was opposite of almost everyone else.

Most coaches made things difficult for their opponent by developing a lot of complex plays and schemes elaborately tailored to fit a multitude of tricky concepts. Leach didn't like that, because while it might have made things more complicated for the defense, it also made things complicated for his own players.

His approach was simple: fewer plays, more formations.

"That way," Leach said, "you don't have to teach a player a new assignment every single time, just a new place to stand."

Basically Leach's players learned a few plays, then drilled them relentlessly as they practiced running them out of myriad different formations.

The premise of the Air Raid offense is simple: allocate receivers across the field at varying depths with significant space between them, making it impossible for a defense to cover all of them—or stretch itself thin attempting to do so. The wishbone offense had used the running game to stretch out defenses horizontally, and used all of its skill players to do so. The Air Raid did likewise, with the additional benefit of stretching a defense not only horizontally, but also vertically. Leach liked to say it was "changing the geometry of the game."

There are more defensive players than there are receivers, but since receivers can run short, intermediate, or long routes, the dimensions of defensive positioning can become challenging. The Air Raid offense is so pass-heavy that linebackers, cornerbacks, and safeties almost never get a break from the receivers. They're chasing someone almost every single snap.

It's simple.

It's relentless.

More than being a mood of optimism, as Michael Lewis wrote, the Air Raid was an insistence that things could be improved from the status quo. It was a rebellion.

At first glance, it also seemed wildly unbalanced—throw, throw, and throw some more—but Leach didn't see it that way. He knew as well as anyone that a good offense is a balanced offense, but to Leach, "balance" didn't mean what most people seemed to think it meant: "There's nothing balanced about the fifty percent run, fifty percent pass," he once said, "because that's fifty percent stupid. When you have five skill positions, if all five of them are contributing to the offensive effort, then that's balanced. But this notion that if you hand it to one guy fifty percent of the time and you throw it to a combination of two guys fifty percent and you're really balanced, then you proudly pat yourself on the back and tell yourself that, well, then, you're delusional."

To Mike Leach, "balance" meant that every player who could make plays was given the opportunity to do so. Balance meant stressing out the defense as much as possible. Balance meant using the whole field. Balance meant using everything and everyone you had. That's what Leach did. It was as though he saw parts of the field that others could not and thought of ways to use them that did not occur to anybody else. He wondered why others passed so little, why he should remain committed to the run when there were so many more ways to attack through the air.

And he imagined ways to maximize his aerial attack that were not directly related to it, such as when he changed what seemed to be one of the most basic, unchangeable aspects of any offense: the amount of space between offensive linemen. Traditional offensive lines had the linemen bunched together practically shoulder to shoulder. Better for protecting the quarterback and running backs in the backfield, it seemed. Leach, however, spread them as far apart as the rules allowed, sometimes up to six feet. At a glance, this appears disastrous—a full two yards suddenly existed between blockers, seemingly giving rushers all the room in the world to invade the backfield. If the defensive players rushed through those gaps, however, they would be funneled toward the middle of the field, allowing an easy handoff or pitch to the running back, who would then have a wide-open path around the outside. Leach knew that the defensive linemen would be forced to line up more or less in line with the now-expanded offensive line, which effectively created more distance between them and the quarterback, giving the quarterback more time to throw.

As for the receivers themselves: with four receivers spread

across the line of scrimmage, Leach's offense could do just about anything.

One play, you send all the receivers deep. The next play, you do the exact same thing, except then you have one or two receivers dart across the middle in a "mesh" play. Then the next play: three receivers bolt down the field, one simply stays at the line of scrimmage for a quick gain. And the halfback is always available out of the backfield in that formation, too, either for a quick out pass or to make a surprise run up the field himself.

Sometimes—more often than you might think—receivers were given a simple command along with their route: "Just get open."

There was a wonderful philosophy at the core of all of this, too: not only was Leach making football more fun by getting more players involved and playing at a faster pace, but he was also showing his players just how much he trusted them. The traditional way of coaching—developing a slew of complex plays and ordering players to learn them—lorded the coach's authority over players. Leach's way of coaching—throwing a few cool plays into a bunch of different formations and telling players that they could do with them more or less what they wanted to once the ball was snapped—showed the players how much he believed in them.

And for all this, Leach once claimed not to even have an official playbook. Leach's reasoning: "All a playbook does is document what you do." Now he says that of course he had a playbook, but it wasn't something he religiously adhered to. Rather, Leach's playbook was like a set of guidelines to riff on. To teach his players, he mainly used film and on-field repetition. He and his coaching staff drilled the plays over and over—and over and over again—to make sure they knew how to execute them. This was all better than playbooks, to Leach. Playbooks were tedious and made players' brains lazy, keeping them from concentrating on the field when it was time to learn. Without a playbook, they had to *really* focus: "You're taking off their little swimming wings," Leach said. "We're going to be swimming in some pretty rough waters, so you'd better know how to stay afloat."

The Red Raiders didn't worry about trying to outsmart the defense. They just wanted to out-execute them. Rather than trying to be cleverer than the other team, Leach preached that the true goal was to simply do what they did better than the other team did what they did. And what Leach did was keep defenses off balance, either repeatedly lining up in the same formation only to use a different play every time, or line up in different formations only to run the same play out of it every time. And in Mike Leach's offense, the options were virtually endless for a smart and capable quarterback teamed with a smart and capable coach.

Lincoln asked question after question, and he learned so much so quickly that Leach assigned Lincoln to be his scout team quarterback, a rare position of trust for a freshman. To many, it's not a glamorous position, but the scout team's job is to get the defensive starters ready for their next opponent, so the players have to be sharp. Leach chose Lincoln because he saw the same things in him that Lincoln's people back home in Muleshoe had seen.

Lincoln wasn't just smart for Muleshoe. He was just smart.

In the days after sitting through the ninety-minute lecture on the intricacies of dip tobacco, Lincoln watched as Leach rewrote some of his own plays in real time.

By this point in his career, Leach had committed to the four-receiver spread and stuck his quarterback in shotgun all the time. He took the tight end and lined him up to the right, and he moved the split end to the left. He quit worrying about whether the offense was symmetrical. He gave the quarterback the option to change the play at the line of scrimmage, and he committed to never backing down from a challenge. No "bunker mentality," as he put it. Attack, attack, attack: "Okay, they're blitzing from our left side. Good, good. Then let's throw a slant right behind it."

Leach's Air Raid concepts now began clicking on a level like never before.

This seems due in large part to three developments: Kliff Kingsbury was now in his third year as Leach's quarterback, so he was comfortable with the new system; Leach had discovered one of the brightest diamonds in the rough ever in unrecruited receiver Wes Welker; and Leach began experimenting more with his offense, in part to maximize Welker's talents.

One of the biggest changes he made was what he did with the concept known as Four Verticals. So far he'd used it only as a deep-pass concept, sending all four receivers sprinting down the field. "We got to thinking about all this space we weren't utilizing," Leach writes in his book *Swing Your Sword*. His imagination took a basic concept and transformed it by having his quarterback and receivers study the defense *on the move*, working out various points in the receivers' routes for them to decide whether to keep sprinting downfield or to stop and turn one way or another, responding to the defense. "The execution of this requires months and even years of practice," Leach writes. "However, the space is always there, and it's impossible for the defense to cover."

The *Smart Football* blogger Chris B. Brown called Leach a "backyard coach." He writes: "This is not an uncommon theme in football: great players often do as much to make the game evolve (from both protagonist as well as antagonist perspectives) as coaches. And the great leap forward for Texas Tech and Leach in 2002–03 was largely sparked by a happenstance combination of this read-on-the-run four verticals plus Wes Welker plus Mike Leach: it was the perfect marriage of the greatest backyard play in football (get open) with one of the greatest backyard players of all time in Welker with maybe the greatest backyard coach to ever roam an actual, honest-to-god Division I sideline."

With Welker, who had gone unrecruited out of high school, turning out to be a shockingly great receiver, Leach's natural creativity and impulse to keep growing his Air Raid concepts led to a breakthrough in its evolution. He started creating plays designed almost solely for Welker to do his thing and get open. If the defense used a zone scheme to cover spaces of the field, the Air Raid would find pockets in the space. If the defense shifted to man-to-man, then they'd just run the coverage ragged until the inevitable lapse from confusion or fatigue. They wore defensive players out not through brute force, the way old running attacks did, but rather through exhausting speed.

What made Leach's Air Raid offense so successful wasn't just its relentlessness, or its high-octane energy, or some sort of magical complexity. In fact, the opposite: its simplicity. That, more than maybe anything, was what Lincoln loved about it. It was simple, so it was efficient. In simplicity, there was room for infinite creativity.

"The beauty at Tech," Lincoln says, "was the consistency. The almost obsessive devotion to what we were doing."

The offense exploded, a long-simmering revolution in college football erupted, and Leach firmly established the Air Raid as the future of football. The Red Raiders threw the ball all over the place. Kingsbury ended up passing for 5,017 total yards and forty-five touchdowns and won the Sammy Baugh Trophy, which goes to the country's best passer every year. Tech went 9–5 overall, 5–3 in the Big 12, outscored its opponents 537–439, and averaged 38.4 points per game, sixth-highest in the country. In the Tangerine Bowl, against Clemson, the Red Raiders racked up 555 yards of total offense and Kingsbury threw for 375 yards and three touchdowns, carrying Tech to its first bowl game win in seven years. The final score: Texas Tech 55, Clemson 15.

Meanwhile, Lincoln was doing all he could to prove himself, to fix his arm, to create the future he saw for himself. On the practice fields and in team meetings and in quarterback position group sessions, he asked question after question after question. He put in his work in the weight room, whose wall of windows looked out over the practice field, where he was working hard to go from scout team to true backup to, one day, starting quarterback.

But his arm wasn't getting stronger. The damage done by the injury was beginning to seem insurmountable. Nothing worked. He couldn't get back to his over-the-top form. "I knew that I just physically wasn't what I used to be," Lincoln says. "And I knew, mentally, I could do it. And that was frustrating for me . . . I couldn't throw it as good, as a senior in high school, or a freshman in college, as I could as a seventh grader. It was just different. And that part was frustrating for me. I felt like I could compete at that level."

Dana Holgorsen, the inside receivers coach, went to Lincoln one day and said, "You know, you're not a very good quarterback, but you're asking a lot of really, really smart questions."

Lincoln, he added, should consider coaching.

Lincoln didn't listen.

He kept playing. Kept dreaming. Kept working, lifting, rehabbing. And he just kept struggling. Receivers would run their routes perfectly, but he couldn't get them the ball. Team morale was slipping. Receivers started getting frustrated when Lincoln was their quarterback during throwing drills or scrimmages. Whereas Lincoln in high school would get mad about receivers not catching his perfect passes, now receivers were getting mad about not getting passes after running perfect routes.

Despite Lincoln's glaring physical limitations, however, Leach loved him. Arm strength wasn't a top priority for him when he evaluated quarterbacks, and he thought it was a mistake when others made it one. "The reason teams struggle when evaluating quarterbacks is that sometimes their priorities are out of order," he once said. "They get caught up in arm strength, size, and speed. Things that are easy to measure. 'Did you see the guy throw it through the goalposts while kneeling at midfield?' That's great, but last time I checked you don't throw passes in games from your knees. I've got defensive ends with great arm strength, but they aren't accurate. I bet they would love to play quarterback. Arm strength is about sixth on the list of what I look for in a quarterback. First, I want to see how accurate he is, and if he can make good decisions. Then I want to see if he's tough, has good feet, and has leadership qualities. After all of that, then I'll consider how much arm strength and speed he has. If he isn't accurate and doesn't make good decisions, then he isn't going to be very good at bringing out the best in your other players . . . My guy had better be smart, because I'm going to let him check from goal line to goal line. I can't have a guy with below-average intelligence."

That's what Leach loved about Lincoln: his intelligence. All of the questions he'd been asking, his obsessive search for the *why* behind the plays. "I was gonna cut him," Leach says, "but he had a good grasp of kind of the why on every play. *Okay, this happens so that this will happen, and when that and that happen, this will happen, too.* And he just sorta understood the layers and the dimensions of the passing game, for a young guy, very quickly."

His arm, however—his arm just wasn't getting better. In the summer of 2003, before Lincoln's sophomore season, Holgorsen and Sonny Dykes, the outside receivers coach, met with Leach about it. "An intervention," Holgorsen said.

He's awful, they said. *Team morale is low because you're giving this kid reps. Our receivers are running routes knowing there's zero chance the ball is gonna get to them.*

Leach was torn. He loved Lincoln, but he also knew that Lincoln didn't have what it took physically to be the quarterback Leach needed. "Physically, he wasn't what we were looking for at quarterback," Leach says. "Funky throwing motion. Sidearm. Inaccurate. Weak. Pushed the ball. Kinda loopy. Basically, he did everything pretty good as far as knowing what to *do.* Disciplined. But weak arm."

But Leach had an idea, one that could be a win for everyone. "I've always tried to be as broad-minded as possible," he says. Above all, he says, "I want smart people." And he was always looking for smart people to add to his coaching staff. "That's always got to be the first thing you do," he once said, "because that determines what kind of success you're going to have. You have to find the right people who believe in what you do and who are willing to work hard. Once you have the right guys around you, then you can start focusing on everything else."

One Friday morning while Lincoln was in the weight room, Leach called Lincoln into his office. Leach wanted to talk to him in private.

Lincoln walked in and shook Leach's hand and sat down. The practice fields lay wide and green beyond the office windows.

Leach had just cut two quarterbacks. "I got nine guys," Leach told him. "I can't keep everybody. And I got these guys, they're on scholarship. So I gotta keep those right there. We're only looking for one. And you don't happen to be that one."

"But," Leach went on, "great news. I got an opening here. You can work with me."

4

Decisions

MIKE LEACH SAW THAT Lincoln Riley had a future as a coach, and Leach knew what the struggle to become a coach was like. His journey had been hard. He and his wife, Sharon—with their young daughter—had once lived in a college dorm. He made $3,000 a year at his first coaching job. At Iowa Wesleyan, he'd made $13,000 and lived in a moldy, mildewed trailer. Eventually, at Valdosta State, they'd graduated to a two-bedroom apartment, but by then they also had a second daughter, and he was still earning less than $40,000. He'd taken classes so that he could defer his student loan payments.

All that, after having moved from job to job to job for years.

He calls it a "nomadic existence," adding, "The hours are brutal. The recruiting travel is insane. . . . I'd be on the road three weeks at a time." He says, "Even if you are fortunate enough to rise up the college ranks, your family is going to end up moving around a lot. . . . The question isn't if you're gonna move, it's when you're gonna move."

At Valdosta, he and Sharon shared a Cadillac he'd bought before he decided to become a coach; now the car had two hundred thousand miles on it. Leach rode a bike to work. He wasn't able to buy a house until he got to Kentucky, when he was thirty-six years old. But he'd learned a lot in that time, a lot that a smart young man like Lincoln could put to good use. He was offering Lincoln a leg up on the rest of his life. Lincoln, clearly, would never be a quarterback, but Leach thought he could be one hell of a coach. "He seemed like a real smart guy eager to learn," Leach says. "And . . . I figured, *Well what the heck, I can roll the dice with this guy.* Because this wasn't just a garden variety student assistant. He was gonna be my personal assistant. Go where I go."

The advantages this gave Lincoln were incalculable: he was going to be right in the middle of everything happening with the team, from the head coach's perspective. "For good or bad," Leach says, "whatever the pulse of our team was, he was gonna be right in the center of it."

There was a downside to it: "The bad of it is, the hours are ridiculous," Leach says. "So you needed a guy smart enough to balance his academics, as well as basically follow me around, and tend to me."

All that said, a job like this—personal assistant to college football's newest sensation of a coach—was a once-in-a-lifetime chance for a nineteen-year-old kid. "I'm thinking, you know, he's gonna be excited about this," Leach says. "Because it's a heck of an opportunity. . . . I'll take a heck of a lot more walk-on quarterbacks than I'll take a guy to be my personal assistant."

So Leach laid this out for Lincoln, and Lincoln's reaction was . . . subdued, to say the least. Where Leach saw the great opportunity he was offering, Lincoln saw a coach taking away his opportunity to play. Lincoln recalls, "He gave me the option—*Look, you can compete to be the third quarterback and go from there, but I've really kind of seen that, being a head coach, I could use somebody to help me with the quarterbacks, especially the young quarterbacks, and I'd be interested in having you do this . . . if you wanted to be a coach.* And we talked about it. And when he first brought it up . . . I wasn't ready to stop playing . . . And I was like, *Hell no.*"

Leach says, "He explains to me what I'm missing out on, and how, you know, he's the guy that can lead us to the promised land, and I don't understand the full picture of it."

Lincoln wasn't a jerk about it. "He was real polite," Leach says. "Lincoln's always real polite, you know?"

But Lincoln didn't want to listen.

So they kept talking.

Leach told Lincoln, "You can contribute more than that if you're helping me with the coaching. And not only that, but you're setting yourself up for a great career. Not that you can't do that if you don't finish playing. But this would give you an earlier start, and this would be a unique opportunity, because we throw the ball more than anybody. Not only do we throw the ball more than anybody, but people are adopting our offense. There's a bunch of other ones you can go get tied up into, and nobody cares about those offenses."

They talked for about an hour.

When Lincoln left, he remained unconvinced.

"He said he had to go think about it," Leach says. "Had to go talk to some people."

Leach couldn't believe it.

"I wasn't pissed," he says. "Because you know, people, it takes a while for stuff to sink in, you know? At least, it always did with me . . . But I'm thinking, this opportunity—there's people been coaching for ten years that would walk on glass to come do this. And I got this kid who's eighteen or nineteen, and he's *thinking about* whether to do this—or walk on? This is basically an invitation—there's twenty-four hours in a day, and you might as well spend it with me. Now, who wouldn't wanna do that?"

Here, Leach was beginning to do more than show Lincoln how to just be himself—he was also showing Lincoln who he really was. And as much as he wanted to be a quarterback, Lincoln just wasn't one anymore. But that would take some time to accept. It's hard work, letting go of who we think we are to become who we really are.

Lincoln got in his truck and went for a drive.

He drove out of Lubbock on Highway 87 South, and he drove for hours. It's a drive that feels like driving in a painting, a drive that's good for thinking, for feeling pain, and seeking answers, and finding the strength to let things go. The road takes you past all manner of West Texas life. The Hallelujah Trail Cowboy Church. Hardin Creek. Venison World. A prison. Kelly Creek. Maverick Creek. Freeman Creek. Eden. And then you still have five more hours to go.

Much of the road is two-lane, even though it's highway, but there's ample shoulder on the side of the road, and it's common West Texas courtesy for bigger vehicles to pull over and allow smaller ones to get by. Cell service is in and out, mostly out. You pass through a few more small towns like Eden. You pass ranch after ranch. Brodeck Ranch. RFS Ranch. Panther Creek Ranch. Creek after creek, too. Tiger Creek. Lost Creek. You pass cattle resting in the shade of overgrown mesquite trees. You drive over hills on winding roads that weave around valleys, some of which look like scaled-down Grand Canyons. A few hours in, on the way out of Llano, the two-lane highway gives way to a breathtaking horizon that makes you think of God.

And then, not far from the destination, you pass a church that has a sign out front: GOD IS OUR STEERING WHEEL, NOT OUR SPARE TIRE.

Soon after that, about seven hours into the drive, you hit Kingsland, and then you're only five minutes out. Suddenly the drive doesn't feel like it was as long as it was. Long drives don't feel as long here as they do other places, especially once you get where you're going. Distance feels different like that in West Texas.

You come to a small side road that leads to a dirt road that leads you where you're going. You follow the dirt road—somehow even the dirt seems brighter under the Texas sky—and come upon a village of mobile homes. Follow the road through the village and follow the signs, and shortly you come upon the only paved portion of the area, a boat ramp just past a large gasoline drum and a red trailer that serves as an office. The boat ramp dips into the water next to a couple of decks with some tables and chairs overlooking the water and giving way to docks for the boats. The water takes over from there, lying across the horizon before the wild trees and brush on the opposite shore. The water is a beautiful blue-green and you just want to dive into it under the hot Texas sun.

This is Woody's Fisherman's Haven in Horseshoe Bay, part of Lake Lyndon B. Johnson, formed where the Colorado and Llano Rivers meet. It's a quiet little nook of southwest Texas about an hour north of Austin. Lincoln's parents have a mobile home here, their personal vacation spot. There's not much here, in a good way. The trailers, and a trailer with an office, and another trailer with a cooler full of treats and some other lake gear for sale. Lincoln learned to water-ski here.

And now, with Leach's words rolling around his mind, he'd come here to think.

"My little getaway spot," he calls it.

He spent the weekend here. He made a few phone calls. His parents. Coaches. Friends. He even called the folks at the smaller schools who'd recruited him, to see if they still wanted him. All the responses came back more or less the same. On the one hand, if he really wanted to keep playing football, to keep being a quarterback, he likely could if he transferred to a smaller school. But he had the perfect opportunity, right now, to do something for his future that he'd never get to do again.

"I just kept thinking, *I want to play*," he says. "But something in the back of my mind was like, *But you might not get a chance like this*."

What it really came down to was this: Was he ready to grow up?

We often know what to do before we feel we can do it. It takes a while for what makes sense to our head to work its way into our heart.

Lincoln went out on the boat and floated around the bay. "Fished some," he says. "Skied some. Just kinda got away from it all. Just kinda to clear my head . . . Just trying to get the emotion out of it in the beginning, and just try to think about it as clear-headed as I could."

Get the emotion out of it.

Don't chase the linebacker.

That's what had happened that day four years earlier in Amarillo. That pass. That perfect pass. That interception by that linebacker. He'd done everything right and something had gone wrong anyway, and that's why he was hurt now.

Except that wasn't completely true.

Throwing an interception isn't what dislocated his shoulder.

What went wrong wasn't what hurt him.

What hurt him was how he'd reacted.

What hurt him was chasing the linebacker.

What hurt him was hitting the linebacker as hard as he could when he caught him.

The interception had upset him, and he wanted to do something with the pain and anger that caused, and the release of chasing and hitting the linebacker had felt good, damn good. It wasn't smart, but he was pissed.

But now it was hurting him for the rest of his life.

"He could've really taken off, career-wise, had he not done that," his high school coach David Wood says. "I think with his brains and size, he could've been as good as any college quarterback there was, really."

Lincoln looked ahead at the rest of his life and tried to see the world ahead of him. He could transfer, become a quarterback somewhere else, and keep playing the game he loved. Or he could start learning what it meant to be a coach.

"I thought I would like coaching," he says. "I knew I loved it. And I knew I loved the college level."

A few of the people he talked to told him the same thing, more or less—that he'd probably never get an opportunity like this again, but it also meant he was going to have to go ahead and grow up.

That wasn't Lincoln's worry. "I wasn't scared to go ahead and grow up," he says. "I wasn't the guy that felt like I needed the college experience for four years. That part of it really had no effect on me."

What had an effect on him was the fact that to become a football coach, he had to quit being a football player. It was a pure and simple thing, and it hurt.

It's the same thing that inevitably hurts every athlete. It's the day he realizes he can no longer play the game he loves the way he loves to. It's when he realizes that his body can no longer do the things he knows how to do so well in his mind. It is a time of real grief.

An athlete spends his life in the game, and that doesn't just mean the time he puts into it, but the energy he gives to it, the passion he gives to it, the way he chooses the game over one thing after another over and over again. A man so committed to his game is a man in love. And when the man and his game must part ways, the harshest pain may be that it is never the game's fault. The game is still there. The game hasn't gone anywhere. The man just can't be part of it anymore, because he is no longer the man he once was. As the sportswriter John Feinstein once observed: "Athletes die twice."

Lincoln was in mourning.

"It took a little bit," he says. "It took some time to talk myself into it."

When the weekend was over, Lincoln got back in his truck and drove back to Lubbock. Back past the ranches and the creeks and the cattle, back around the valleys that look like miniature Grand Canyons, back through Eden.

Same as it's a good drive for thinking and sitting with pain and asking questions about it, it's a good drive for sitting with answers you've found and making peace with them. Sometimes the best thing to do is just let life take whatever it's taking and go. Be smart. Learn from whatever made things go the way you didn't want them to go. Breathe. Someone once said that Anger is just Sad's bodyguard, anyway. Let yourself be sad. Breathe some more. Let life do whatever it's doing to you in the moment. Make as clearheaded a decision as you can from there. Make the most of what you still have left. Of the gifts you still possess. Sometimes the strongest thing to do is just stay calm. Accept what is, rather than rage against what you wish wasn't. *Don't chase the linebacker.*

Somewhere between Horseshoe Bay and Lubbock, Lincoln knew what he'd do.

"I settled on it when I was driving back," he says.

Maybe he couldn't do what he wanted to do, and maybe he couldn't chase his dreams anymore, but he could help other guys chase theirs.

Back in Lubbock, he told Leach he'd take the job.

"I knew I was taking a gamble with him in the first place," Leach says. "You talk about unproven—unproven as a quarterback—you're even more unproven as somebody I can deal with. Of course, I can always fire him if I get tired of him, so I took comfort in that."

5

Work

By the time Lincoln Riley became Mike Leach's full-time student assistant in the fall of 2003, his girlfriend, Caitlin Buckley, had joined him in Lubbock as a freshman at Texas Tech. When Tech's defensive coordinator, Ruffin McNeill, first saw Lincoln with Caitlin, he gave Lincoln a hard time. "I'm always the one on the staff who gets after the young guys, starts picking at them a little bit," McNeill says. "So I saw him and Caitlin walking around, and I said, 'How's somebody as pretty as you going with someone as ugly as that?'"

They'd met in high school. Caitlin was from Dimmitt, a small town some forty-five minutes northeast of Muleshoe, and although their high schools were rivals, they'd first caught each other's eye at basketball games. A year younger than Lincoln, Caitlin was a sweet blue-eyed blonde with a thick Southern accent and a big heart. She shared Lincoln's affection for small-town life. "I think a small town, Southern, you have a sense of community," she says. "Where maybe a large, more urban population is kind of out for themselves. There's only four thousand other people there, and you gotta live together, and make it work. You gotta be real."

She and Lincoln began dating during Lincoln's freshman year

at Tech, which Jody Wood, the wife of Lincoln's high school coach David Wood, remembers well. "The girls all wanted to date the Riley boys," she says. "And then they were like, *Dang, he's dating a Dimmitt girl.*"

Lincoln knew that at some point his playing career would end, and when that day came, he would become a coach. He and Caitlin just figured he would be a high school coach. She knew all about the coaching life—she was the granddaughter of a high school basketball coach named Kenneth Cleveland, a local legend.

Even as Lincoln began working with Leach, they didn't know just how far that would take Lincoln. "He was gonna be a high school coach," Caitlin says. "And I would be the coach's wife. And there would be a little town around us . . ."

She would teach and lead the cheerleaders and drive them to the games. He would coach the team and probably teach some classes, too. "And," she says, "just stay how we grew up. That's just kind of what we had initially thought would be our path. And that would have been great."

But now Lincoln was on the college coaching ladder, and he began to see a whole new world laid out before him. He would soon learn just how hungry he really was.

Across five NCAA divisions, there are fifteen hundred head coaches in college football. Becoming one of them is not easy. Before they become head coaches, they're one of the roughly ten thousand assistant coaches. Below the offensive and defensive coordinator positions, there are position coaches—for quarterbacks, receivers, linemen, and so on. Sometimes a coordinator will also coach a position; for instance, an offensive coordinator might also be the quarterbacks coach. It's not the military or the coal mines, but it's not an easy life for those coaches, and especially for their families. The hours are long. The money's good at the top, which helps—the average head coach's salary at the Division I level is over a million dollars, and some assistant coaches at top programs can earn well into the six figures—but there's rarely job security.

Most begin their careers as student assistants, or enrolling in graduate school and becoming grad assistants. Student/grad assistants are basically unpaid interns working for a team while getting their degree, and theirs is unglamorous work. They break down film, run camps, and generally do whatever the rest of the coaching staff needs them to do or doesn't want to do. They're usually given titles like "assistant video coordinator."

If you want to become a coach, you start there. For people who don't understand how the system works, it's not the sort of thing parents might fully understand or brag about to the neighbors. And just because that's how the system works doesn't guarantee future success; it's paying your dues with astonishingly long odds and little immediate return. The lessons it teaches you are invaluable, though: you learn the profession from the ground up and from the inside out. To go from grad assistant to head coach is a long process that will take years and appear grueling to anyone other than those who love it. As in most professions, some rise faster than others due to a fortuitous blend of unique ability, connections, and luck, but even for them, the road is demanding and all-consuming.

All that said: for a young guy like Lincoln, who really loves football and wants to become a coach, a student assistant job is the first step toward the dream. It can suck, but in the way that teaches you things you need to know.

And Lincoln had already skipped a step or two. He was no ordinary student assistant. "Those guys are a dime a dozen," Leach says. "Most student assistants will just get sandwiches, get coffee, you know?" Lincoln was going to be on Leach's hip—figuratively speaking—pretty much whenever he wasn't in class or sleeping. And Leach didn't want sandwiches from Lincoln. He wanted football. He wanted to see what Lincoln could do with that gifted brain of his. "Lincoln was my direct assistant," he says. "That was unique . . . He was like, literally, my right-hand guy."

It was, indeed, a golden opportunity, a way for Lincoln to make the most of the intelligence with which he was gifted. But intelligence alone would not be enough. Many smart and talented people have their gifts undone by entitlement and laziness. What turns gifts into wealth is work.

And not just the work of time spent, but also sacrifices made, growing pains endured, the comfort of who you are given up for the discomfort of learning what you're capable of.

For starters, that meant crossing an important dividing line: Lincoln had gone from player—from teammate—to member of the coaching staff. Though he'd never been a party guy, he liked beers with teammates as much as the next college kid. That was mostly gone now—partly to create appropriate boundaries, but also because of the demands of the job.

"That wasn't part of life that I missed that much," he says. "I really didn't. As I was doing that, I didn't find myself, when we were in the office late, wishing I was at a party, or, you know, doing whatever most young guys do at that age. That didn't tug on me very much."

What tugged on him was learning what he could do next with this game that he so loved. It gave his active mind something to run with, and seemed to sate the hunger in his heart.

Lincoln didn't say much the first couple of years working for Leach, not unless he had to. "He was quiet—he was a listener, you know," Leach says. "He was a listener, but you gotta understand, at a fairly young age . . . he was together enough that I felt like he could handle it."

Lincoln asked smart questions when he didn't understand something, but maybe even more important, he didn't bullshit Leach by trying to seem smarter or more competent than he was. Leach could trust him. "I can't stand dishonest people," Leach says. "And Lincoln—he's a very straightforward, loyal, honest guy. And honest, loyal people generally move further."

This honesty is a hallmark of Lincoln's success, because in this world there's too much to learn too quickly for you to go anywhere fast if you're not honest with yourself. You can't fake your way through this world. It tests you too harshly. And honesty came naturally to him. Like all boys making the turn from their teens into their twenties and beginning to experiment with the kind of men they might one day become, Lincoln seemed to unconsciously fall back on what he knew best, which was the honesty on which his parents raised him—and the work ethic along with it.

"If you're going to be successful in this business, you have to work crazy hard," Leach says. "And he did work crazy hard."

Ruffin McNeill agrees. "He was just a hard worker," McNeill says. "Getting his elbows and knees dirty was no problem. My ethos is *earned not given*. And you saw him not get a dime, but work like he was getting a hundred thousand a year."

"There wasn't any of me having to tell him, *Do this, do that, be here, be there*," Leach says. "He was a very organized guy. And a clear-thinking guy. And as time went on, I could put more and more on him, and I could just have him handle things."

As a result, Lincoln embodied how to get ahead in the world. "In his case," Leach says, "the most important thing you do is, you gotta get your hands around enough stuff, and then do it all confidently enough . . . to where it's extremely inconvenient to function without you. Lincoln's one of those guys. And that happened fairly quickly."

The more work Leach gave Lincoln to handle, the better he became at handling everything. "He did so many things so well," Leach says. "Especially with regard to me and my job."

Lincoln's responsibilities for Leach were, in classic Leach fashion, free-flowing and often open-ended. "His job," Leach says, "was to tend to anything I needed."

This was time-consuming, to say the least. The work demanded a hundred hours some weeks. No matter. "He was always available," Leach says.

Leach and Lincoln worked on everything together: breaking down film, planning practices, developing new plays, on and on. And Leach was quickly impressed by his new assistant's perceptiveness. "Even though he was a young guy, he was smart and insightful," Leach recalls. "We'd watch film, we'd break down opponents, put the script together, put practice together, the whole thing. He's just a brilliant guy. He's one of those guys who will think of stuff before you think of it."

That expanded beyond film preparation and analysis. "It's not just simply about *Okay, when do we meet the quarterbacks? What plays do we run?* Because I got all these other things, too: the fundraising, the PR, the administrative stuff. He would be somewhat administrative, despite the fact that he was nineteen."

Leach started having Lincoln give instructions not only to the players, but also to the other coaches on staff. "I'd say, go down there and gather up those guys and tell them this," Leach says. "And he didn't seem to have a big problem doing it, whether it was the players or the coaches. Now once in a while, the coaches may have come down with some complaint whether I'm watching film or whatever, but he didn't have a problem delivering the message, and just understanding [what I needed] if I had him, *Here, I need you to handle this, I need to go speak to such and such*. He really didn't have any problem with it. He'd just do what was necessary. Step up and say what I asked him to say, or organize what I asked him to organize."

There was little limit to what sort of tasks Leach could give Lincoln to accomplish. "Announcements or stuff I need people to attend," Leach says. "Some issue in the weight room or workouts or academics . . . Or like recruiting calls, I . . . said I wanted to personally see [the coaching staff's] recruiting logs each week just to make sure they were recruiting like I hired them to do."

Lincoln was professional about it, too. "He was always a very mature guy," Leach says. "One of those guys where you can tell he logged a lot of time with adults growing up. You know?"

Lincoln actively sought not only to do what he was told, but also to create his own contributions. When Leach gave him a task, Lincoln did not blindly do what he was told. He would talk things through with Leach first. "He would think carefully about it," Leach says. "It was, *Let me see if I can help decide. Let me see if I can contribute something to help* . . . And he would. I certainly didn't accept all of his ideas any more than I ever have anybody else's, whether they are better than mine or worse. But if I thought they were better, I accepted them." Seemingly anything Leach gave Lincoln to do, Lincoln sought to improve. "There'd be a chart or something," Leach recalls, "and he would make a better chart."

Because of how much Leach came to trust him, Lincoln soon became more than a personal assistant: he became an integral part of Leach's process. He began spending games in the coaches' box above the stadium, where he sat beside Dana Holgorsen, Leach's co-offensive coordinator. Though Leach called the plays, he relied on Holgorsen to provide him the bird's-eye view. "[Lincoln] was up there in the box beside Dana, learning a lot," Leach says. "He was the guy that would chart things for Dana . . . and Dana was the guy I'd talk to."

Lincoln charted critical information that he would then feed to Holgorsen so that Holgorsen could in turn feed it to Leach: down and difference of yardage to first down, defensive play calls, whether the defense blitzed or not, what coverage they were in, and if the defense "stunted"—a term meaning the defensive linemen quickly switched positions just before or after a snap in an attempt to confuse the offensive line.

This was enormous responsibility to place in the hands of such a young student assistant. "Sometimes, it's tough getting guys at that age to just show up," Leach says. "They don't show up too many times, you pack up their locker and cut 'em, just like you would a player."

Beyond that, Leach came to lean on Lincoln for one thing above all. "His single biggest role," Leach says, "was as a sounding board. Anything on my mind, he would sit there and bat it back and forth and play devil's advocate. Offer better ideas. *What's a better route than this one?* Or, *I don't think I like this, what do you think of this?* Well, *it's bad because*—you know, you just bat things back and forth."

Leach and Lincoln spent hours in the coach's office and in conference rooms talking concepts and ideas and brainstorming new wrinkles on the playbook. And the more they worked together, the more in sync they became, to the point where they would sit down to watch film and find themselves reading each other's minds. "Bringing up something at the same time the other is thinking about it," Leach says. "Our efforts really complemented one another."

Their efforts complemented one another more, perhaps, than Leach first imagined when he offered Lincoln the job. "I was good at a bunch of concepts," Leach says. "He was good at, how are we gonna organize it all? He'd be very helpful at stringing it all together." Lincoln seemed to have a preternatural feel for the forces at work between bodies on football fields, the ways they pulled and pushed each other around, the way one receiver's route pulled a safety away from another receiver while pushing a linebacker away from yet another, and the ways these pushes and pulls created empty space on the field, the open grass of the field bending and flowing around players like water.

And so began an era in which the Red Raiders, in the words of Chris Brown at *Smart Football*, "blitzkrieged the previously conservative Big 12 Conference."

In 2003, Tech's new quarterback, B. J. Symons, set the NCAA record for most passing yards in a season, breaking Kliff Kingsbury's record from the season before.

In 2004, another new quarterback, Sonny Cumbie, led the Red Raiders to a win over No. 4 California in the Holiday Bowl.

In 2005, yet another new quarterback, Cody Hodges, led the NCAA in passing and Tech as a team led the whole NCAA in passing. The Red Raiders were also the No. 4–ranked scoring offense with 39.4 points per game, and No. 6 in total offense, with 495 yards per game. Hodges was No. 2 in the nation with 396 yards per game.

Tech frequently led the Big 12—one of the monster conferences in college football—in passing yards and total offense. The Red Raiders made innovative tweaks not only to their myriad passing routes but also to the basic, underappreciated aspects of the game, such as the offensive line. They spread their offensive linemen as far apart as they could at scrimmage, which pushed defensive linemen farther away from the quarterback and more readily exposed line-backers or defensive backs who might be trying to sneak up for a blitz. They committed to running virtually every play out of the shotgun, which gave the quarterback yet more time while also letting him see the field better. They *hurried*, too, committing to getting off as many plays as possible every game, exhausting defenses and creating overwhelming momentum for themselves.

"We were kind of the black sheep," Lincoln says. "We were doing something there that was so unique and I think other people did not know what to make of it."

It all came from those long days and nights reviewing film and batting ideas back and forth with Lincoln. "He got to be right there as we did it," Leach says. "And whether he agreed with everything or not, he was part of helping install it, teach it, reinforce stuff right there on the field. Some is by trial and error. Some just takes off immediately. And some wasn't a good idea to begin with."

But the good ideas were *really* good.

In 2006, Tech was ranked No. 8 in the nation, No. 3 in passing offense, and No. 6 in total offense. They were a legitimate contender for a national championship.

By then, the football world had officially woken up to what Mike Leach was doing—and it was freaking people out. Jim Schwartz, coaching the NFL's Tennessee Titans, remembered feeling anxiety as he studied Tech's game film in 2005. Speaking about the Tech offensive line in particular—which would sometimes stretch as many as fifteen yards across the field—Scwhartz told a writer, "It scares people."

In 2006, Lincoln graduated from Texas Tech, but he remained on Leach's coaching staff. But even as he was settling into the coaching life, he became involved with his hometown team again, too. His old coach from Muleshoe High School, David Wood, was trying to learn more about what Tech was doing, in hopes of installing a similar spread offense of his own. One day that summer, he drove to Lubbock with his coaching staff to learn from the great man himself.

They congregated in the big team meeting room with Mike Leach, who was happy to talk to anyone who wanted to learn about his new offense. Leach started breaking down the offense for them, but after about five minutes, he stopped. "You know," he said, "Lincoln's from Muleshoe, and y'all know him, and he can tell you just as much about the offense as I can, so I'm going to turn it over to him."

Wood wasn't happy. "I really want to hear it from the man," he says. "Because at the time I really didn't know how much Lincoln knew . . . I wanted to get it straight from the horse's mouth."

Wood's frustration quickly faded. "Once Lincoln started talking, we got so much more out of Lincoln than we ever could have from Leach," he says. "Because Leach, he would hold back on some of the things he was talking about and not give us the full extended play or philosophy behind it or whatever. As soon as Lincoln started talking, it was a completely different atmosphere . . . We all relaxed more, and we didn't have to try to draw information out. Lincoln was providing anything we were asking. And he just spent, I don't know, three or four hours with us. It was just a completely different tone and experience than with Leach. Which I appreciate Leach doing that for us. But when Lincoln took over then . . . the whole coaching staff knew that Lincoln was the real deal."

The offense was so simple: "See the green grass," Wood says. "And get the ball to the green grass. Whether it's the run game, the pass game, it's simple. It's backyard football. Run where they ain't. Throw where they ain't."

Lincoln also taught them small, simple tricks. "Decoying," Wood says. "Decoy calls were incredibly advantageous to us. You get a quarterback who, he's going like this, and he just glances over there, and he makes a dummy call, and everyone says, hey, watch over here, watch over here . . . And that's what Lincoln said. He said, *Hey, say something when you're under center all the time. Say something whether it's dummy or not. Then they'll never know. If all you gotta do is talk when you're gonna change a play, they'll pick that up.*"

Lincoln also cautioned them against trying to mix the old with the new. Wood says, "One thing Lincoln said is, *If you really want to make this work, you can't mix this offense with your other offenses. Just do this. Just do this. You won't have time. The way you practice, you won't have time to practice.*"

That fall, Lincoln's kid brother, Garrett, a junior, became Muleshoe's starting quarterback. Lincoln, for years, had been helping Garrett as much as he could. Locals would regularly spot them on the field practicing together.

Garrett's senior year, he became a better quarterback than Lincoln ever was.

"One thing Leach told us is he had certain players he could [give]—he called it the green light," Wood says. "That means the quarterback can change it at any time that he feels like there's a better play and could get us the results of that situation, where a first down or whatever the deal was, he had the opportunity to make that change. Well, Garrett did it quite a bit. He changed the plays. Of course, we had certain things he could change, he couldn't call just any play. But he had the green light to change things, and it was through the learning of Lincoln and what he was looking at."

His senior year, Garrett was named Texas's AP Offensive Player of the Year for his division, the first of three Muleshoe quarterbacks to win this honor. Muleshoe football had become a bona fide force to be reckoned with. "It was all after we changed to the spread," Wood says.

Back in Lubbock, as the 2007 season rolled around, Lincoln saw the spread becoming a bigger part of football as he looked ahead. "We went year after year of not having the best talent and breaking all these records offensively and number one offense in the country year after year after year after year," Lincoln says. "And none of our other offensive coaches were getting any opportunities."

That's the mark of a respected and successful head coach as much as any success his own team has: how many of his assistant coaches get better job offers elsewhere. One of Leach's assistants, Art Briles, had become the head coach at Houston, but otherwise, that was it. "And," Lincoln says, "I remember, as a young coach, thinking, *I'm pretty sure if a couple guys can get opportunities, this can catch fire, but is anybody going to get a shot? Is there ever going to be any movement?*"

That year, Lincoln earned a substantial promotion, taking his next big step forward: Mike Leach named him Texas Tech's receivers coach. Lincoln was just twenty-three years old. "He was the youngest full-time assistant in America," Leach says. "Maybe ever."

6

Wunderkind

WHEN LINCOLN BECAME THE Texas Tech receivers coach, his father, Mike, told a reporter, "I don't think they would have had to pay him. He loved the job and he was used to working for nothing."

Even so, it wasn't a naturally smooth transition.

"I got a lot of crap on that," Mike Leach says. "There was some professional jealousy on that, too. Some guys feel gypped because this young guy got elevated at a younger age than they did."

And it wasn't just one or two guys, either. "Four guys are coming in," Leach says. "I got tired of it and I said, listen . . . there's people with twenty years' experience—I don't care about the years' experience they have. They didn't have five years' experience with me day and night, at my elbow. So even if you make the experience argument, Lincoln had more experience than they did."

At first, Lincoln didn't necessarily have the magic touch. He recalls that like many young men in their early twenties, he possessed a confidence in his ideas that was tremendous and unearned, and he presented those ideas with great passion and lack of tact. This created more than one toxic exchange, as he remembers it. "I had to learn there's a right way and a wrong way to do things," Lincoln says. "And I did some things the wrong way."

He was learning that his hunger was good, but only until he allowed his hunger to express itself in unhelpful fashion. And this hunger would grow strongest when he had an idea that he knew would work but that ran counter to the status quo. When it came time for communicating such ideas, he did so with "just pure aggressiveness," he recalls. "And probably a little bit of arrogance."

It's worth noting, though, that Leach says Lincoln wasn't as bad as he remembers. "I think he was probably just a little insecure," Leach says, "because he was a young guy."

Ruffin McNeill agrees; he doesn't recall Lincoln ever acting out of order. "I looked at it as confidence," he says. "He had confidence in his ability. He had confidence in his knowledge. And the suggestions, you've got to have some courage, too. With confidence comes courage, and with courage comes confidence. So it didn't bother me at all . . . And the coaches that were offended by it, that's their own fault. But I like seeing a young coach that has all those ideas."

Lincoln was probably more concerned with his demeanor than anyone else, hyperaware that the way he carried himself affected those around him. He held himself to a different standard. Hunger can be useful and productive and can lead to greatness, same as it can cause you to eat yourself alive. "I had so much tunnel vision if I had a good idea and I knew it could help," he says. "I never really thought about any ramifications. I have a good idea? I'm gonna speak up. I put people in the corner, and I didn't handle it well. So I had to learn that early."

Early on in anyone's career—especially a coach's career—it's all about finding the line between not stepping on toes or hurting feelings while making sure your thoughts get heard and your vision pursued. "You're always searching for that line," Leach says. "I mean, that's just part of the deal, no matter what you do."

Lincoln was dealing with some of the biggest names and most successful people in college football, a situation that could have been deeply intimidating for an inexperienced coach. "I think he covered it quite well," Leach says. "He was a guy who was very practical. You told him to do something, and once he understood what you wanted and how to do it, the bottom line—you embrace it, and he'd go do it. He wasn't a guy that hesitated. He wouldn't flinch at the task, you know?"

Lincoln handled himself with calm strength with the players and staff, too. Pranks and teasing and various acts of tomfoolery were commonplace at Texas Tech. For instance, table-topping: one person would kneel on all fours behind an unsuspecting victim as an accomplice then shoved said victim, sending him tumbling backward to the ground. "Yeah, they would do that stuff to him," Leach says. "But . . . he's not one of those guys who would fly off the handle and say, *You have to call me Coach Riley*, or nothing like that. He would just laugh it off and roll with it."

Leach and Lincoln had their disagreements at times, such as when Leach brought in the wide receiver Adam James in 2006. Adam's father, Craig James, had been a running back for the New England Patriots and then went on to a successful career as a broadcaster. Adam hadn't been recruited much, and Craig James persuaded Leach to take a flyer on the kid. Lincoln—and others on the coaching staff—had been skeptical of the decision, to put it mildly. "We adamantly doubted his talent" is how Lincoln once put it.

Adam grayshirted for the fall of 2006, meaning that he was invited to join the team, but not until the spring semester of his freshman year. And when he began working out with the team in the spring of 2007, Lincoln said, "[We] came to see that Adam actually had enough talent to help us out"—but also that he displayed poor work habits and attitude. "I . . . worried about Adam's effect on my other players," Lincoln said, describing him as having a "weak and conceited attitude."

Lincoln went on to describe Adam this way: "He has an unbelievable sense of entitlement because of who his father is; one that hurts himself and people around him."

Even so, the 2007 season went well for the Red Raiders. They were ranked No. 3 in the nation. They also led all major college teams in passing (more than 470 yards per game), ranked No. 2 overall in total offense (nearly 530 yards per game), and No. 7 in scoring (40.9 points per game). Quarterback Graham Harrell led the nation in total offense—and, with Lincoln as his position coach, wide receiver Michael Crabtree won the Biletnikoff Award, presented each year to the best wide receiver in college football. Lincoln's first year as a coach could not have gone much better. "And I'm just sitting there thinking, *All these guys think this is hard; this is easy*," Lincoln told a reporter once, laughing. "*My guy's catching three touchdowns every game. I'm the greatest receivers coach who ever walked on the planet*."

Leach raved about Lincoln to people such as his mentor, Donnie Duncan, with whom Lincoln had also become acquainted. "Lincoln was my right-hand guy for years, so he would've been in the room and overheard conversations between me and Donnie Duncan nonstop," Leach says. "Sometimes when some crisis is taking place, sometimes a social call. And then, you know, Donnie said, *Well, who's on your staff?*"

In 2008, the Red Raiders put together the best season in school history. They went 11–1, including a 39–33 win against Texas, the school's first win against a No. 1 team. That game was a huge moment for Tech; it was the premier game of the day in college football and the first time ESPN's *College GameDay* had ever broadcast from Lubbock. Some ten thousand students camped out near the stadium during the week prior, their tents circling the arena. Leach ordered them all pizza. Both teams were 8–0 entering the game, and Texas, led by the Heisman Trophy–winning quarterback Colt McCoy, seemed bound for a national championship. That the Longhorns lost to Tech was unfathomable. The Red Raiders, historically, were nobodies, whereas Texas was a college football giant. The game would later be memorialized as "when Michael Crabtree and Texas Tech broke Texas's heart," and people would talk about the game for years to come. It was a defining moment in the Mike Leach era. "They had some mojo out there in West Texas, where teams did seem to play a little bit differently," Texas defensive back Blake Gideon told a reporter. "Teams that would be hot that knocked off one or two teams would go through [Lubbock] . . . and they'd be a shell of themselves."

The Red Raiders went on to play in the Cotton Bowl, and even though they lost to No. 20 Mississippi, it was a phenomenal season. Michael Crabtree was named an All-American and won his second Biletnikoff Award, the only receiver ever to win it twice. "Any time," Lincoln told a reporter, "not just in football but in life, that you can do something that nobody else has ever done, you're on the right track."

And Lincoln got to share all of this with his kid brother, Garrett, who'd joined the Texas Tech team as a walk-on quarterback.

In the meantime, Lincoln was also playing a critical role for the Muleshoe High School team, aiding them on a quest for an undefeated season and a state championship.

Lincoln frequently spoke with David Wood throughout the 2008 season, advising him on Muleshoe's new offense. Mostly, they discussed plays. "Combinations, and depth of a receiver on a certain route, or something like that," Wood recalls.

One example: The team was having trouble with a drag route, in which a receiver crosses the field over the middle. Wood's receiver kept getting jammed up by linebackers. Lincoln told Wood that he was letting the receiver go too far downfield. *Just have him run straight across the offensive line*, Lincoln said. By the time he was crossing the line, the offensive linemen would already be drifting back into the pocket to deal with the pass rush, but the linebackers wouldn't be close. The receiver would be wide open. "It made all the difference in the world," Wood says.

Wood would regularly send film for Lincoln to watch, knowing there was a problem but not quite able to identify it himself. Sometimes a quarterback was waiting too long for one receiver to get open and missing other receivers who were already open. Other times a receiver running his route was accidentally bringing his defenders with him, jamming up the route of another receiver who could have been open had the first receiver gone in a different direction. "And he'd tweak it," Wood says, "and sure enough, he was usually right. He could see how it was all fitting together, how all the routes are fitting together . . . and he could say, *This one guy is messing the whole thing up*."

Lincoln stayed in close contact with Wood as the Mules moved through the playoffs. "He was involved a lot," Wood says. "Anytime we had a question, we'd pick up the phone and call him."

And then, as the team prepared for the state championship game, the town held a pep rally, for which Lincoln made the drive back to Muleshoe. He was to be the guest speaker. Lincoln walked back into his old hometown gym, where he was given quite the introduction by David Jenkins, the recently retired high school principal. Jenkins called him "a young man who has qualities that impress me more, probably, than anyone I have ever associated with in my almost forty years of education," and he went on to say, "I've never seen a young man that was as competitive as he was, or displayed the leadership that he had."

As he took the mic, Lincoln said, in an embarrassed drawl, "I don't know if I'm worthy of that introduction. I'm just glad if I don't pass out giving a speech up here."

But Lincoln knew what he needed to say. After introductory remarks praising the coaching staff and the team's achievements, he turned to the players, drawing on his own experience during Texas Tech's own chase for a championship. "Just do what you got here," he said. "Don't change anything. Just because this is a state championship game doesn't mean you have to try any harder, do anything more than you do every time. We always tell guys before every game, *We don't need any superheroes.* We need everybody to do your job, and do what you've done all year. That's why you're fourteen and O. That's why you're in a state championship game. Because you're a damn good football team."

"Seeing you guys in the state championship—it's very special," Lincoln went on. "I'll leave you with this one thing. I think it's very important. When you get out there between those lines tomorrow night, don't waste one second. Get out there the very first snap, the kickoff or kickoff return, those boys from Kirbyville will be on the opposite side of you—get out there and hit them in the mouth from the very first snap."

The crowd erupted at that, electrified, roaring louder than it had all night, drowning some of Lincoln's last words before he concluded, "Take it home, and make us all proud."

Two days later, Muleshoe beat Kirbyville by a score of 48–26, and their quarterback threw for three touchdowns to put him at sixty-one for the season, just three shy of the state record. He went on to be named the state's Player of the Year for his division. His name was Wes Wood, and he was Coach Wood's son.

By 2009, Texas Tech had established itself as a true force in college football, and Lincoln had established himself as a young man who was going places. "Donnie [Duncan] and I would talk," Charlie Sadler said, "and he asked me what I thought about Lincoln. I identified Lincoln as one of the top young coaches. He's highly intelligent, knows what he's doing."

Gil Brandt, a Dallas Cowboys executive for nearly three decades before retiring to become an analyst, marveled at what he saw when he spent time at Texas Tech's practices. He told a reporter that Lincoln was "the next great young coach in college football."

And soon Lincoln would be granted yet another incredible opportunity, one on par with when Mike Leach first offered him a job as his personal assistant six years earlier. Once again, the opportunity would change the course of his life. Once again, it would teach him things he did not know he did not know. But once again, it would come about as a result of impulsive decisions made in anger, so once again, first, it would hurt.

7

Chaos

As THE 2009 SEASON got under way, Lincoln called Adam James into his office and informed him that his practice performance had been poor and his effort lackluster, and as a result he was being demoted from second team to third.

Mike Leach would later recall in his book *Swing Your Sword* that Adam "stormed out of the office" and yelled "Fuck this!" in a lobby full of people. Leach also said that Adam "rammed through the door of the football office so hard that the door split and came off the hinges. It cost us eleven hundred dollars to fix." He would also say that his biggest regret from his time at Texas Tech was not cutting Adam from the team.

This was the same Adam James whom Leach had recruited to Tech at the insistence of his father, Craig James—the same Adam James whom Lincoln had found to possess an "unbelievable sense of entitlement" that "hurts himself and people around him."

The damage Adam's sense of entitlement could do was about to get a lot worse.

"Adam," Lincoln said, "is the kind of person that makes excuses or blames people for things that go wrong in his life."

And not only that, when things did go wrong, he responded to such setbacks by lashing out and then getting his father involved. After storming out of Lincoln's office, his father was the first person he called.

Turns out that not only was Craig James a former NFL running back and a famous football broadcaster, he was also, in Leach's words, "the ultimate Little League dad."

After Adam called him, Craig James called Tommy McVay, the director of football operations at Texas Tech, and questioned the coaches' mental state, insisting that they were, as Leach recalls, "screwing" his son. Next, Craig James called Lincoln and left a voicemail that went something like this, in Leach's recollection: "You don't know what you're doing! Adam James is the best player at the wide receiver position . . . If you've got the balls to call me back, and I don't think you do, call me back."

Texas Tech ended up having a solid season in 2009, though not quite as strong as their on-fire campaign the year before. The Red Raiders finished with a respectable 8–4 record and ranked in the Top 25, earning a spot in the Valero Alamo Bowl against Michigan State.

As they prepared for the bowl game, however, the toxic situation with Adam James was only getting worse. Throughout the season, Lincoln and Leach had continued to have problems with Adam. Graham Harrell, a Texas Tech quarterback, once wrote in an email, "During the season [Adam] was often 'injured' (it usually seemed like a very minor injury that could keep him out of practice but never out of any other activity, including games) so he would not participate in some drills in practice."

For his part, Adam frequently complained that the coaching staff singled him out for unfair treatment. "In the locker room and away from the facility," Harrell said, "Adam used any opportunity he had to tell other players how he was being treated unfairly, how the coaches did not give him a fair chance, and how we did not have to do everything the coaches told us because they had no option but to play some of us."

Harrell would disagree with Adam—"When I heard these kinds of things I usually tried to put an end to them," he said—but it did little to stop him. "Adam pretty consistently talked bad about the coaches or downplayed the importance of working hard," Harrell said.

About a week and a half prior to the Alamo Bowl, Lincoln and Leach felt that Adam was being lazy during practice and decided he needed some discipline. They sent him to "Muscle Beach," a part of the practice field where strength coach Bennie Wylie managed injured players and administered discipline through workouts. Wylie made Adam and another receiver run laps and stadium stairs, but he felt Adam wasn't taking the drills seriously. When Wylie also called him out for being lazy, Adam told him he didn't know what he was doing.

Meanwhile, the other receiver, who was disciplined alongside Adam for his own reasons, had no complaint. "[He] agreed that his effort wasn't his best," Lincoln said of that player, "and had a good attitude with Bennie and also in meeting with me after practice."

When Lincoln spoke with Adam after practice, "it was very clear to me that Adam did not agree with the punishment," he said, "and believed that we were just mis-assessing his effort." In fact, Adam told Lincoln that he wasn't doing his job as a coach—that none of the coaches were doing their jobs—and that his effort was fine.

None of this surprised Lincoln. "Just another example," he said, "of Adam thinking that he knows more about coaching than people who have been coaching for their entire lives."

A couple practices later, Adam showed up twenty minutes late and wearing street clothes, a backwards cap, and sunglasses. Street clothes at practice and backwards caps were against team rules, which mandated that players dress for practice regardless of injury and participate to the extent the trainers permitted. When Leach asked Adam just what the hell he was doing, Adam said he had a concussion. Team trainer Steve Pincock confirmed to Leach that Adam had a concussion, hence the sunglasses on account of the resulting sensitivity to light, but Pincock had no further explanation for the remainder of Adam's chosen attire.

The facts of what, exactly, happened next remain a source of contention among all involved, and it would reverberate throughout all their lives.

Leach says he told Pincock to "put [Adam] somewhere dark and have him do something," and that's the last Leach had to do with it, according to the coach. "I wanted him off the field so he wouldn't be a distraction," Leach wrote in his book.

Pincock told Adam to go to a large equipment garage and rest there. In the garage, there was an electrical closet, which Pincock later said he explicitly told Adam not to enter. Adam proceeded to enter the closet and shoot a video on his cell phone in which he acted as though he'd been locked in there by the coaching staff. "Even having that phone with him during practice time was against team policy," Leach said, "but he ignored that rule, too, and used it to make his own little *Blair Witch Project* where he was seen whispering and scanning the electrical closet. He was specifically told *not* to be in that area, but there he was, acting like a captive."

Then Adam sent the video to his father.

Craig James proceeded to tell anyone who'd listen to him that Adam had been forced to stand in an electrical closet for three hours.

In no small part because of Craig James's influence as a broadcaster, the story quickly took off.

Texas Tech launched an investigation into the whole situation.

Specifics aside, what seems to have happened is that an immature kid got embarrassed, his overbearing father escalated everything, a coach who doesn't take shit didn't take shit, and all manner of chaos ensued. Leach's staff sided with him, Adam's friends sided with him, Craig James sided with his son, and ultimately, the only people who truly know what it was all about are those who were there that day. Leach has a theory that the whole thing wasn't really about Adam James at all, but rather that Texas Tech used the situation to get revenge on Leach for contentious salary negotiations earlier in the year—and to have an excuse to fire him before an $800,000 bonus vested on December 31.

You can take all of them at their word or none of them at their word. The only thing that can be said with reasonable certainty is this: every year, coaches at all levels deal with players they regard as disrespectful, lazy, and entitled, and their helicopter parents with them, and most of those coaches have expressed displeasure with those players in a profane manner at one point or another. That is the way of this world. Whatever Leach's intentions were for Adam James that day, it seems that Adam was disrespectful and Leach reacted accordingly—but it does not appear Leach ordered Adam locked in a closet, which was the claim that sparked the whole controversy.

As the bowl game approached, Leach went about his business more or less as usual, traveling to New York City for several days for fundraisers, dinners, and media appearances. The Red Raiders flew to San Antonio, with Leach planning to fly down from New York, but soon after, Texas Tech suspended Leach over the Adam James allegations. He vowed to fight the suspension, but as of that moment he was barred from coaching the team for the Alamo Bowl.

Ruffin was informed of this news while everyone was settling into the hotel, about thirty minutes before a scheduled team meeting. "I'm not sure what's gonna happen," Ruffin remembers saying at the meeting, "but we're taking over right now."

He would be the interim head coach, and, turning to Lincoln, he said, "Linc, I'll run the defense and run the game, and the offense—well, you got it."

Running the offense in practice at just twenty-five years old— that was one thing. But being the official interim offensive coordinator? For a bowl game? That was going to be played in less than a week?

"When he first told me," Lincoln says, "I was like, *Oh, shit.*"

As Leach fought the suspension, university officials told him that if he signed a letter of apology, he could keep his job—but he refused. Instead, he filed a lawsuit against the university.

In reply, they handed him a letter of termination.

Just like that, Mike Leach was fired.

Oh, shit, indeed.

Lincoln Riley and Ruffin McNeill now had to prepare for a bowl game while facing the very real possibility that they would soon be out of a job themselves. That's how it goes in college football. When the head coach gets fired, the rest of the staff generally does, too. They both hoped Ruffin would get the head coaching job in Leach's place, but they weren't naive—they knew the university would likely want to move on from the whole fiasco, which would mean hiring a new coach, who would likely want to hire his own staff. On top of all that stress, Lincoln was also a young husband with a young wife, and children likely not too far in their future.

"You're coaching and then you're wondering, *How am I going to take care of my family next year?*" Lincoln said. "There was lot going on at that point."

Meanwhile, Lincoln had to think about running the offense—which included coaching the player whose actions had set these events in motion. Adam James was still part of the team. "It was like a soap opera," Lincoln later recalled.

And yet, for all his frustration with Adam and the situation at large, Lincoln still wanted to coach him as well as he could regardless of his feelings—and he really didn't like the fact that some fans were actively threatening Adam and Craig James and their family. That was unacceptable. "We're on different sides of the fence on this deal," Lincoln told reporters, "but he's still my player. All the threats on him and his family are completely ridiculous. I told him if he needs help as far as feeling in danger, I'll help him any way I can."

As maddening as the whole situation had become, above all, it was heartbreaking. "A lot of us guys had been there coaching since 2000," Lincoln recalls. "And there's 2009—and the previous year, we had a great chance to win the national championship. We all felt like we had been a part of bringing that program so far, and then just to see it all crumbling down like that, we were just like, *this isn't necessary.* It was ugly. It was sad."

The heartbreak over what was happening to Mike Leach, the frustration with Adam James, the fear of what fate awaited him following the game—Lincoln had a lot of emotions to manage. Meanwhile, there was football to be coached.

Lincoln looked to Ruffin for support. Twenty-five years older than Lincoln, Ruffin had an affable and laid-back personality that belied a sharp intellect, all of which provided a warm and grounding contrast to Lincoln's coiled intensity. Ruffin kept his instructions simple when it came to Lincoln and the offense, telling him, "Just call it. Do what you want to do. Change what you want to change. Go for it."

In other words, for better and worse, Lincoln had full control of the offense.

It helped Lincoln, too, for him to simply empathize with his new interim head coach—Ruffin was trusting Lincoln a great deal, and whatever stress Lincoln felt, Ruffin had to feel even more. "[Ruffin] was in the toughest position," Lincoln says.

Even so, Lincoln said, "Professionally, toughest thing I've ever had to do. Don't know that I'll ever have to do anything tougher. Biggest mix of emotions I've ever had . . . It was just so many things pulling you so many different ways."

And it didn't help that he had media swarming everywhere, reporters constantly asking him questions about everything. "It was crazy," he said. "You kind of had to catch your breath, settle your emotions."

Amid the chaos, however, as often happens when all seems to be falling apart, other things were falling into place that would only be fully revealed later, as relationships began to form that would ultimately shape the trajectory of Lincoln's life.

That week, Lincoln received a phone call from Donnie Duncan, the senior associate commissioner of the Big 12 Conference—the man who was Mike Leach's mentor, and a good friend of Lincoln's colleague Charlie Sadler, Texas Tech's defensive ends coach. Char-lie had urged Donnie to call Lincoln and Ruffin to help talk them through this. And if there was a man to lean on, it was Donnie Duncan.

A broad-shouldered man with a crown of white hair around his balding scalp, Donnie Duncan was similar to Ruffin in his personality, warm and approachable, but also with a sharp mind. "Whatever emotions you're dealing with—and we all had a ton that week—he's able to see through all that and think about things clearly, rationally," Lincoln recalled. "He always keeps an unbeliev-able perspective on things, which is hard to do especially in times like that."

Donnie's perspective came from experience. He wasn't just the senior associate commissioner of the Big 12 Conference, he was a man who'd done about everything there was to do in football. When Mike Leach said Donnie knew the ropes, that was under-stating things. Donnie had lived and worked at all levels of college football for decades. Lincoln says, "I don't know that anybody in this game's history has had the amount of perspective and wore all the different hats that he did."

Donnie had grown up in Celeste, Texas, a tiny town of about eight hundred people a little over an hour northeast of Dallas. Like Lincoln, he'd been an All-District quarterback for his local high school. He was a four-year letterman quarterback at Austin Col-lege, too, where he also lettered in baseball for four years and won several awards for his athletic prowess. The guy had been a stud.

He started coaching in 1962 as an assistant for Dublin High School in Texas. Not long after that, he became an assistant coach at Tarleton State University before taking his first head coaching job at Honey Grove High School, where his teams went 20–3–1 and won two district titles. A couple more small college coaching jobs later, Donnie caught his first big break when Barry Switzer hired him to be an assistant coach at Oklahoma in 1973. Donnie coached for Switzer for five years, in which time the Sooners went 62–6–2 and won six Big 8 Conference titles, plus two national championships.

Donnie then became the head coach at Iowa State, but he lasted only four seasons there, posting an 18–24–2 record, and he decided coaching wasn't for him. After spending a couple of years working as an executive director for bowl games, he returned to Oklahoma as the athletic director. Teaming up with DeLoss Dodds, his counterpart at the University of Texas, he then drove the creation of the Big 12 Conference. In 1997, he became the conference's director of football operations. He also served on the TV committee for the College Football Association, chaired the NCAA Special Events Committee—overseeing All-Star and bowl games—and he would later serve on the research committee that made the case for college football playoffs. He was named by *Sporting News* as one of the ten most powerful people in all of college sports.

"His mind for college football is a treasure," Lincoln said.

And now Donnie was helping Lincoln through one of the most trying times of his young life. His advice was more than welcome. "Obviously, we were in new positions that week, and a lot going on," Lincoln said. "He just reached out to help us and be a calming sense of guidance."

Ruffin had a similar assessment of Donnie's acumen. "He was a thousand for a thousand on giving you advice," Ruffin says. "He'd say, *Hey now, tomorrow, they're going to ask you this question, this question, and this question . . . What are some of your answers? And here are some answers to think about.* And I'm doggoned—I'm sitting in the interviews the very next day, and those same four or five he told me came up."

Lincoln said, "He would predict things before they happened. He could always see two or three steps ahead."

Donnie reminded Lincoln of the same lessons so many successful people must learn. "He talked about being patient, keeping our heads, and staying focused on the task at hand," Lincoln said. "And—not worrying about the things we can't control. He settled us and calmed us."

Ultimately, there was only one thing Lincoln could control in the chaos: how he chose to prepare for the game. And so he chose thoughtfully. During practices he worked the sidelines with the same intensity and focus he imagined he would need during the game, getting acclimated to that perspective after years spent in the coach's box above the field. "I'd been in the box for two years, I think," Lincoln said. "So it was a little bit different getting down on the field. Even when you see it every day in practice, it's different when you've been up there and you get back down."

And when he wasn't at practice, Lincoln locked himself in his hotel room, going over plays and poring over his game plan. "I never left," he told a reporter.

As the week ticked by, Lincoln and Ruffin began to feel, against all odds, as though everything just might click into place. "We had a great week of practice," Ruffin says. "A *great* week of practice."

He and Lincoln were working well together, and Ruffin only grew more impressed with the kid. "He listens so well," the older man says. "And he is always searching for knowledge—how to make things better. How to make a masterpiece."

Lincoln, in turn, felt stabilized by Ruffin's steady presence. "He just handled it like a guy that was ready to be a head coach, and didn't flinch," Lincoln recalls. "He was ready for it. And his calmness and confidence really helped me . . . He had a great feel for the team that week, and what they needed, and he handled those guys well, and the way he handled it rubbed off on all of us."

Then it was game day, and all there was left to do was play. *If I could survive this,* Lincoln recalls thinking, *I could survive a lot.*

More than 5.5 million households tuned in to watch the game on January 2, 2010. No previous Alamo Bowl had been watched by more people, and no bowl game broadcast by ESPN had ever received higher ratings.

And the way Lincoln handled it was, in a word from Leach, "outstanding."

"From the get-go," said wide receiver Lyle Leong, "his swag that he had, just the look on his face, was like, *We got it.* The way he called plays, he had it. From the first play to the end play, he called a great game, and everything flowed together. We didn't miss a beat."

The Red Raider offense put up 468 passing yards and three passing touchdowns to go with 137 rushing yards and two rushing touchdowns. They lost starting quarterback Tyler Potts to injury, and then Steven Sheffield came in with the Red Raiders trailing 31–27 in the fourth quarter. They closed out the game victorious, 41–31.

Considering the circumstances, you might call it a masterpiece.

"I should have recorded it, how smooth and precise he was with the calls," Ruffin says. "He went from the call to the booth. And he said, *Ruff, got your play coming right now,* so he ran and slipped the receiver in the backfield, and the quarterback up the F seam, we call it, up, the back acts like a linebacker, and he got him. Anyway, he did a great job calling it that day."

"I learned a lot about myself through that whole deal," Lincoln says. "That was a unique situation and a tough test that showed me I could do that."

Surely, he and Ruffin thought, their future was now secure.

"We thought we would get the job at Texas Tech, really," Ruffin says.

Instead, just a couple weeks later, Texas Tech hired Tommy Tuberville, who promptly fired pretty much everyone who'd worked for Mike Leach.

Welcome to the world of college football coaching. People in the business like to say you're not really a coach until you've been fired. This is a wildly underappreciated aspect of the coaching paradigm: there's virtually no true job security. And when head coaches get fired, their staff gets fired, too.

In a matter of weeks, one of the nation's most popular underdog football teams, one that Mike Leach had built from nothing into a national championship contender, was undone.

That the situation devolved as it did, as quickly as it did, was stunning. Mike Leach still gets heated about it all, but to Lincoln, it came down to just one word: "Sad."

Sad as it was, Lincoln had no time to waste. His whole life was suddenly completely changed. He had to find a new job, and a good one, and quickly. He jumped on one plane after another, flying around the country to interview for various positions.

Then one day, while he was somewhere in Texas or Mississippi—he can't remember exactly—Ruffin McNeill phoned him.

Ruffin was calling from a small town called Greenville, North Carolina, at a school called East Carolina University. It was his alma mater, and he'd just been hired as their head coach. Lincoln was one of his first calls.

"Hey, Linc, got the job. You comin'?"

"I'll be there."

Lincoln took a flight to Greenville the next morning, and he marked the occasion with uncharacteristic formality by walking into Ruffin's office carrying a suitcase and wearing a slick gray suit with a tie. They both laughed hard.

Lincoln was Ruffin's first hire. Ruffin says, "I told the athletic director, *I don't want no more gray hair. There's enough gray hair on the staff. Lincoln will do a great job. Just watch.*"

At twenty-six years old, Lincoln Riley was now the youngest offensive coordinator in the country, and East Carolina University was about to become his personal canvas.

8

Greenville

ONE WINDOW IN LINCOLN'S new office in Greenville overlooked the practice fields, and another gave him a clear view of Dowdy Ficklen Stadium, home to the East Carolina University Pirates. Located in the middle of Greenville—THE HEART OF PIRATE COUNTRY, as it says across a bridge down the street—his office took up a corner of the second floor of the Ward Sports Medicine Building, a simple brick structure located on the edge of campus.

In a lot of ways, Lincoln had a dream job. At twenty-six years old, he was making $275,000 a year, and he was in charge of a Division I offense. He even had fresh digs, as the team locker room on the Ward Building's first floor had just been renovated. It had 125 custom-made lockers with a natural wood veneer finish and solid wood edges, and new carpet in the Pirates' signature color, purple. The stadium itself had been newly improved, too, with seven thousand seats added to create a new student section behind the west end zone, which was named the Boneyard.

But just because it was a dream job didn't mean it would be an easy job. One of Lincoln's first days in town, a local coach and Pirate Club booster club member named Harold Robinson burst into Lincoln's corner office and declared that Lincoln would have to prove to him that he could make adjustments at halftime in order for Robinson to accept him at his young age.

This was more or less the prevailing sentiment regarding Lincoln's arrival. Young is young, people were skeptical of him—if not outright cynical—and he heard about it. The citizens of Greenville were a passionate bunch, especially when it came to Pirate football, and this was the sort of small town in which every emotion the locals might have about their team feels heightened. What the Pirates lacked in prestige and accomplishment, their fans made up for in sheer zealotry. Back in 1999, when East Carolina defeated No. 9 Miami, Pirate fans stormed the field and tore down the goalposts, despite repeated pleas from the public address announcer.

Greenville is smaller than Lubbock, just twenty-five square miles, with a population of about ninety thousand, and the town can feel like its own little world. If Muleshoe is a rural island in the desert sea that is West Texas, then Greenville is a larger island in the middle of a rural archipelago in the plains of eastern North Carolina. There's a similar sense of isolation, largely because of Greenville's location. Beach towns like Morehead City and Emerald Isle lie roughly ninety miles east, and the Triangle of Raleigh, Durham, and Chapel Hill roughly ninety miles west. In between, there are vast fields, some full of corn, others of cotton, others nothing more than green grass or brown dirt, and many of them are dotted or lined with distant trees. Not unlike the plains of West Texas, these fields evoke a sense of serenity one moment and a sense of confinement the next. Even as the Triangle has become one of the country's booming economic regions, that boom hasn't really reached Greenville, and frequently its citizens are drawn away by the pull of the city. Just to get to Greenville, you typically either fly into the town's tiny airport—the only flights to and from which go through Charlotte—or you fly into Raleigh and drive the rest of the way.

There are worse places to live, no doubt, but Greenville isn't the easiest place to live. The town sits in an eternal flood zone, downstream of multiple rivers, including the Tar River running through downtown. Hurricanes have swamped Greenville and the surrounding areas several times over the last fifty years and regularly leave chaos in their wake, creating millions of dollars of damage and displacing dozens if not hundreds of families. That game in 1999, when East Carolina beat Miami, came in the wake of Hurricane Floyd, one of the most devastating storms to hit the region in decades. The Pirates had to play in Raleigh instead of Greenville that week—Dowdy Ficklen Stadium was in disrepair—and although tearing down the Wolfpack goalposts was inconsiderate, the fans' passion simply overflowed in the symbolism of the victory: the Pirates had defeated the Hurricanes.

There is a small but vibrant and earnest community of entrepreneurs in town doing good work, and in recent years, the downtown area has undergone a renaissance of sorts, with some trendy restaurants and new businesses being built, and town officials finally making good on promises to enhance the roads in order to improve traffic around town. But nonetheless, the town can sometimes feel restricted by its own design, the infrastructure not well suited for growth. Though things are slowly getting better, downtown has little parking, and despite some recent improvements, the town's roads speak to the fact that city planners of yore seemingly never expected Greenville to even reach the size it had. Despite the town's small population, traffic is often terrible—it can take you half an hour to drive a few miles across town. Locals can rattle off plenty of reasons to love the place—vibrant outdoor activities, a great family atmosphere, a low cost of living—and all these things have merit, but Greenville can at times feel more like a place you learn to make your peace with, even if you dream of living somewhere else.

If you like quiet small-town life, then you'll love Greenville, but if you dream of more, you may feel out of place there. And yet for all of this—and maybe because of it—Pirate football has been something to hold on to. When Lincoln and Ruffin arrived in 2010, the Pirates were not the best football team in the country—and they've sometimes been among the worst—but there were people in the town that possessed deep, real love for the Pirates regardless of how well they performed. They knew they weren't *great*, but that didn't stop many of the fans from imagining that they *could* be, and in a lot of ways, it was the *desire* for greatness that gave them joy as much as any time the team actually showed flashes of it.

In this way, Greenville was a window into part of college football's soul that is rarely seen.

It's easy to see the love fans have for college football's better teams and understand the passion of people in places like Tuscaloosa, Gainesville, Columbus, Norman, and Happy Valley. It's easy to see why coaches go into the profession when you witness such passion, even reverence, for the teams that play the game. Likewise, it's easy to understand the skeptics and the cynics who scoff at such passion, dismissing it all as silly escapism, if not woeful debauchery. Yet that barely scratches the surface of what college football really means—it cannot possibly take measure of the true depth of its soul.

That depth you find in a place like Greenville.

College football is in many ways the true regional identity sport of the country. This is an aspect of college football that doesn't often get seen but is no less important than what happens in powerhouse programs like Alabama and Oklahoma. College football towns provide a delightful slice of Americana in all of its fantastic peculiarities. The universities and colleges that make up these towns are woven into the fabric and psychologies of their communities far more than professional sports organizations.

That spirit is a part of Lincoln's journey, one that college football fans know all too well.

Pirate football fans have been more passionate than many of the fans of college football's big, famous, successful programs. It took deeper love to love something the way they loved this team when it was so inconsistent for them in return. And the reasons they loved the team could be seen in how they reacted to the team's recent run of success.

On Lincoln and Ruffin's arrival, the Pirates were on an unusually strong streak, coming off back-to-back conference championships. For the first time in school history, a coach had left because he received a better offer from another school. For the previous five seasons, their coach had been Skip Holtz, son of Lou Holtz, the legendary coach turned analyst who has been inducted into the College Football Hall of Fame. Skip coached the Pirates to conference championships in 2008 and 2009 and three straight bowl games before South Florida hired him away.

The locals had developed high expectations. But those expectations often ran up against a university that doesn't have a budget to compete with the larger schools that surround it, such as North Carolina, Duke, North Carolina State, and Wake Forest. When Lincoln and Ruffin arrived in 2010, East Carolina allocated less than $170,000 per year for recruiting costs, which ranked the school in the bottom half of the country and dead last in its conference. Even tiny Appalachian State spent more on recruiting. East Carolina also earned less than any other public school in its conference in revenue, topping out at a little less than $36 million one year. For comparison's sake, the University of Texas made some $136 million in revenue that same year.

But their fans? The people who live in Greenville?

The people of Greenville are a passionate lot, and what happens in Greenville carries with it a feeling of significance disproportionate to its importance to the rest of the world at large. The town has a way of sometimes feeling like the whole world, for better and for worse.

For a coaching prodigy like Lincoln Riley, it would be an ideal testing ground, because whatever he did here, whatever successes and failures he experienced, the town would reflect them back to him, and he would feel it. For the people of Greenville, their relationship with winning could be an insecure and adolescent one— the more they won, the more they partied, and the more they wanted. This is not uncommon among fan bases like East Carolina's. They could be a fickle bunch, too. Even as they began to consistently win games under Skip Holtz, Greenville fans found reason to be dissatisfied. The stadium was actually filling up for games, but East Carolina fans still sometimes complained that the *way* Holtz was winning all these games was boring. "The one thing everyone hated about Skip," says Nathan Summers, who covered the team for the *Daily Reflector*, the town newspaper, "was that they just ground out these wins . . . It was a very slow, methodical process, and fans always hated the offense."

If there's one thing people in Greenville do know how to do, however, it's have fun. Sometimes they take things more seriously than they need to, but they always work with what they've got to have a good time. An unofficial Pirate football motto is "Win or Lose We Still Booze." The tailgating around here is choice, and although there aren't many bars in town, the ones that are here make their existence count. In 2019, a downtown bar called Sup

Dogs won the Barstool Sports Best College Bar "tournament," each round decided by fan voting. Barstool called it "the biggest upset in college bar competition history." In 2020, Sups won again. So, yeah, the Pirates know how to party. The university does its part, too, by having a local actor dress in full, authentic pirate garb and lead the team onto the field every game, and by having its cheerleaders fire off an honest-to-God cannon behind the end zone after the Pirates score. During games, the fans will chant the team colors back and forth at each other: "Purple! Gold! Purple! Gold!"

They weren't fully satisfied by winning in the Skip Holtz era, even if they were winning more than ever before, because they wanted the winning to be fun. Ultimately, that's what they'd be left with when the game was over: how much fun they had. Winning is great, but what's the point if you're not having any fun?

That was one thing Ruffin McNeill promised that he and Lincoln would deliver.

They would make Pirate football fun.

"He said when he got here that they were going to completely revamp the way fans saw games, and the way that we as reporters saw games," Summers says. "And we were gonna see this awesome version of football, and it was gonna be high-scoring, and they were gonna blow some teams out."

To win games, first they would have to win over the team.

The first day of practice, as Lincoln introduced himself to everyone, the way the team's star senior wide receiver Dwayne Harris reacted to him reflects pretty much everyone else's reaction, too. "I'm standing there," he says, "looking at this kinda skinny white dude, and I just keep thinkin', *This dude is only four years older than me, and he's trying to teach us how to play football?*"

Dwayne was planning to have a killer year, establish himself as an elite college receiver, and get drafted into the NFL. This was no time for experiments. The rest of his life was on the line.

The players knew that Lincoln was bringing in some kind of brand-new offense, they knew he was extremely young, and they didn't know how to feel about it.

"The first few days," Lincoln recalled, "there was some confusion."

He made time in those first few days to meet with all the offensive players and lay out his new offense and what would be expected of them. "The receivers and the quarterbacks looked like they just got their first date," he said. "The running backs and the tight ends looked like their dogs just got ran over."

Lincoln spent extra time with Dwayne in particular—he was a star player and a team leader, and there needed to be mutual trust between them. "He started breaking down what he had planned for me as a receiver," Dwayne says, "and what he did for Crab [Michael Crabtree], who had a great career at Texas Tech . . . My respect for him grew. He could understand where I was coming from as a player."

Ruffin and Lincoln were also blessed with a quarterback named Dominique Davis, who happened to be a great fit for their offense. As a redshirt freshman for Boston College in 2007, Dominique had started in the ACC championship game, but then he was suspended for academic issues. He transferred to a junior college, then found his way to East Carolina in time to establish himself as the Pirates' starter. He was six foot three and 215 pounds, passed well and ran well, and was just the kind of guy Lincoln could work with in the Air Raid offense. His high school had even run a spread offense. "He's a fantastic leader," Lincoln said. "He holds the group together. He's the glue of the thing. He has a great demeanor about him for a quarterback, kind of a relaxed and confident demeanor. He's done a really good job on the intangible things."

As Lincoln worked with the team, "I think they settled down and saw what we were going to do," he said. Even the running backs and tight ends who'd looked at him like he'd run over their dogs came to see his ultimate plan, which was, he said, "Give guys the chance to touch the ball and make plays."

Almost immediately after getting hired, Lincoln hit the recruiting trail, too. He would need just the right types of players to do what he wanted to do, and Skip Holtz hadn't exactly been recruiting players suitable to the spread offense.

While in Atlanta to scout a quarterback, Lincoln received film of another quarterback, a two-star recruit out of Houston named Shane Carden. Lincoln's former Texas Tech colleagues B. J. Symons and Dana Holgorsen had told him and Ruffin about Shane. Symons had been training the kid. "B.J. had one of the greatest years in college football that one he started for us there," Ruffin says. "And B.J. was training Shane. So Shane understood the system, the concepts of what we do."

Never mind that Holgorsen had become the offensive coordinator for the University of Houston, which was East Carolina's conference rival; he told Lincoln and Ruffin that Shane was good, and even said, "He will beat U of H's butt. Y'all need to take this kid."

Lincoln watched the film in his hotel room, and what he saw was simple. "I thought he was a playmaker," he said. "I thought when he got outside of the pocket, he made things happen."

Lincoln and Ruffin invited Shane to campus for a visit. It was a day of unusually intense winter weather in North Carolina. Some snow had recently come through—which was rare—and even though it was clearing out, it left the town and the campus coated in an icy sheen.

Ruffin was out of town but called Shane ahead of time, made some small talk, welcomed him to campus—and then said, "I'm your new dad."

"I haven't heard anything like that before," Shane said, "and I've talked to a lot of coaches."

He liked it, and he liked Lincoln as they talked, too. Lincoln's story was one that resonated, and Shane liked the offense. "I loved the coaches and the offense we were going to run," he said.

Shane accepted a scholarship and was redshirted for the 2010 season, which was Dominique Davis's senior year.

Lincoln also wanted to take a risk on a completely overlooked receiver from right in Greenville's backyard. His name was Justin Hardy. He was a scrawny five-foot-ten, 160-pound kid from West Craven High School in Vanceboro, a tiny town about a half hour southeast of Greenville. He'd even quit playing receiver to become West Craven's quarterback his senior year. The only reason Lincoln had heard of him at all was because Justin's coach, Kevin Yost, personally had delivered a video to the East Carolina offices shortly before Lincoln arrived.

Watching the video, Lincoln saw the potential for greatness in the smallest of details. Justin's hands, for starters, were huge despite his small frame, ten inches from middle finger to wrist, nine from thumb to pinky. Not only that, but he knew how to use them, catching passes with ease. Lincoln showed the tape to Ruffin, who agreed. "He has some of the best hands I've seen in thirty-four years of coaching," Ruffin later said.

Justin also had great feet and an impressive ability to shimmy-shake his way free at the line of scrimmage. He ran routes with laser precision, leaving defenders helpless to stop him. He was a smart and dedicated student as well, holding a 3.8 high school GPA. And yet he had no scholarship offers except to Division II Fayetteville State, where he'd already committed.

Lincoln wanted him. He and Ruffin persuaded Justin to bail on Fayetteville State and join East Carolina as a preferred walk-on. Like Shane Carden, Justin would redshirt the 2010 season, but the two would soon become a huge part of what Lincoln hoped to accomplish.

Meanwhile, Lincoln and Ruffin continued to consult Donnie Duncan regularly for advice, sometimes as often as once a week. "He was my number one mentor growing up," Lincoln says. Lincoln would visit Donnie whenever he could, sometimes during recruiting trips to Dallas, sometimes just to visit. "Anytime I was in Texas," Lincoln said, "I would stay with him for a couple of days." Big 12 associate commissioner John Underwood, a close friend of Donnie's, once told a reporter, "Donnie always made sure to see [Lincoln and Ruffin] a couple times a year. Anytime they wanted to bounce something off of someone, Donnie was the person that they talked to . . . It was their mutual love and admiration for college football. They embraced what's good for it."

And, Underwood said, "Donnie recognized Lincoln's ability. Recognized his unique talents in the game of football. Donnie said he would become a head coach at an early age."

East Carolina's first game of the 2010 season fell on Lincoln's twenty-seventh birthday, September 5: a home game against Tulsa. It was a rare nationally televised game for the Pirates, airing on ESPN2, and some fifty thousand fans filled Dowdy Ficklen Stadium, ready to see if Ruffin and Lincoln would live up to their hype.

The lead changed twelve different times during the game, and would be described by an Associated Press writer as "a wacky . . . shootout in which defense seemed optional."

The Pirates led by a thin margin at halftime, 17–16, and Lincoln came into the locker room unsatisfied but optimistic. Dwayne Harris remembers, "He said, *We're gonna change a couple things around*, and he said, *The second half is our half. We already know what we can and can't do, and so here's what we're gonna do . . .*"

The second half was explosive. Both teams would combine for more than eleven hundred yards of total offense, with the two quarterbacks each throwing for nearly four hundred yards. And the game ended in thrilling and dramatic fashion: The Pirates were losing 49–44 with five seconds left in the game and the ball on the Tulsa 33-yard line on fourth down with ten yards to go. Lincoln called a Hail Mary. Dominique Davis took the snap out of the shotgun—virtually all their plays were out of the shotgun—and dropped back to around the 40, scrambled to his left to avoid a pass rusher, and then slung the ball downfield to the end zone as he got chased by another rusher. He threw in the direction of six-foot-eight, 260-pound tight end Justin Jones, who came down with the ball in the middle of a crowd of quickly dismayed Tulsa defenders.

Touchdown.

Game: Pirates.

Later, Dominique said that was his birthday present for Lincoln.

"That was the greatest experience of my life," the quarterback said afterward. "There were probably people in the stands—our fans—who thought the game was over. But I told the team, 'Just trust.' As soon as I let it go, I knew he was going to catch it."

The Pirates got flagged for excessive celebration, and they didn't even bother to kick the extra point; they just took a knee, and the game was theirs.

East Carolina also got a strong performance from running back Jonathan Williams, who finished with nearly a hundred yards and a touchdown. As for Dwayne Harris, the star receiver finished with seven catches for 121 yards and two touchdowns. But the hero of the game was Dominique Davis, who finished with 383 yards passing, five passing touchdowns, just one interception, and another rushing touchdown.

"So then," Dwayne says, "I was like, *Okay. I'm in.*"

The rest of Pirate Nation was with him.

It was a perfect and fitting first game that set the tone for Lincoln and Ruffin's time at East Carolina: full of ups and downs and strong performances and mistakes and recoveries from said mistakes, featuring a few marquee players. Justin Hardy, though just a redshirt, was already paying his dues—he even played quarterback for the scout team. One week in October, he mimicked Russell Wilson, then a star quarterback for North Carolina State University, as the Pirates prepared for their game against the Wolfpack. When Wilson and the Wolfpack came to Greenville, the Pirates sent them home with a 33–27 loss after Wilson threw an interception in overtime.

Justin Hardy and Shane Carden also began working very well together on the scout team, showing flashes of fantastic future potential. Shane called his mom one week just raving, "Mom, there's this guy named Justin Hardy, and I think he's a walk-on, but I don't know how, because this dude's a freak." Shane later said, "He stood out big time, and I knew he was going to do big things."

And on the varsity, Dwayne Harris came to share the same

opinion of Lincoln that's been held by people at all stages of Lincoln's life, from Debbie Conner to David Wood to Mike Leach to Ruffin McNeill: "Lincoln Riley is a football genius."

He goes on, "He's an offensive mastermind, and at that young of an age, and being that knowledgeable about the game of football, amazed me. That's how he got a lot of the guys' respect at ECU—because he knew the game, and he was a genius at it. And we bought in . . . [Lincoln] drew up plays, created plays, and . . . you go out and run it, and like, nobody can stop it."

His opinion of Lincoln had fully reversed from when they first met.

Lincoln also displayed a unique ability to connect with his players, one that felt like real love. "Honestly, he was my guy," Dwayne says. "Him and his wife, they were always inviting me over to the house to cook, and he would do that one-on-one relationship with his players. And that's how we both had a great relationship. I can call him about anything, and that's just how it rolls for us."

That came naturally to Lincoln, a part of just being himself, and he was encouraged to be that way more simply by watching Ruffin McNeill. "The way he relates to players . . . he just has a way with players that was always real impressive to me," Lincoln says. "Could kinda reach them on a different level. Great passion for it."

Lincoln had seen this at Texas Tech, but becoming a head coach only amplified these attributes in Ruffin.

"They are my sons, and it's not lip service," Ruffin once said. "They know that. I love them more than I love them as a football player. I love the person inside the uniform."

He could be hard on them when he needed to be, but he was often downright affectionate. "I don't know if you could ever replicate it," Lincoln says. "Just a constant energy level with those guys and a passionate understanding and caring about them. He could push them, man. He could press their buttons. And so at the end of the day they respond. And he's just got a great way about people, man. He's one of those guys you just love being around."

As the year went on, players developed a deep appreciation for Ruffin and Lincoln. "I'll go out and give my all for them," Dwayne Harris says. His relationship with Lincoln grew to a point that Dwayne would call Lincoln or walk into his office whenever the urge struck, and Lincoln would make himself available to talk, even if only for a few minutes. "No matter what it was," he recalls, "if I just needed to sit down, and talk about stuff, he was there to be a coach, but also a mentor, to teach me and guide me, to tell me how I could work on my game, work on being a better person in life. He did so much . . . He always told me I could be as good as I wanted to be, as long as I put the work in. Like, *You have the talent. You remind me of Crab in certain ways. You got the talent, you just gotta put the work in to be great.* We never got to arguing on the sideline or anything like that."

That mattered as much to Dwayne as any of Lincoln's offensive schemes: "When you build a relationship like that," he says, "we don't question the trust we have for each other. You still believe in your heart that he believes in you."

In many ways, the season was still one befitting an East Carolina football team. They beat some teams they shouldn't have, like Russell Wilson and North Carolina State, along with Tulsa, who went on to finish 10–3 and ranked No. 24 in the country. They also lost games they probably should have won, such as when they lost by twenty-four points to Rice, which finished near the bottom of the Conference USA standings. East Carolina finished 6–7 for the season and 5–3 in their division. That was good enough for second place, behind No. 21 Central Florida, and they made a bowl game, the Military Bowl against Maryland—but then lost by thirty points.

There was much to be improved upon, but there had also been moments of pure, dazzling entertainment. Lincoln and Ruffin had a challenge ahead of them to make their team more consistent in its performance—but they had also given East Carolina fans what they had promised. They made Pirate football fun.

The Pirates set twenty-nine team and individual records that season. Dominique Davis was named Conference USA's Newcomer of the Year. Dwayne Harris broke the thousand-yard receiving mark for the first time in his career and got drafted by the NFL, where he would play for ten seasons.

Dwayne Harris would be leaving, but Lincoln had promising players coming up behind him. For 2011, Justin Hardy would no longer be a redshirt walk-on, having earned himself a scholarship. Lincoln saw him as a sort of hybrid between Michael Crabtree and Wes Welker, once telling a reporter, "Justin catches the ball like Crabtree in the sense that it's effortless. He's not the fastest receiver on the field, but he plays at a high speed like Welker. There's just never any hesitation or confusion in the way he plays."

But Lincoln would soon find a steep mountain to climb, when East Carolina kicked off the 2011 season by losing four of its first five games.

"That," he says, "was a hard year."

He would be forced to make changes to the offense. "We did a few things different, but we were a lot like we were at Tech," Lincoln says. "Those first two years especially."

Beyond the field, Lincoln would also have to change himself as a coach, and as a man. His second year at East Carolina would be one of the most challenging and formative years of his career, one in which he began hurting himself again—and he would inadvertently pass that pain along to his players.

9

Reset

THE HARD, SIMPLE TRUTH was that East Carolina didn't have players that were as good as many of the teams they were playing against, but Lincoln was coaching them and developing game plans as though they did. It might be more shocking that his game plans almost worked sometimes, and there were tantalizing moments that teased great success awaiting over the horizon. Take, for instance, the performance of Justin Hardy. He was lifted from the scout team for the 2011 season, and he entered the Pirates' season opener against No. 12 South Carolina in the first quarter. They were playing in Charlotte at the Carolina Panthers' stadium, and the arena was full with some fifty-eight thousand people. Hardy, unfazed, caught a slant pattern, put a spin move on a defender, and dived into the end zone to score the first touchdown of the game.

That game ended badly—the Pirates lost 56–37—but their second game of the season the following week, at home against No. 11 Virginia Tech, showed more promise. They competed well throughout the game in front of fifty thousand fans and were a threat to the end before losing by a single touchdown, 17–10.

They finally beat the University of Alabama at Birmingham—but only barely, 29–23, and UAB was a bad team that would go on to finish the year 3–9.

North Carolina was next. The Tar Heels were always a difficult opponent, and the Pirates lost, 35–20.

After that, No. 18 Houston destroyed them, 56–3.

Yes, 3.

The problem wasn't just that the Pirates were outmatched. They were also just playing flat-out bad football at times, and on top of that, they were losing key players to injuries seemingly every week. "We had a million injuries and didn't play well," Lincoln says. "Like, every single week, it was a starter going down for the season."

They had all the passion in the world to match it, but passion won't make you faster, stronger, bigger than the other guys. Lincoln thought he was used to that because they had dealt with a similar situation at Texas Tech, but he hadn't accounted for how sharp the disparity could be at a lesser program like East Carolina. "At times at Tech, we were outmanned," he says. "We played better teams. But we weren't outmanned at the level we were at, say, ECU when we were playing North Carolina or Virginia Tech."

The fans started grumbling about the accumulating losses. Tension built with every passing week, and Lincoln was feeling it. Nobody was more displeased with how things were going than he was. So he coached *harder*. "I kept thinking, *if I work harder, if I do this and that, we can flip it around and do it*," he recalls.

The way he describes it, he coached the way football coaches had traditionally coached their teams when they struggled. He pushed them harder. And eventually his frustration and exhaustion gave way to anger. He handled the team's failures the same way most immature leaders handle their subordinates when things aren't going well: he criticized more, pushed them more, demanded simply *more*. And not only from them, but also from himself. And when they lost, he would sink into the anger, wallowing in a pool of broody misery. "He used to be, like, the worst loser ever," Caitlin says. "It was awful when he first started coaching. You didn't—we didn't talk. It was not fun. Not that he was ugly. Just nobody wanted to be around him. To talk about it."

He spent more time in his office, reviewing film, brainstorming, trying to will something successful into existence as the sun rose over the practice field out one window and set behind the stadium out the other.

Failure breeds fear, which breeds a desire for control. Lincoln makes it sound like he tried to control things by choosing to work harder, to *try* harder, to do *more*, even as it became counterproductive. He wasn't the first coach to make this mistake, and he wouldn't be the last. Such an approach feels dedicated, committed, passionate—and it is, but in a blind, zealous kind of way, not unlike the way Lincoln's crazy freshman coach sought to motivate his players by head-butting them so hard he made himself bleed.

Ruffin would pump the brakes on Lincoln here and there, but Ruffin also had some insight about it: this was something Lincoln was going to have to sort out on his own. From his many years of coaching, Ruffin knew that everyone struggles sometimes. He also knew that there were only two ways to handle it when a coach was struggling. "You try to interfere with that, which some people do," he says. Or, he goes on, "Believe in him."

Believe in him. Not only to succeed, but to learn when he was failing. That may be the sign of ultimate trust. Rather than preach at Lincoln how to be better, Ruffin trusted that he would learn the lessons he needed to when he was able to. "He gave me a lot of room to make mistakes," Lincoln recalls. "Especially early there. And believed in me—believed in what we were doing."

Ruffin believed in Lincoln even as he locked himself away in his office, worked more hours, pushed his players harder, pushed himself harder, and—when none of that produced the results that he wanted—brooded more. Lincoln would even call reporters who criticized him, arguing about one thing or another, or just explaining his side of things, trying to get them to see what he was trying to do on certain plays. His nerves were wearing raw, his skin thin. And he started feeling drained, losing the life, the fire, that the game had always given him.

"I just didn't have my same energy levels," he says. "My energy got zapped."

In a way, he was chasing the linebacker again.

In high school, when that linebacker intercepted that pass, Lincoln was angry that the success he had expected—a pass caught for a touchdown—had become a failure. He responded in anger, and in that anger, he made a damaging mistake. If only someone could have stopped him right there on the field, before he tackled the linebacker and tore his shoulder apart.

In Greenville, someone did.

Many people offered sound advice and insight throughout the season. His father. His wife. Mike Leach. Ruffin. Donnie Duncan. Gil Brandt, who was also becoming something of a mentor for Lincoln.

But it was Harold Robinson, the retired high school coach, the head of the East Carolina booster club—the Greenville native who had first told Lincoln how he'd have to prove himself—who got through to Lincoln with a calming message that moved him perhaps most of all that year. "I remember him pulling me off to the side," Lincoln says. "And he could tell I was in the dumps."

Harold told Lincoln: "Hey, you can only, you know, do so much as a coach. You can't do it for them. You can't do anything more than give it your best."

Lincoln took that advice to heart, and he would remember it for years to come. "I needed that at that time," he says.

In trying to work and push himself and his players so hard, he was also slipping away from one of the foremost things he'd first learned under Mike Leach: *Just be yourself.* Even—especially—when dealing with your players, even being as young as he was. "As a coach, you have to be yourself," he says. "I don't factor my age into it a whole lot when I made a decision on how to deal with them, and at the end of the day you're their coach and they either respect you or they don't. You have to be yourself."

Lincoln seemed to have lost touch with the boy who was raised in Muleshoe, Texas, on kindness and honesty and hope—lost touch with the boy who grew up just loving to invent mind-bending plays in a field full of caliche rocks. Compared to that kid, he had become something of a brooding workaholic—and being a brooding workaholic hadn't been what brought him great grades as a kid. He hadn't been a brooding workaholic when he became a star high school quarterback—even after he'd ruined his throwing shoulder. He'd been mature, serious sometimes, and he worked at the game—but that work was born of love, and he'd played his best when he played out of that love. Same for when he'd gotten his shot at Texas Tech. He'd taken it seriously, but he'd been having fun learning what it took to be great at coaching the game he loved.

Now, Lincoln seemed to have stopped having fun. "That was a

hard year," he says. "I wasn't very happy." Passion can sometimes toxify into something damaging, into one day after another of figuratively head-butting oneself and, sometimes, one's players. "I didn't see it in the moment," Lincoln says, "but looking back, yeah. Guys watch their leader, and they watch their coaches. So I certainly wasn't giving them a very good vibe there for a while."

He had been so obsessed with making things work on the field that he had forgotten to think about what made things work for his players.

"He has learned," Caitlin says, "that everybody feeds off of him, and the way you react is how everybody is gonna react. Whether it's our family, whether it's the other coaches—if he learns and moves forward then that's what others will do."

The way Lincoln moved forward reflected the love he had for the players more than it did the frustration he felt at things not going the way he wanted. This was a shift back toward himself— and back toward the way Ruffin loved their players, too—like sons, like family, same as he had made Dwayne Harris feel just a year before. "He treated me like family at ECU," Dwayne says, "and I think that goes a long way, when someone treats you like family, and they genuinely care about you . . . Ruff and Linc—I love them to death. I would do anything for them."

"There's a balance needed for coaches," Ruffin says. "Especially in the beginning of a coaching career, it's totally different. There's immediate feedback in this business. So you have to find a balance . . . And he did. He loves football. He loves coaching, the strategy part of it. But when things are not going perfectly, that's when you have to be able to fix it. As long as you're yourself . . . you can fix whatever you need to be fixed, whatever needs to be fixed, but it comes from having balance. He has it now."

Lincoln also, of course, adjusted his strategies on the football field.

Love is vital, but love alone does not win football games.

And he couldn't keep doing things the way he'd done them at Texas Tech. He would not forsake all the things that had helped him get here, but he would have to transform them. "Still . . . devoted to what you're doing offensively," he says, "and . . . whatever you're going to do, believing in it, and not changing if you have a bad game. But I also started seeing that, *Hey, we get different kinds of players, we're playing against different kinds of competition*."

He would have to adapt—and grow.

"Some guys think, *If I'm flexible, that's a weakness*," Ruffin says. "Nope. If you're flexible, that's a major strength . . . You get your different philosophies in line, but there's also room to be flexible in each of those philosophies . . . Not many coaches can do that—be able to adjust that system to fit the strengths of the kids that you have right then. That's a big learning deal."

Lincoln made some changes, two in particular.

The first change: he took the Air Raid offense as he knew it and put it through a metamorphosis.

Mike Leach's original Air Raid was built on passing almost exclusively, with the run as a convenient option here and there.

Lincoln began to rebuild it with a greater focus on running the ball.

"I think a lot of the base concepts and way of thinking, at Tech, it was a lot different," Lincoln says. "We were gonna be the same at Tech no matter who we recruited and who we played with. The beauty at Tech was the consistency—the almost obsessive devotion to what we were doing. But we didn't change much week to week, year to year. We just kinda—*Here's what we're doing and here we go*, and we just got really good at it. And then I still had that mentality in the early years at ECU."

His first season at East Carolina, the Pirates had passed 68 percent of their plays and run only 32 percent of the time.

By the end of Lincoln's second season, that ratio had shifted by more than 10 percentage points, to 57–43.

Lincoln started to add new formations to the Air Raid offense that he'd come up with himself, that had nothing to do with what Mike Leach had taught him. Mainly, that meant adding not one but two tight ends, and sometimes even adding multiple halfbacks in the backfield. He also incorporated more complex plays. Where the Air Raid offense is fairly simple—line up a bunch of receivers and have them run a bunch of different routes to keep the defense off balance—Lincoln added motions and shifts in which players move around more prior to the snap, throwing defenses even more off kilter.

He would spend days locked in a room with his staff, studying the Air Raid playbook and developing new concepts based on it. He brought in coaches he'd worked with at Texas Tech, and they meshed well with other longtime East Carolina assistant coaches. And he worked closely with Ruffin and the other coaches to ensure they made the most out of what their players could do rather than expecting too much of them. "You really had to work your hind parts off to do that," Ruffin says. "And you learn how to be flexible ... to be able to adjust to your strengths and what a kid can do."

And in those rooms with his coaches, he made sure not to do what he felt he'd done at Texas Tech as a younger man—just railroad everyone with his own ideas. Mike Leach, after all, had listened to everyone who had something to say, even Lincoln when he was just nineteen years old. Lincoln, in turn, did the same with his staff. He listened. "He gave everybody on offense a chance to have an opinion," said inside receivers coach Donnie Kirkpatrick. "He listened to those opinions, he grew from those, and then he made final decisions."

In addition to overhauling his offense, Lincoln also changed the way he worked with his players. He took to heart what Harold Robinson had said: *You can't go out there and do it for them.*

Lincoln took it further, too: he made sure he saw things from his players' perspective.

He remembered what it felt like to be a struggling college football player.

He remembered what he had needed at the time, and it sure wasn't a coach screaming at him and belittling him. He remembered feeling the full weight of his inadequacy. A young man who feels inadequate already doesn't need someone else telling him to be less inadequate, getting angry at him for his inadequacy—he needs someone who cares about him, someone who will help build him up. Someone who believes in him.

Lincoln let his heart be soft again.

He stopped figuratively head-butting himself and his players.

"We turned it around at the end of the season," he says, "and played a little better."

The Pirates went 4–3 the rest of the season and that felt good, but two of those losses felt particularly brutal. The first was a 48–28 blowout loss to Southern Mississippi at home, and the second was the final game of the season against Marshall, an overtime loss against a team they could have beaten. They were still outmatched.

"They didn't have any answers for that situation," says Nathan Summers of the *Daily Reflector*. "They pulled out all their tricks in that game, and they went three and out in that first possession in overtime. And it was clear they were not gonna win that game."

"He took that to heart," Summers recalls.

Still, despite how much work there still was to do, and despite that year being his hardest year as a coach, and despite all the team's struggles, 2011 was still East Carolina's all-time fifth-best season in total passing yards. And the receiver Lincoln had believed in, Justin Hardy, was named to the conference All-Freshman team, finishing with six touchdowns and 658 yards on sixty-four receptions in ten games played.

"I'm lucky to be here," Justin would say later.

What Lincoln had seen in those old high school tapes had become abundantly clear after Justin joined the team. "The first rep, the first drill he ever did, the first day of two-a-days," Lincoln told a reporter. "When you see it, you see it. It was just an easy, simple catching drill. Sometimes you just see something with guys. Not like it was hard to see, like I'm some visionary, none of that. It was just very obvious he had some big-league skills."

It had been a rough year, but good things still happened, and important lessons had been learned.

That year, Lincoln learned who he was *not*—he was not a brooding workaholic performance-obsessed coach who figuratively beat himself and those around into working *harder*, dammit, to leave *nothing* on the table—no, those were parts of him that had begun to take hold, but in the way a coach had once taken hold of his face mask before head-butting him in order to draw his own blood before a freshman football practice. They *felt* good sometimes, and they were *energizing* in a way, but they were not exactly healthy. They got his players' attention, but they didn't make his players better.

That year was like a reset that reshaped Lincoln into the kind of coach he was meant to be.

That year, Lincoln says, "I grew up."

So much of growing up is less about learning more, and more about unlearning unhealthy habits in order to connect with who you really are. Lincoln had been figuratively head-butting himself most of the season and having little to show for it beyond the pain. He left that behind and moved forward accordingly.

"I'm more steady now," he says. "Not the crazy ups or the crazy downs. I don't feel like I get as riled up either way now."

10

Magic

SHANE CARDEN, NOW A redshirt sophomore, narrowly lost a quarterback competition in the 2012 preseason, edged out by redshirt junior Rio Johnson, who performed respectably in East Carolina's first game of the season, a 35–13 win over Appalachian State. But then the Pirates went to Charlotte, where, in front of seventy-seven thousand fans, they faced No. 9 South Carolina in the Carolina Panthers' stadium, and things did not get off to a good start. Through the first half, the formidable South Carolina defense, led by superstar defensive end Jadeveon Clowney, made easy work of the Pirate offense—Johnson threw two interceptions, and the Pirates failed to score a point, entering halftime trailing 21–0.

Shane, who had filled out to become a six-foot-two, 215-pound gunslinger, was coming off the bench.

The Pirates had possession to start the second half, and Shane was fired up. "I came running out of the tunnel real excited," he said.

Then, on the second play of the half, on his first pass, he threw an interception.

For the Pirates' next possession, Johnson was back in the game, and Shane was back on the bench.

That might be my only pass this season, he thought. *This can't really happen this way.*

Johnson promptly threw another interception, which was returned for a touchdown. With the Pirates trailing 28–0, with little to lose and curious what the promising gunslinger could do, Lincoln put Shane in once again.

On the next series, Shane threw just one pass, and it was incomplete, and the Pirates punted the ball away after just five plays, but it was, technically, progress.

After the Pirates' defense forced the Gamecocks to punt, Shane took the field, and this time, on the first play, he completed his first pass, a fourteen-yarder to Jabril Solomon. He completed six more passes on the drive, including one on fourth down with six yards to go, and the Pirates were able to kick a field goal.

On the Pirates' next possession, Shane completed four out of five passes as he led the Pirates eighty-two yards down the field, including two passes to his former scout team buddy Justin Hardy, one for twelve yards and the other for thirty-four—and a touchdown.

The game ultimately ended in a 48–10 defeat, but it marked the beginning of what would become a fantastic era of East Carolina football.

After that game, Lincoln went to Ruffin to discuss starting Shane for their next game, against Southern Mississippi.

"It took about ten seconds," Lincoln said later.

Shane Carden was in.

The Pirates won the Southern Miss game by a score of 24–14. They weren't playing well, and their offense wasn't clicking the way Lincoln wanted, but Shane did his job, passing for 171 yards and a touchdown with no interceptions. His touchdown pass was once again to Justin, with whom he connected five times for ninety-two yards. Lincoln was pleased with the way Shane handled himself and the team throughout, later describing his performance as "really impressive."

"We played poorly offensively," Lincoln said, "but he had a good feel for *We're not that great offensively right now. We're on the road. We're playing great defensively.* We were up most of the game, but he made just enough plays that we could win. He was really smart about it."

Next, however, the Pirates went to Chapel Hill to face North Carolina, and once again their fearsome rival dominated them: the Tar Heels won 27–6. Shane threw for just 124 yards, with no touchdowns or interceptions, and finished with a quarterback rating of 26.3. He was sacked five times and fumbled on one of those sacks. It was a simply miserable game. "I remember sitting outside the locker room at North Carolina," Shane later recalled to a reporter. "We sat out there and [Lincoln] gave me confidence. He just connected with me. He helped me understand that I was a young quarterback, but I would learn."

The learning would take time and test patience. After the North Carolina game, the Pirates won a tight game against the University of Texas, El Paso, 28–18. It was not a particularly promising victory, as the Miners were one of the weaker CUSA teams—they would go on to finish the season 3–9 overall and 2–6 in conference. The next week, the Pirates lost badly to the University of Central Florida by a score of 40–20.

That put their record at 3–3 for the season, and the Pirates still felt adrift and not quite able to find their way. Nathan Summers, the *Daily Reflector* sportswriter, wrote a column about it, echoing what many in Greenville were starting to feel at the time: that Lincoln's offense was running its course, becoming predictable and— heaven forbid—even boring.

"A lot of teams were scheming against the spread," Summers

recalls, "and . . . blitzing the defensive ends when they went empty backfield, and common, you know, just football stuff."

He adds, "They were dangerously close to revisiting that Marshall moment . . . where they had maybe run out of tricks."

There was plenty of opportunity for Lincoln to revert to the brooding, overworking coach he had become the season before. But instead of getting angry and pushing himself and everyone around him to the breaking point, Lincoln would remember to dial all that back, all those old-school football philosophies—and just do what he did best: He thought. He dreamed. He created. "To be able to win and produce there, we had to adapt," he says.

He stayed in those rooms with Donnie Kirkpatrick and the rest, brainstorming—and listening—as he created ways for his offense to evolve. In particular, he started using what's known as a run-pass option. It's a play that's called as a run but has a passing option if the quarterback, after reading the defense, determines that throwing would be better.

"I started to believe more—you gotta adapt to what your players do well," Lincoln says. "Have a base system you believe in, and a base concept you believe in, and ideas, but also having the flexibility to adapt to what your players do well year in and year out."

Lincoln was determined that East Carolina would not run out of tricks. He believed in Shane Carden and Justin Hardy and the rest, and he believed in what they were doing, and he believed that any day now, it would begin to click.

Lincoln and Ruffin spent hours every week talking through the offense and defense alike, one playing off the other. "I would go in," Ruffin says, "and say, *Linc, here's the things that would hurt me defensively . . . I'll tell you things, Linc, that bother me on defense.* And then just never tell him what to do, but sit and watch it. And I watch it and go, *Okay, that's gonna be good.* Because then I couldn't figure them out. Always looked at it from that point of view—calling plays against it. So he added to it, added two back, added offset back, added tight end, tight end flex . . . He just kept adding."

"We started adapting more," Lincoln says, "and marrying some of those old throw principles we believed in with more play action, with more run game, with a few more formations—and yeah, we kinda found a little niche there, and that kinda kept expanding."

When it came time for Lincoln to implement the changes they developed with the team, Ruffin gave him the room to do so his way, even encouraging him to take the lead in team meetings. "We talked about this, him at a young age, when you are a volunteer, think of yourself as a graduate assistant," he says. "If you're a full-time coach, prepare to be an offensive coordinator. And when it happens, you'll be ready for it, and when you're an offensive coordinator, get ready to be a head coach. So as a coordinator, he conducted offensive meetings just as if he was a head coach."

Ruffin began handing Lincoln more responsibility, too. He had him planning practices and running team meetings, to the point where people began to joke that Lincoln was the real head coach. This was by design, Ruffin says. He, like Donnie Duncan, saw the greatness in Lincoln's future and wanted to help him reach it. "I think that's part of our duty, if I'm in a position to do that," he says. "Everybody can't do that because they're nervous about that guy taking his job. I'm not and I wasn't then . . . It's part of our duty in this business to train them, and to pay it forward. Sharing responsibilities. Sharing opportunities. And the only way you become a head coach is practice as a head coach."

Following the loss to Central Florida, the Pirates turned a corner and began to look like all that Lincoln thought they were. They were back home at Dowdy Ficklen Stadium in front of forty-five thousand fans, and facing a strong Memphis team. It could have been a tough game.

On the opening possession, on the third play of the game, Shane threw a sixty-seven-yard touchdown pass to Justin.

On their second possession a few minutes later, he hit Justin for a thirty-nine-yard touchdown pass.

The Pirates proceeded to dominate the rest of the game as well. Shane finished with 308 passing yards and five touchdowns, three of which were to Justin, who finished with 137 receiving yards.

The final score was 41–7.

As the game ended and the teams left the field, Lincoln locked eyes with Nathan Summers, who was standing behind the end zone. "He was at the twenty-yard line," Summers recalls, "and he sorta had a grin on his face and he sorta didn't, and he's looking at me in a kinda weird way . . ."

Lincoln ran straight at Summers, grabbed him by his shirt, and "He was, like, shaking me," Summers recalls. "Like, *Was that exciting enough for you, Nate?!* And then he just ran off. I didn't know how to take it."

A couple of days later, when Summers saw Lincoln at practice, he asked him, "Were you pissed at me at all?"

"Naw, man!" Lincoln replied, shooting him a grin. "I was just excited!"

The Pirates finished the season strong, with an 8–5 overall record and 7–1 in their conference division, tied for first place as division co-champions. Shane Carden finished with three thousand passing yards and twenty-three passing touchdowns, while Justin Hardy finished with eleven hundred passing yards and eleven touchdowns—and just a glimpse of greatness to come.

And on top of all that, Lincoln had become a father. That December, Caitlin gave birth to their daughter Sloan.

As the 2013 season approached, the vibe around East Carolina football had demonstrably changed. A freshman scholarship wide receiver named Isaiah Jones arrived. Six foot one, and better known as Zay, he hailed from Stephen F. Austin High School in Austin, Texas. He had sent his high school highlight tape to East Carolina because his father, Robert, had played there. In fact, Robert Jones, a linebacker, had been the school's only consensus All-American. Lincoln and Ruffin loved what they saw on the tape, and Ruffin called Zay right away. "He really believed in me when a lot of people didn't," he says. "A lot of people didn't see my potential. They saw an average player with average speed . . . A lot of people told me I wouldn't play Division I football." In fact, the only other Division I program to offer him a scholarship was Arkansas State. But Zay Jones would be Exhibit A for one of Lincoln's greatest gifts, perhaps even greater than what he could scheme up for a playbook: his ability to identify players with potential who had gone overlooked by others, and to help them not only to play up to their potential, but also to surpass the potential they thought they had.

"He just really vibed well with the players," Zay says. "You could just tell he genuinely loved us. And I really just believed and trusted in him."

Lincoln saw Zay Jones as an ideal counterpoint to Justin Hardy, giving the Pirates another immediate NFL-level threat, and he convinced Zay that he was ready to be a starter, even as a true freshman. Zay wasn't sure. "Lincoln wasn't afraid to play me as a freshman," he says. "That's the thing . . . freshmen really don't go in there and just start right away. That's not really common. So to have Lincoln trust me, like—*No, this kid out of high school, at eighteen years old . . . is ready.* Threw me in the fire, just knew I could handle it, and I just trusted him. Like, *You know what, coach? You feel like I can do this? I'm gonna do it.*"

In the first game of the season, Zay caught a touchdown pass. He caught four more over the course of the season, had nine receptions in two separate games, eight in two others, and twice reached the hundred-yard mark. He did things he didn't know he was capable of.

The Pirates went on to have their best season yet in terms of wins—they finished 10–3 and won a bowl game. "Lincoln Riley's presence is rare," Zay says. "His aura and his persona is unmatched. The level of energy that he *exuberates* is *phenomenal*. Lincoln just had a different swagger."

And the rest of the team produced a monstrous and gorgeously balanced set of statistics: East Carolina was the only team on its level to have a four-thousand-yard passer in Shane Carden, a one-thousand-yard receiver in Justin Hardy, *and* a one-thousand-yard rusher in Vintavious Cooper.

For all his energy and swagger, however, Lincoln was also a stickler for discipline when he felt the situation called for it. Vintavious Cooper, a senior, was late to a team meeting leading up to the final game of the season, and team rules mandated that he be benched to start the next game. Ruffin was inclined to let it slide. The next game was Senior Night, after all. But Lincoln insisted, Ruffin recalls, "and he said, *Ruff, this is what we've done our whole time here.* It may be tough, and he was exactly right . . . There comes a point in any type of organization where accountability applies to everyone."

Job offers began rolling in for Lincoln. Assistant positions at major programs. North Carolina. Texas. Notre Dame. As he decided how to respond, Lincoln did what he was learning to do best: he listened. He listened to Ruffin McNeill, who of course didn't want him to leave but still wanted the best for him. Mike Leach. Donnie Duncan. "Lincoln wanted to make the right move," Leach says.

The Notre Dame job was particularly tempting. "I said, *Listen, I know it's Notre Dame,*" Leach recalls, "*but you control your destiny to a far greater degree there at East Carolina than you will at Notre Dame. You're just another guy at Notre Dame.*"

This wasn't just about finding a better job. This was about finding the right job. A job that challenged him but also made the most of his gifts. Lincoln possessed unique talent, unique ability, and a unique opportunity to control his destiny, as Leach put it. "So he turns it down," Leach says. "Which took some nuts, too. And he didn't get caught up in money."

Ruffin recalls that Lincoln "had job offers that probably could pay him two or three, even four times as much as I could. He told them no, to stay with me by my side. To stay with us . . . And so a lot of that, Donnie had to do with."

Donnie Duncan was becoming one of Lincoln's primary advisers, one of the men he trusted most to help him make big choices. "I consulted him on every major career decision," Lincoln said.

"We fed off of [Donnie's] knowledge and wisdom," Ruffin says. "I had him come down to our games as much as possible."

And whenever Lincoln was in Dallas for recruiting, he would visit Donnie, and they would take to the water. Donnie shared Lincoln's love for it. They would get in a car and drive forty miles outside of Dallas, to Lake Grapevine, and set off on Donnie's boat—which, at thirty-seven feet, was really more like a small yacht. "We would get out there on the water, take some food out there, and would stay up all night," Lincoln has said. "Just he and I, nobody else, and just sit there and soak it all in."

They talked about everything. Contract negotiations. Career choices. Compliance. Dealing with boosters. Dealing with the media. They'd talk about all Lincoln could do, and all that Donnie saw for him two or three steps ahead. "What an incredible learning environment," Lincoln has said. "Very little of it had to do with football. He was, in essence, I think, preparing me to be a head coach without me actually knowing it."

Donnie told Lincoln to be patient, to wait not only for the right move but also for the right moment. "Donnie trained both of us," Ruffin said, "and patience was a big thing . . . Patience is the key."

In the meantime, Lincoln remained focused on landing the right players for his evolving Air Raid schemes—Shane Carden's senior year was coming up, and the time had arrived to begin training a proper replacement. Lincoln had his eye on a new quarterback he thought could be special, too. He was a transfer quarterback, having played at Texas Tech as a true freshman, and Zay Jones knew him from high school. His name was Baker Mayfield.

Lincoln and Baker reminded Zay of each other. "Lincoln's ambitious," he says. "Ready to get after it. Aggressive . . . He's a risk-taker . . . And Baker's one of those fearless quarterbacks, too. Baker's got some swagger with him. Baker's got confidence. He knows that he's the man. He knows that he's a dominant play-maker."

Lincoln called Baker a couple of times, and they talked. It turned out they did have a lot in common. Baker had grown up as a dreaming young kid in Texas, too, and was also a little bit different from most people around him. Though he was raised just outside Austin, home to the University of Texas, he grew up a die-hard fan of Texas's archrival, the University of Oklahoma.

Baker and his older brother, Matt, both wore Oklahoma gear for class pictures in elementary school, and Baker would flash the upside-down Hook 'Em Horns sign—utterly offensive to anyone loyal to the Longhorns. He grew up fighting with classmates about it.

Baker came by his love of the Sooners through his father, James, who had played high school football for Rex Norris, a future assistant coach for Oklahoma under Barry Switzer. And James Mayfield was close friends with several members of Oklahoma's coaching staff, such as Mike Jones, who helped teach Baker how to throw a football. "That little runt," Jones said. "He used to wear me out playing football . . . Baker was a competing son of a gun at a very young age. He loved OU football, loved to hear me tell stories about OU and football."

Baker grew up tailgating with his father in a parking lot across from the stadium before Oklahoma football games and watching the games from the sidelines, and he met several Oklahoma football players along the way. They might as well have been gods, and Baker wanted to be one of them one day. Even as he enrolled at Lake Travis High School, less than twenty miles from the University of Texas campus, Baker saw himself as a future Sooner.

But Baker was overlooked—he was tiny, just five foot two as a freshman, and even though he had grown eight inches by his sophomore year, he was still small next to the other quarterbacks on the roster. By his junior year, he was still a backup. "It was a hard time for me," he later said.

The first game that year, the team's starting quarterback got hurt, so Baker went in and threw for three hundred yards and rushed for another hundred. He then went 25–2 in two years as the Lake Travis starter, passed for six thousand yards and sixty-seven touchdowns total, and won a 4A state championship. But he also went largely unrecruited. So Baker decided to walk on at Texas Tech in 2013—same as Lincoln had done twelve years earlier. Now coached by former Red Raider quarterback Kliff Kingsbury, Texas Tech remained a solid football program where Baker thought he could play, and the in-state tuition eased the financial burden on his parents.

He didn't even get to pick his jersey number there, and he was handed number 6.

He made the team, earned a spot as the backup quarterback, and then the starter got hurt, making Baker the first walk-on true freshman to start a season opener in any of college football's "Power 5" conferences.

His first game, he threw for 413 yards and four touchdowns.

Texas Tech won its next four games as well, with Baker at quarterback.

But in his fifth game, a 54–16 win over Kansas, Baker sprained his knee and had to sit out for the next few weeks.

In that time, something seemed to sour between him and Kingsbury. "All of a sudden," Baker later said, "it was as if I hadn't played for him, hadn't done anything for him. It was just different after I got hurt."

James Mayfield later told people that Kingsbury "completely withdrew contact" and "didn't talk to Baker. He didn't include Baker in the meetings."

Baker recovered and played a few more games, finished the season with 2,315 passing yards and twelve touchdowns, and he was named the Big 12 Conference's freshman offensive player of the year. But he said Kingsbury would not guarantee him the starting job as a sophomore, nor even a scholarship. "That was the final straw for me," Baker said.

He said screw it, he was leaving Tech.

In their first conversation about a possible transfer to East Carolina, Baker and Lincoln talked a bit about Lincoln's career and how it had ended, and the way that that experience had influenced the way he cared about coaching his players now: "He cares so much because he wanted it so bad," Baker says. "And he still does. I respect that."

But in the end, Baker told Lincoln that he was going to walk on at his dream school, Oklahoma.

Oklahoma had just won the Sugar Bowl in a stunning upset of Alabama, and they'd been led by Trevor Knight, a freshman quarterback who had played lights-out and been named the game's most valuable player. "Trevor Knight's going to be there for three years," Lincoln said. "Are you crazy?"

Baker would not be moved. His dream was to play at Oklahoma.

Lincoln said all right and wished him the best of luck, and soon thereafter, Baker did what he said he was going to do. He went to Norman, where he enrolled at the University of Oklahoma without first so much as speaking with a member of the coaching staff.

As the 2014 season approached, Lincoln and Ruffin were preparing under the heavy weight of terrible news: Donnie Duncan had been diagnosed with terminal cancer. "Oh, that was tough," Ruffin says. "Tough is not even the right word . . . It was devastating."

Donnie's relationship with Ruffin and Lincoln had become a source of life, a way of giving him goals to keep moving toward. "It was something that kept him going," Lincoln said.

Donnie told them, "Do not pity me. That will not help me heal."

"From that point on," Ruffin says, "we never did. We just talked as much as we could."

And they set out to make East Carolina football as great as they thought it could be.

As the season got under way, it quickly became clear that Lincoln wouldn't be at East Carolina much longer. The only questions were where he would be going next, and how much the Pirates would accomplish in the meantime. And that season, Lincoln's coaching finesse and foresight went on full display. The Pirates' first game was against North Carolina Central, a team they typically dispatched with ease. They started the game slow, however, and were trailing 7–3 late in the first quarter. "We had been struggling," Zay recalls. "We were a little bit behind . . . and Lincoln was like, *Screw it . . .*"

He called a play named "Magic," in which Shane Carden handed off to one guy who sprinted one way only to then hand it off to Justin Hardy, who sprinted the other way, and then Justin—a former quarterback—would get around the edge to launch a bomb downfield to Zay.

A double-handoff reverse pass.

Just a little something to get the juices flowing.

And it worked.

Justin hit Zay for a forty-one-yard touchdown pass.

"And," Zay says, "we went on to blow out that game."

They won 56–7.

For their second game the Pirates traveled to No. 21 South Carolina and played in front of eighty thousand people in Williams-Brice Stadium. "We didn't play our best," Shane said after. They'd felt they had a real chance to win the game but ended up losing, 33–23.

"Everyone was pretty bummed after the game," Shane said. "Coach Riley grabbed myself, Justin Hardy, and a couple other guys before we even got off the field."

Lincoln was already thinking ahead. "He told us the rest of the guys would be looking at us and how we handled this loss," Shane said. "He told us to stay up, because the next couple games would define our season."

The next game was in Blacksburg against No. 17 Virginia Tech. Lincoln reveled in the matchup against the Hokies because Bud Foster's defense was a lot like Lincoln's offense in one way that Lincoln loved. As Nathan Summers of the *Daily Reflector* put it, "[Lincoln] said his unit and Foster's parallel one another in that neither one is based in deception, and that both are rooted in out-executing the opposition."

But Virginia Tech was killing East Carolina early with a relentless, devastating blitz. Lincoln and Shane easily could have panicked, but they didn't. Lincoln believed in himself and his quarterback, so he stuck up a figurative middle finger at Virginia Tech and all of its blitzing and had Shane start throwing deep over and over again, each play a race between Shane finding an open man before the pass rushers got to him. Lincoln kept calling aggressive pass plays—with all the blitzing, there was bound to be open grass somewhere, and Shane kept finding it. He threw for 427 yards and three touchdowns, and East Carolina pulled off the upset, 28–21.

Ruffin McNeill loves that story and what it illustrates about Lincoln. "That's a small thing," he says, "but it's a big thing. Everybody feared the pressure, but he didn't. He took advantage of it."

But nothing could prepare anyone for what happened the week after that.

North Carolina came to Greenville, and the Pirates played what may well have been the single most memorable game ever played in Dowdy Ficklen Stadium, putting up 35 points in the first half and 35 more in the second. They racked up 789 yards of total offense. They won by a final score of 70–41. Even the sunset was absurd in its beauty that night, the sky becoming a breathtaking blend of

Pirate purple and fiery golden orange. People around Greenville have pictures of the stadium and the score of the game and the sky above it from that night framed in their offices and homes like works of art.

East Carolina was ranked in the national Top 25 after that game, for the first time since Ruffin and Lincoln came to town.

Afterward, Shane Carden recalled the Pirates' loss to South Carolina. "I think back to that moment," he said, "and how he handled it, because he knew we could have easily hung our heads and let it affect us negatively."

The Pirates kept winning.

Three weeks later, they were 7–1 and ranked No. 18.

Old habits didn't couldn't completely die—just as quickly, the Pirates inexplicably lost to Temple, a middling conference opponent, and then came Cincinnati. With time running down and East Carolina trailing 45–39, Lincoln called several pass plays in the red zone that kept the clock from running down more. He eventually got his touchdown, but he had also appeared to badly mismanage the clock—more than a minute remained. Cincinnati had time to go downfield, kick a field goal, and take home the win.

That loss knocked the Pirates out of the Top 25, and Lincoln's picture ran on the front page of the local sports section that week, in which he appeared exhausted and weathered in a heavy pullover coat. "The fans were calling him out," Nate Summers says. "You know, we're talking about it. 'Pirate Nation,' quote unquote, was in just a huge uproar about it. The fans knew they were that good of a team and the fans expected you know, this magic ride. They saw that this was their chance to have that kind of a season."

The loss apparently ate at Lincoln so much that he was still stewing on it a week later. While in an airport on a bye week recruiting trip, he picked up his phone and called Nate Summers.

"I could just tell he had been drinking," Summers recalls.

"I wanna talk about this goddamn Cincinnati thing, man," Lincoln began. "It's driving me nuts."

"He laid out all this stuff about play calling," Summers says. "And he was just so damn passionate about it."

They talked for an hour.

The Pirates won their next two games, then lost the season finale and their subsequent bowl game.

But as frustrating as losses like that could be, there was no denying how much better things had gotten in Greenville.

In five seasons as East Carolina's offensive coordinator, Lincoln's teams ranked No. 1 through 5 in the school's record books for total passing, not to mention a slew of other records. The team was setting so many records that breaking records started to feel routine. "We get a record here or there," Shane Carden told a reporter. "We just kind of look at each other and say, 'Well, we had no idea.' It just kind of comes."

The Pirates weren't just breaking their own records; they were becoming a national force. They ranked in the nation's top twenty for passing four times in those five years, the top twenty-five for total offense three times, and the top fifteen for scoring three times.

Ruffin and Lincoln may not have won as many games as Skip Holtz had—they didn't even win a conference championship—but they electrified Greenville and elevated Pirate football to a level never seen before. They had done more than make football fun again in Greenville. They had put the Pirates on the map. And they had done it by bringing together players that had gone overlooked everywhere else, and showing them just how good they could be. Assistant coach Donnie Kirkpatrick described their process like this: "We really try to put emphasis on it a lot like the NFL does with free agents. I really think we spend more time as a coaching staff evaluating and talking about the potential walk-on kids than the kids we sign."

Justin Hardy put it another way: "We find the players that nobody else wants," he said. "That's the kind of mentality we have. We're the team that nobody else wants."

And throughout the 2014 season, Shane Carden and Justin Hardy were experiencing personal success beyond anything either of them could have imagined. Fans loved the swagger Shane brought to Pirate football; he even tattooed the Dowdy Ficklen Stadium midfield logo on the inside of his biceps: a pirate skull inside the outline of the state of North Carolina.

And Justin remained the stoic one, the silent ninja somehow always losing his defenders, always sneaking into empty space, a Michael Crabtree–Wes Welker hybrid that no man could stop. ESPN started running highlights of their plays. Their identities coalesced into a hashtag that became their shared alter ego: "#Cardy." They became a national sensation. Shane had passed for more than three thousand yards and thirty-one touchdowns as a sophomore, and in each of his next two seasons, he passed for more than four thousand yards—the only Pirate quarterback ever to do so, and he did it twice. He was the conference MVP in 2013, and in 2014— after East Carolina switched to the American Conference—he was the conference offensive player of the year. He finished his career with 12,244 passing yards—a school record, and by miles—and claimed school records for single-game, season, and career marks in *every passing category*.

Justin, meanwhile, finished his career with 4,541 yards and

thirty-five touchdowns on 387 receptions—setting the NCAA all-time record for career receptions. "He's benefited from this offense just like Crabtree and any other receiver, because this offense creates opportunities," Lincoln told a reporter. "But make no mistake: this guy would be a starter anywhere in the country. If things go his way and he continues to stay healthy and humble, he's going to start for somebody for the next several years."

The Atlanta Falcons selected Justin in the fourth round of that year's NFL draft, and he's still with them today.

Two years later, Zay Jones would break his record for receptions, with 399.

As had become the norm, after the 2014 season Lincoln received several calls from schools wanting to interview him for various jobs, even getting a call from a coach with one of the most famous names in all of college football: Stoops. It was from Mark Stoops, the head coach at the University of Kentucky and the brother of Bob Stoops, the legendary coach at the University of Oklahoma.

Mark wanted to interview Lincoln about becoming his offensive coordinator.

As with all the other offers so far, however, Lincoln and the Wildcats ultimately didn't work out.

Not long after that, another call came in.

This call was from Bob.

This was Oklahoma.

11

Norman

BOB STOOPS WAS ONE of college football's kings. He was an Oklahoma icon, and one of the rare coaches who seemed to actually have some semblance of job security. Now he was looking for someone who could help him protect his legacy.

Stoops had orchestrated a remarkable turnaround in Norman. Before his arrival, the Sooners had fallen far from the dominance they had enjoyed in the 1970s and '80s under Barry Switzer, when they were regularly at the top of their conference and won three national championships. Switzer's tenure came to an abrupt end in 1988 after various scandals hit the team, and Oklahoma football began a steady decline. "In the nineties, they were just a joke," says Jason Kersey, a reporter who has covered the team for the *Daily Oklahoman* and the *Athletic*.

The joke bottomed out in 1998 after three straight losing seasons, and the university went looking for someone to turn things around.

They found Stoops at the University of Florida, where he'd been the defensive coordinator for three years under head coach Steve Spurrier. The Gators had finished No. 5 in the country with a 10–2 record in 1998, and they beat Syracuse in the Orange Bowl. That was recommendation enough. Stoops was in.

One of his first moves was to hire a good offensive coordinator, and he knew just the guy he wanted.

Mike Leach.

At the time, Leach was Hal Mumme's offensive coordinator at Kentucky, where they were making the Air Raid offense officially a "thing." The team itself was only okay in 1998—they'd gone 7–5—but that was solid for Kentucky, and they had turned quarterback Tim Couch into a Heisman winner and No. 1 overall draft pick. The Wildcats' offense was the talk of college football, and Stoops wanted that offense for himself, so he hired Leach.

Leach installed his Air Raid offense and a new era for Oklahoma football began. The Sooners went 7–5 in 1999, which was a solid improvement for a first-year head coach taking over a struggling program—but their offense was so impressive that Leach got hired away after just that one season to become the head coach at Texas Tech.

Stoops gave an assistant coach the offensive coordinator job and had him basically run the same offense Leach had installed the year before. Oklahoma started the 2000 season No. 19 in the country and went undefeated to win the national championship, with quarterback Josh Heupel playing so well he was named an All-American, a Heisman runner-up, and All–Everything Else.

From there, Stoops kept the Sooners near the top of college football. They won seven conference championships over the next twelve years. They produced superstar college players like running back Adrian Peterson and Heisman Trophy–winning quarterback Sam Bradford. Between 2001 and 2014, Stoops had five twelve-win seasons, four eleven-win seasons, and two ten-win seasons. The Sooners finished first or tied for first in their division eight times and were regularly ranked among the top ten teams in the country. Stoops's 2008 team was the highest-scoring team in college football history.

But in January 2015, Stoops wasn't happy with how things were going. Granted, in 2013 they'd gone 11–2 and won the Sugar Bowl. But the following year, the Sooners went 8–5, and the season had felt miserable by Oklahoma standards. They'd started off ranked No. 4 in the country, and they finished out of the Top 25, with a 40–6 loss to Clemson. "It was incredibly disappointing and deflating to take a major step backwards," Stoops later wrote in his book *No Excuses*. That season "might have been my most difficult at OU."

Stoops worried that things would get worse if he didn't make a big move. What bothered him wasn't just that the team had struggled—everyone has a down year here or there—but why they were struggling. Oklahoma's offense had moved away from what had originally made it great and "started chasing the next shiny new thing." They had a great running back in Samaje Perine, who racked up 1,713 yards and twenty-one touchdowns behind the Sooners' monstrous offensive line, but something just wasn't working.

So Stoops fired his offensive coordinator and went looking for a new one.

He wanted to reconnect with what had made his offense great in the beginning. "I just didn't feel we were operating our offensive system the way I felt it ought to be done," he wrote. "I thought we had drifted too far from the Hal Mumme–like system we had started with years earlier."

He had a few possibilities in mind—older, more experienced coaches.

This was a big decision. Nobody knew this at the time, but

Stoops was contemplating retirement. He was still young—just fifty-four—but he was quietly looking for a way out of the coaching game. He felt that there was more to life than coaching football, and he wanted to find out what it was. He also wanted the program to be in good enough shape for him to leave without things falling apart the way they had after Barry Switzer's departure decades earlier.

He called Mike Leach to get his advice. Leach gave him one name: Lincoln Riley. "Lincoln wasn't on his radar," Leach says. "I specifically told him Lincoln was the one he needed to hire."

Stoops had noticed Lincoln at the time of the Alamo Bowl in January 2010, when Lincoln had taken over Texas Tech's offense after Leach was fired. And as he looked deeper into his résumé, he loved what Lincoln had done with East Carolina. "Watching them play South Carolina and take them to the wire," he said, "watching them in their bowl game put up points and yards and move the ball against Florida. That was primary, and then . . . anyone you ask about Lincoln, they were excited about him."

So Stoops called Ruffin McNeill to ask for permission to interview Lincoln.

"He was selling him to me," Stoops later recalled. "I said, 'Ruffin, I've read all about him.' But that's the kind of guy Ruffin is. He felt that it was a good opportunity for him. He was all for it."

"I was so proud for him," Ruffin says.

So Stoops called Lincoln and set up an interview.

"I told him, *Look . . . you gotta talk to him*," Mike Leach recalls. "*And if he offers you the job, you gotta take it.*"

Meanwhile, Leach wasn't the only one lobbying for Lincoln to get the job at Oklahoma. Donnie Duncan was calling Max Weitzenhoffer, a university regent, who later recalled Donnie telling him, "We should hire Lincoln . . . He was the best out there and a perfect fit both as a coach and person to be the eventual coach here."

Not just the best offensive coordinator.

The best eventual coach.

And then, as Stoops was waiting for Lincoln to arrive for his interview, he got a call from Gil Brandt. Stoops was good friends with Brandt, too. "He said, 'Bob, there's a guy that you ought to research, check into and check out,'" Stoops recalled. "I said, 'Gil, he's going to walk in my office in five minutes.'"

When Lincoln met with Bob Stoops, the coaches' offices were situated in trailers parked across the street from the Oklahoma stadium; the team's offices and locker rooms were in the midst of their multimillion-dollar makeover. The stadium loomed large over the trailers, a fitting visual for what it meant for Lincoln to be there.

Their interview went well, too. "I was impressed," Stoops says. "I was impressed by the certainty of what he wanted to do, and his poise, and just the way he communicated, and the confidence, and the direction of his offense. And—he was so sure of what he wanted to do."

A week went by before Lincoln heard from Stoops, and he thought he hadn't gotten the job. "I really was going to be crushed if I didn't get it," he said later. "I knew this was perfect, the one I wanted as badly as any job I've ever interviewed for."

There were a lot of reasons why. "It's something that my wife and I have been very picky about for the last few years," Lincoln said later. "We were first looking for a great person. I was able to have that with Ruffin McNeill over the last several years at East

Carolina, and I know what [I'd be] getting into working at Oklahoma with Coach Stoops."

Then there was the football of it all. "It's honestly hard to match it," he said. "Coming into a program like this, coming to a place that is very committed to what we are going to be doing offensively, were things that were very important to me."

Oklahoma spends more than $1 million on recruiting alone. The renovations being made to the football facilities were going to update the offices, training facilities, and weight room, as well as enclose the south end zone to bring the stadium's seating capacity to 83,400—all to the tune of $160 million. This was a place devoted to its football.

And on top of all that, Norman wasn't all that far from Muleshoe. "Getting back close to home was a bonus, too," Lincoln said.

As Stoops considered things, Mike Leach stayed in his ear. "I fully endorsed Lincoln," Leach says. "Not just one call, a number of calls, with Bob. Bob had other people in mind. I said, *No, hire Lincoln.* 'What about this guy?' *No, hire Lincoln.* 'What about the other guy?' *No, hire Lincoln.* 'What about'—*No, hire Lincoln . . .* Bob was going to hire somebody else. And I said, *No, you're out of your mind. Here's who you need to hire.*"

Lincoln was on his way to a coaches' convention and had just landed at Love Field in Dallas when Stoops called to offer him the job.

And so it was official: Lincoln Riley, the dreaming kid from Muleshoe in the middle of nowhere, at just thirty-one years old, was going to be the offensive coordinator for Bob Stoops and the legendary University of Oklahoma.

"The very first day I walked onto campus at Oklahoma," Lincoln said, "my initial feeling wasn't awe or excitement. I felt pressure. I felt a sense of responsibility. OU is a place where that's just always present. You don't need to say it or even acknowledge it—it's just *there*."

In some ways, Norman felt a lot like Greenville. Both places had their small-town quirks. Norman's name started as a joke back in the 1870s. A young surveyor named Abner Norman was surveying the area for the U.S. government, and his crew jokingly carved a sign on an elm tree that said "Norman's Camp." When railways began service to the area and settlers began arriving in the late 1880s, people saw the tree and made that the name of their new town.

Like Greenville, Norman is a small college town with a similar population—about 120,000 to Greenville's 90,000—but it's nowhere near as isolated. Around 1960, after Interstate 35 was completed, the drive to nearby Oklahoma City suddenly became a quick half hour. This allows Norman to exist as a small town while still reaping the economic and cultural benefits that come with living in the vicinity of a metropolis. Plus, Dallas lies just three hours south. There's a lot of life around there.

So while Oklahoma football is big, there's a lot more going on. Norman doesn't feel like an island, and likely for that reason above all others, there's a sense of steadiness to the fandom here, a sense of security.

Yet with that security comes expectation: if you are part of the Sooners football program, you are here to perform, to produce results. Greenville had been a place for learning, for experimenting, for making mistakes. Norman was a place you either showed up or shoved off.

Not that Lincoln needed the motivation of a Power 5 fan base to make sure he performed. Oklahoma was the opportunity he'd been waiting for. The school nickname was deeply appropriate for his own experience: "Sooners" was the name given in the late 1800s to the settlers who sneaked into Oklahoma before it was officially opened for settlement. They were people who arrived somewhere before they were expected to be there.

Still, the juxtaposition between Norman and the towns Lincoln had been through—Muleshoe, Lubbock, Greenville—felt significant. Norman was in many ways the quintessential college football town. Everything about it felt like what someone who loved football and the small town life would call home.

Gaylord Family Memorial Stadium rises prominently from the edge of downtown. A few blocks away, the campus merges with a downtown area known as Campus Corner. That's where you can find restaurants, bars, souvenir shops, and the like. There's Louie's, a low-key burger joint and bar that's perhaps most famous for Bob Stoops's having invested in its opening years ago. Other popular locales include Seven Forty Seven, the Roof, and O'Connell's. A little way down the road from Campus Corner is the Mont. Locals will tell you that you haven't officially visited Norman until you've been to the Mont and had a drink called the Swirl: one part sangria, one part margarita, one part Everclear. If you have more than one, get a ride home.

The people of Norman are warm and friendly in all the ways that fit small-town stereotypes, and likewise, there is a gentle power to the fandom there. As in Greenville, the town parties on game days, and yet the partying in Norman feels somehow less intense than in Greenville. In Greenville, it can feel as if the partying is the point and the football is adjacent or even secondary to it. In Norman, it's all about the football, with partying as a nice addition.

Traditions run deep and rich in Norman, too. Where the Pirates have, well, a pirate on the field, in Norman you have two white ponies named Boomer and Sooner who pull the Sooner Schooner around the field—a replica of the covered wagons (or "prairie schooners") that settlers of the area used in the nineteenth century. Jets perform flyovers during the national anthem. During games, fans chant back and forth at each other, one side shouting "Boomer!" at the other, which shouts "Sooner!" in response. And outside the stadium, there is Heisman Park, home to regal bronze statues of every Sooner player who has won a Heisman Trophy.

It feels like the difference between living somewhere that *wants* success and a place that *knows* it. To want success is to feel that you don't quite have it. To know success is to have done the work and expect it to arrive. It's a small difference, but that gap between wanting and knowing has a profound effect on people and a town.

In Norman, greatness is simply known, the way love is known from a good romantic partner. It feels like a mature relationship with winning. There's a confidence to the football enthusiasm there. It's not a matter of wondering whether their team will be good, or even great—it's a matter of how great. Excellence feels familiar here. That's a different sort of pressure to live up to: an all-time great program's earned expectation of greatness.

Soon after Lincoln arrived in Norman, Donnie Duncan arranged a dinner between Lincoln and an Oklahoma legend: Barry Switzer. Donnie believed in Lincoln enough that, even then, he was telling people that Lincoln wasn't simply going to do well as Oklahoma's offensive coordinator; he described Lincoln as "our future coach." And so it was only right that the future coach meet the former coach who was known around town as the King.

It was January 2015, the night before Lincoln's first winter workout with Bob Stoops and the rest of the team. "And you don't tell Barry Switzer no," Lincoln later recalled. They went to an Italian restaurant, Benvenuti's, downtown. "We get to the restaurant," Lincoln said. "We're having a great dinner. I'm laughing, he's telling stories. We had a great mutual connection with Donnie. We were talking about OU. It's starting to get pretty late. We've got a bottle of wine open. I think it's some of his wine, actually. We're moving through that. It gets to be ten o'clock. I say, 'Coach, this is awesome, but I have to go. I have a five-thirty a.m. workout.' It's my first official team deal at OU."

Switzer pulled out his phone and called Stoops. "Why," he asked, "are you having a five-thirty a.m. workout?"

Lincoln made it in the next morning on time, but, he said, "I was a little foggy."

Had he been motivated solely by his own personal ambition, by such things as winning games, conquering college football's giants, and claiming rings, the pressure Lincoln faced as he met his new team could have felt crushing. He was still just thirty-one years old.

This was a young man who simply didn't feel pressure, and yet when he stepped onto Oklahoma's campus, he said he felt pressure all the same. And nobody—no matter how old their soul, no matter how wise their mentors, no matter how lucky their stars—can long withstand unrealistic expectations the likes of which such a job can place upon them.

"Things have happened for me quickly," he reflected. "I have worked hard and I have also been very, very fortunate to work for some great people and to learn from some great people . . . Just to be associated with the people that I've been lucky enough to be around, I've just been the luckiest coach in the world. I've been able to learn from those guys at such a young age, and they've taken a very unselfish interest in me, and they've certainly helped me get to this point."

And he was thinking about those things in large part because of Donnie Duncan.

Donnie had become one of the most important people in his life. "The relationship," he said, "really, really grew to a father-to-son relationship."

For Lincoln to be taking this job at Oklahoma had a particular significance. "That," Lincoln said, "was probably like a dream for [Donnie]—and for me—to come back to the place that was most special to him. He's always spoken so much about his love for this place."

Donnie was beloved by those who knew him, but some felt he hadn't done right by Oklahoma football during his time as athletic director in the 1990s. That was the decade when Oklahoma suddenly wasn't good at football anymore, between Switzer's departure and Stoops's arrival—and it happened under the command of three different head coaches, all of whom Donnie had hired. The first, Gary Gibbs, was a solid hire but just didn't win enough games. After him, Howard Schnellenberger lasted just a single season. Next, James Blake was fired after three consecutive losing seasons. Before Blake's last season, Donnie left Oklahoma to create and lead the Big 12 Conference.

And so—from a sports narrative standpoint, anyway—Lincoln doing well for Oklahoma would provide a measure of redemption for Donnie Duncan: "If Riley turns out to be a worthy caretaker of such a tradition," wrote Berry Tramel, a local sports columnist, "consider it a debt repaid in full."

Lincoln cared about doing well by Donnie, too, of course, but his desire to do well cut deeper than mere gridiron redemption.

Donnie's cancer was taking a nasty turn, and Donnie was beginning to deteriorate. Fading was the vibrant presence he had once
been, his hair going white and thin, his skin ashen and vulnerable,
small bumps becoming big bruises, his frame turning haggard and
frail.

After Lincoln was hired, Donnie told a friend he just wanted
to make it to the following January, to see the Sooners play their
bowl game at the end of the season. He wanted to see what Lincoln
would do with this team.

12

Baker

LINCOLN FACED MORE THAN just the challenge of living up to expectations—he also faced the challenge of changing how things were done at Oklahoma, similar to what Mike Leach had faced sixteen years earlier. The Sooner fan base wasn't nearly as negative as it had been when Leach first brought the Air Raid to Norman, but they had their reservations, because Oklahoma had once again become a running-focused team. The sportswriter Jason Kersey says, "They really didn't want to go back to a Mike Leach offense, because people were worried . . . They had these running backs, and I think the concern was, *Does he play with a fullback? Does he use tight ends?*"

But more importantly, Lincoln's own players had their doubts.

Sooner center Ty Darlington, a brilliant player and team leader who Lincoln once described as "the smartest person in the room," had not been impressed when he watched East Carolina's performance in the 2014 Birmingham Bowl. Shane Carden threw sixty-eight passes that day. "I was petrified," Ty said. "I was not a fan." The thought of passing sixty-eight times in one game—Ty said it was "unfathomable" and even "nauseating."

When Ty heard the news that Lincoln had been hired as Oklahoma's new offensive coordinator, his first thought was, *Well, there goes the run game.* His second thought: *Samaje Perine is doomed.*

Ty's assessment did not improve when he opened his new playbook in the spring of 2015. A self-described "brainiac," he liked complexity and deception and out-thinking the other team. He said, "I tend to be attracted to intricate offensive schemes rife with checks and audibles, predicated on finding the absolute *perfect* play for that particular defense."

And so, he said, "When I opened the new playbook, I felt almost insulted."

He was almost insulted because of the very thing that made Lincoln's version of the Air Raid work so well: "It's brutally simple."

As the Oklahoma players began learning their new offense, Ty was far from the only skeptic. There was significant concern about how much the team was focusing on passing.

But this is what made Lincoln Lincoln: he didn't come to Oklahoma determined to make players do things his way, which would have been a perfectly natural impulse. Head-butting them into submission, if you will. After all, he had made East Carolina one of the best offenses in the country, with far less talent to work with—an argument could be made that there was no reason for the Sooners to doubt him. But instead he was just going to show them what the offense could do. He was going to do what he did best: rewrite a formula. "One of the beautiful things in this offense," Lincoln said at the time, "is that it can become whatever we need it to become."

As a kid in Muleshoe, drawing up plays with childlike joy in fields full of caliche rocks, he had seen nothing but possibility. Likewise, now in Norman, Lincoln could create a dynamic air attack that bordered on chaotic balanced by an aggressive, even intimidating, smashmouth running game. All the pieces were there. He not only had quarterbacks with great potential, and receivers like Dede Westbrook who could do all sorts of great things—he also had a monstrous offensive line anchored around a brilliant center, and explosive running backs in the likes of Samaje Perine and Rodney Anderson, athletes built not only for elite college football but also for the NFL. Lincoln had no plans to abandon Oklahoma's running game at all. If anything, Shane Carden throwing sixty-eight times in a bowl game aside, running the ball had become a vital part of his game plan at East Carolina. In his final season there, the offense ran the ball on 48 percent of its plays. And here, in Norman, he had NFL-caliber talent at every position, and there was a lot he could do with that.

"There's going to be some games where we have to run it a lot," he said. "And there's going to be some games where people load up on us, that we're going to have to throw the ball well . . . This is an unselfish offense. Everyone will get involved. Not always, every ballgame. But throughout the year? A lot of people will get involved. If they stay unselfish and play hard, the mentality will be right."

His hard times at East Carolina—the way he had to learn to evolve and adapt with the personnel at his disposal—had prepared him well for taking over the Oklahoma offense. He'd learned how to be more creative, and now he had top-tier talent to work with. He saw the whole world in front of him. And he trusted that soon, if his players trusted him, they would see a whole new world, too. He told them that if they bought in, he would make them the best offense in the nation.

And besides, at least one player was excited about this new direction: the walk-on quarterback who had left Texas Tech two years earlier, whom Lincoln had tried to recruit to East Carolina, whom he had called crazy: Baker Mayfield. Baker already knew the Air Raid, having run a version of it at Texas Tech under Kliff Kingsbury, so he bought in right away. "Obviously it was a lot of fun for me," he says. "I got to throw a lot. I had been in an offense like that before."

In some ways, Baker was eerily reminiscent of Lincoln when Lincoln had been younger. Walk-on. Thought differently than most people around him. Worked harder than most people around him. Seemed driven by impulses that even he didn't seem to fully understand sometimes. Chip on the shoulder. Could come off as arrogant, which belied a sensitivity that, with proper management, could be leveraged for greatness. And willing to do anything to go after his dreams.

True to his word, Baker had just shown up on Oklahoma's campus a year earlier, having enrolled at the school without speaking with anyone in the football department. He didn't meet Bob Stoops until he showed up at a team meal sometime in January 2014. It was their first team meeting of the year. Later, Stoops called Baker's arrival "maybe the strangest thing that's ever happened in my coaching career."

Baker was aware of this strangeness. "People probably thought I was crazy just showing up without talking to the coaches," he said later.

Baker would make the team as a walk-on—Stoops knew the kid could play—but the Big 12 Conference's rules dictated that a player who transfers also had to give up a season of eligibility, so he couldn't actually play in games that fall. This did not suit Baker, who seemed to require competition the way most people require water. "I struggled having to watch from the sidelines," he said. "I struggled with the fact that I could not do anything to help my teammates out. I struggled with the fact that no matter how hard I worked, I would not be able to test my ability on Saturdays.

Although I was at the school I love, I was miserable. I was miserable watching the game I always played but was not allowed to play because I chose to walk on to another school."

When he wasn't practicing, working out, or going to classes, Baker got his fix by playing Halo 3 for hours on end, a video game he loved so much that at one point when he was younger he seriously considered quitting football to become a professional gamer. He also got into intramural sports with some guys he met in his dorm. They played softball, at which Baker excelled, having been a baseball player in high school. He was the team shortstop and displayed "unreal range," according to one of his new friends, Nick Pine, and he hit a lot of home runs. He also played basketball, though another one of his new friends, Brandon Boggs, politely said, "Baker is not nearly as good at basketball." And yes, he played flag football, but he was banned after the second game of the season.

Now that he was eligible for the 2015 season, Baker fully intended to be the Sooners' starting quarterback. "After I served my year of sitting out," he said, "I pushed myself harder than I ever could have imagined."

Problem was, Baker was a good quarterback, but he was only pretty good for Oklahoma. Trevor Knight, the incumbent starter, may not have become the superstar that everyone thought he was destined to be—"solid, not spectacular," to borrow one local newspaper headline—but he'd thrown for twenty-three hundred yards and fourteen touchdowns in 2014, with twelve interceptions. Then there was Cody Thomas, a redshirt sophomore who had performed respectably in a few starts the season before—and who, at six foot five with a strong arm, was built like a prototypical quarterback.

Baker was maybe six feet tall on a good day. He had a good but not great arm, he was athletic but not especially so, and he was smart but had gunslinger tendencies that resulted in some fantastic plays but also some silly interceptions.

Oklahoma had a quarterback competition on its hands. Bob Stoops liked to quote the legendary college basketball coach John Wooden, who said, "Competition is a coach's best friend." And Stoops was going to let Lincoln decide the winner. "Clean slate," he said. "I didn't care about the past. I told Lincoln that whomever he thought was the best quarterback after spring and fall workouts was to be our guy."

Lincoln liked Baker from what he knew about him heading into the spring—he liked the way he played, and he really liked the chip he carried on his shoulder. But he also recognized where Baker fell short. "He had to change in a lot of ways who he was as a player," Lincoln told a local reporter.

Lincoln wasn't the type of coach to head-butt a kid into playing better, but he wasn't going to sugarcoat things, either. From his own experience, he knew all too well how painful it can be to hear that you're not good enough to do the things you want to do more than anything else. But he also knew what was possible once you accepted what you could and could not do. "There are certainly times you gotta have tough conversations and be absolutely real with them, too," he says.

So Lincoln made it clear to Baker that nothing was guaranteed—and Baker responded well. He wanted to be great, and having flaws meant there was room to improve. He appreciated Lincoln's honesty. "I've got a pretty good judge of character," Baker says. "And from the start, I always felt like I could trust him."

To ensure that the three quarterback competitors would have a fair chance, Lincoln decided not to watch any film of any of them. How they performed through the spring and summer would determine who was under center in the fall.

That parking lot where James Mayfield once parked his truck to tailgate before Oklahoma games, where young Baker Mayfield grew up giddy that he was about to go watch gods play football? That parking lot, where Baker's dream began, was now the Everest Training Center, Oklahoma football's indoor training facility, where he was spending all his time chasing that dream. He'd made the team as a walk-on, and he had a chance to go after the starting spot, right there.

Lincoln did make Baker one guarantee. "He was like, *I'm gonna push you*," Baker says. "*The best guy's gonna play. So just take your coaching, and take it one day at a time.*"

13

Mentality

IN APRIL 2015, ABOUT a month after spring practice began, Lincoln walked into the Oklahoma weight room and saw Baker Mayfield looking far more subdued than usual. "We're around these guys so much," he told a local reporter, "even at that time, I could tell something wasn't right."

The night before, Baker's father, James, had called to say that his mom, Gina, had been in a car accident, but wouldn't go into more detail. All Baker knew was that it had happened in South Carolina, on the highway to Hilton Head Island, where Gina was going on vacation with some friends. James seemed to want Baker not to worry, but later that night Baker impulsively checked the Internet to see what he could find. He learned that the driver of a sedan had crossed the highway median, hopped a barrier cable, collided with one car, and then hit the small SUV that Gina's friend was driving, head-on. As the sedan hit yet another vehicle before finally stopping, Gina's SUV was violently rolling off the highway. The driver and passenger in the sedan died at the scene. The rest were at a hospital.

Lincoln arranged for Baker to fly to South Carolina as soon as possible, where Baker would spend the better part of a week, taking turns with his dad and his older brother in the hospital by

Gina's side. She had a lot of recovering to do—busted collarbone, damaged abdominals, intestinal trauma—but she would be okay.

That was an extreme situation, but Lincoln gave that kind of care, on a smaller, daily basis, to as many of his players as he could.

"He just loves these guys," Bob Stoops says. "And that came through immediately."

A lot of coaches say they love their players, say they care about them as human beings first and football players second, say all kinds of things that sound good, but "you can't fool the players," Ty Darlington wrote in a blog post. "They know. They know whether you really care about them as people, or if first and foremost you want to win, no matter the cost. There is no doubt in my mind that Coach Riley cares."

They can feel how much he feels for them.

They can feel how much he once felt what they feel now.

Lincoln busted up his shoulder in high school, was going to play at Texas Tech, it didn't work out. Yeah, he was now a wunderkind coach, but the disappointment still hurt. And he still felt that pain. He knew intimately how precious was the time playing the game. How fragile it could be. He'd been there. He'd tried to do what they were doing and he caught a bad break. He knew what they felt on that field. And he knew something else: the feeling of when it ends. As he had learned at East Carolina, he knew all too well just how important it was to love his players until that day. How important it was to walk them home.

Lincoln showed an acute understanding of just how short football careers usually are. Players are well aware that their careers have expiration dates that nobody actually knows. "He knows football is his job and his career," Baker says, "but for us, one day, it will end."

Lincoln knew this as well as any of them. All his players knew his story. "And that's why," Baker says, "seeing how honest he is, and how much he cares about us, and not just football—you can see that part of it, and that means a lot."

He knew what he was putting them through when he pushed them. He knew what it felt like to be told how much work you have left to do. That mattered to the players. "It does," Baker says. "It does for a lot of guys on the team, actually. I'd probably say almost everybody. If you hadn't been there, then it's kind of a question of, some guys might think, *Well, how do you know what this is like?* . . . He can relate. And that's very, very important."

As spring practice got under way, like all college coaches, Lincoln felt the strain of spending so much time away from his family. Children don't remember how big the house was they grew up in and they don't really care what their daddy does for work, but they remember everything about how Daddy made them feel. Many men, especially ambitious young men, make the mistake of forsaking their family for their work. Lincoln didn't. "You do have to separate it at times," he says. "Like when you go out of town, or one night you turn your phone off and spend time with your family. I certainly try to do that as much as I can."

One of the underrated aspects of being a coach at Oklahoma was that Bob Stoops was a family man at heart, too. As much as a college football coach can be, anyway. "There wasn't a *guard-your-desk* mentality," Lincoln says. There was no honor in working unnecessarily long hours. "That's one thing I learned from Bob," Lincoln says. "You gotta get away from it, too. I think that's a big reason for his consistency and longevity. He was able to get away, and recharge, and spend time with his family."

And Lincoln, same as he had done at East Carolina, sought to blend football with family, so he and Caitlin opened their home to his players in Norman. "We always felt—as soon as we were married and he had a full-time position—we really wanted the players to be around us outside of football," Caitlin says. "We really enjoy having them at our home, even if they are just laying on the couch watching football. But we think it's important to get to see him as a father, as a husband—as somebody who's not just an Xs and Os football coach. We want them to see him as more than just a coach—as a human being—and we want them to know he sees them as human beings, too."

Putting it simply, she says, "Relationships are what make life important, not accolades."

Lincoln welcomed Caitlin and Sloan to the practice fields or the office at least a few times each week. "Everything he does, you could take notes on," Baker says. "The way he carries himself. Every day. As a father, too."

And on those fields, as spring practice unfolded and the players did what Lincoln asked, they began to trust him, and they began to see just what might be possible.

Even the brilliant and skeptical Ty Darlington was coming around on Lincoln's offense, in all its brutal simplicity. He would come to describe what Lincoln was doing as not just simply installing a new offense, but also instilling a new approach to the game, which Ty later termed simply "the Mentality." "I've bought into the system," Ty wrote in a blog post. "I'm seeing the results . . . Sure, there are a variety of tweaks and tricks, but the base system is not difficult to understand whatsoever." He was coming to see what Lincoln had learned long ago from Mike Leach. "A complex offensive system oftentimes leads to doubt, hesitancy, and then underperformance," Ty said.

In Lincoln's offense, Ty saw, "Simplicity breeds confidence."

And that confidence was the key to the whole thing. "Confidence is the foundation of the Mentality," Ty said. "When a player is confident, he can play aggressively and he can play fast. The system itself, with its simple concepts and aggressive, big-play schemes, is designed to develop the same mentality *on the field* that he works so hard to cultivate *off the field.*"

In other words, Lincoln didn't convince his players that every play would work because the plays were perfect. He convinced them that the plays would work because *they* would make them work. "The guys on that offense truly believe that they are unstoppable," Ty wrote, "and that is why they are." He called this the most valuable thing he learned playing under Lincoln: "Mentality is more important than scheme."

It didn't matter what play was called—what mattered was that the players believed they would find success with those plays. Ty wrote, "This is the attitude Coach Riley instituted from Day One: Aggressive, fearless, confident."

What helped instill this confidence was the way that Lincoln made certain his players understood not only how the plays were meant to be run, but also *why.* He showed them the forces at work, the push of the receivers running one way in order to pull the defenders with them, in order to clear the space for another guy coming behind them. He convinced them that they were unstoppable for reasons that had nothing to do with him. That was Lincoln's genius as much as anything he put in the playbook. He wasn't all about himself. He didn't want to convince them to believe in him; he wanted to convince them to believe in themselves, by showing them who they really were.

"His ability to adapt to our personality and get the best out of our players has been huge," Baker says.

His hard times at East Carolina had given him more than just an affinity for creativity on the field—they had also reminded him to remain in touch with those soft parts of his heart that still hurt sometimes. To tap into his pain, let it soften his heart into its most natural state, that of giving more than instruction and coaching—that of giving love. That was what his players needed. They needed to feel heard, seen, felt.

The players believed in *his* belief in them, because they believed that he really knew them. And so much of this came back, in a way, to Lincoln's shoulder.

To his pain.

The thing about putting yourself aside to get to know somebody else is that it means inevitably revealing yourself along the way. Connecting with people requires authentic reciprocity. Lincoln's players got to know him, and as they did, they got to know just how much he had once wanted what they all had, and they saw how this gave him greater empathy for how much they wanted it, too. "He cares so much because he wanted it so bad," Baker says. "And he still does."

And as the offense mastered Lincoln's playbook, they wore their defense out. "Our offense jumped all over our defense," Baker says, "which was supposed to be strong . . . We had so many talented guys."

"We averaged I don't know how many yards per play that spring," he goes on. "Like, holy crap. This is why they brought him in. He knows what he's talking about."

That would become an emotional refrain for the next two seasons as Lincoln steadily grew his players' trust in the system: *Like, holy crap.*

"For me and for everybody, it was like, *this is the real deal*," Baker says. "It was like the words he had told us the whole time since we got there in January and then up until we start spring practice, what, the second week-ish in March—we realized that all the stuff he was saying and preaching for that long, when we got out there for the first day of practice, it was the real deal. If there were doubts in the back of your head—nah, they were gone, because this was real."

As spring rolled into summer, the quarterback competition raged on. "It was just like a prizefight," Lincoln said at the time. "A fifteen-rounder, where there wasn't one big knockout."

As summer took hold, Donnie Duncan's health continued to decline. Lincoln and everyone else began to get the clear sense that he would not be with them much longer. Ruffin McNeill was so upset that when he learned that Donnie was planning to sell his boat, he offered to buy it, even though he had no idea how to pilot a boat himself. He had it transported to Washington, North Carolina, a small town on the Pamlico River half an hour east of Greenville, and he renamed it *Timeout* because Donnie told him that he should think of taking the boat on the river in North Carolina as just that, a timeout.

In July, Steve Hatchell, the president and CEO of the National Football Foundation, announced that Donnie Duncan would receive the foundation's Legacy Award at its annual dinner that December at the Waldorf-Astoria Hotel in New York City for having "spent his entire life involved with the game of football" and having "made an impact at every level."

Donnie told his good friend John Underwood, the associate commissioner of the Big 12 Conference, that there were three things he wanted to live to see before he was gone. He wanted to make it to New York in December, not so much for the award itself but for the chance to see everyone who'd be there. He wanted to see what kind of recruiting class Oklahoma signed for the next season. And he wanted to see how the Sooners finished their first season with Lincoln.

As the summer deepened, Bob Stoops and Lincoln Riley would go back and forth almost daily on who their quarterback would be. "Some days," Stoops said, "we'd get done with practice, and I'd ask Lincoln, who was leading the quarterback derby, which player was our man. One day he'd say, 'Probably Baker.' The next, he'd say, 'Probably Trevor.' And Cody had his moments, too."

Come August, Lincoln had to make a decision. The team needed to know who would be on the field come opening day. His choice was Baker Mayfield.

"At the end, you just had to tally up the punches," Lincoln said. "It came out pretty close . . . They all played very well. Baker was able to minimize his mistakes a fraction more than those guys did, and that's probably the biggest reason we made the decision."

Baker was also showing signs of becoming a remarkable leader. He played with the same magnetism and charisma with which he lived—a video of him impressively executing the "Whip" dance with his teammates quickly went around, endearing him not only to the team but to Sooner Nation at large. He was full of life throughout practices, to the point that Bob Stoops's wife, Carol, even took note of him, telling him well before the final decision was made that she was sure Baker was going to end up being the starting quarterback. Star receiver Dede Westbrook said, "He was a leader in our locker room, *the* leader in our huddle, and probably the hardest-working guy at practice."

It seemed that leadership simply came naturally to Baker, too, because when he found out that Dede, who lived half an hour from campus, didn't have a car, he would go out of his way to give him rides to and from the field, "pick me up at my apartment and drop me off afterwards pretty much every single day," Dede said. "We didn't really even know each other at that time, but he did it like it was no big deal. The only thing he cared about was being a teammate and making our group of guys better."

And then there was the way he played. He and Dede connected beautifully on the field as Baker's ability to read defenses improved, his evasiveness increased, and his passes became more precise. "Baker's a winner, plain and simple," Dede said. "He might not even be human for all I know. Humans aren't that good at everything."

Lincoln later said, "I think that competition was the best thing that could have happened to him."

Baker simply changed in the ways he needed to change. He put in the work. He dedicated himself to changing. And he was able to make the most of that work and that dedication because he also knew his coach believed in him. He played with a passion that bordered on anger—but anger has a way of burning out. It's love that sustains passion, and Baker's heart seemed big and tender under his brash exterior, and what Lincoln offered him was just what Baker needed to unleash his potential. "I felt like he treated me with respect," Baker says. "That's how he talks to you. Like he respects you. Like he really cares. And it's because he really does."

"Your name is on the starting lineup," Stoops told him, "but you've got to keep it there."

Whether Baker kept it there would reflect not only on him, but on Lincoln, too.

Of course, Baker had no intention of losing the job. After all, as he put it, "It's a dream come true."

He could have lost it, though, and easily. He had Trevor Knight waiting behind him, after all, and Cody Thomas waiting behind Trevor, and their quarterback competition had been, in Lincoln's words, like a fifteen-round prizefight. And Baker Mayfield's time as the Sooners' quarterback did not begin well.

14

Reality

OKLAHOMA STARTED THE 2015 season ranked No. 19 in the country and whupped a lowly Akron team in its season opener, winning 41–3 as Baker put up 388 passing yards with three touchdowns.

The next game was bad, though. The Sooners were on the road against No. 23 Tennessee before the largest crowd they had ever played in front of, with 102,455 fans crowded into Neyland Stadium. Going into the fourth quarter they were down 17–3, Baker had thrown two interceptions, and the offense was sputtering. There were a lot of ways things could have gone for Lincoln and Baker at that point. Still, Lincoln believed his faith in his quarterback would be rewarded.

That faith alone spoke volumes to Baker. It's one thing to be told you're good in practice, another thing to be named the starter as an underdog walk-on—and a whole other thing to be that underdog walk-on who then struggles, yet still has his coach keep faith in him. "You get to feel pretty expendable as a player sometimes," Baker says. "There's a lot of pressure to be perfect or risk losing your spot . . . But Lincoln never made me feel that way. He'd remind me how to believe in myself."

At halftime, Lincoln had simply told Baker, "We believe in you.

Relax and go play. We're on the road, and we're going to write a story today."

Then in the third quarter—well, things went from bad to worse. The Sooners failed to so much as reach midfield, and Baker had completed just eight of twenty-five passes for eighty-four yards on the game. The grand Lincoln Riley Experiment couldn't have been off to a worse start. "Most head coaches would've been on the phones, saying, 'What you're doing ain't working,'" Lincoln later said. "[Stoops] never said a word. Never. He believed in me and our offense. When your head coach has that much confidence in what you're doing, that same confidence comes to you, whether you're a player or assistant."

And same as Stoops had faith in Lincoln, Lincoln kept faith in Baker. "He pulled me aside," Baker recalls, "and said, 'Listen, you're here for a reason. You're playing for a reason. Just focus on doing the little things right, and we'll get this done.'"

In the fourth quarter, Baker led two dramatic touchdown drives, including one that ended on a touchdown pass with less than a minute left, to tie the game. Oklahoma ended up winning the game in double overtime. And in that quarter and overtime alone, Baker put up 103 yards with three touchdowns on eleven of fourteen passes, and he added another touchdown rushing. "They didn't crumble under the pressure," Baker later said of his coaches. "They didn't panic . . . They showed how much they trusted me. It goes a long way. What they did resides deeper in me than they'll ever realize."

Three weeks and two solid wins later, Oklahoma was ranked No. 10 in the country as the Sooners went to the Cotton Bowl in Dallas to take on their archrivals, Texas, in front of ninety thousand people. Texas wasn't even ranked that season, destined for a forgettable 5–7 record and not so much as a bowl game.

Oklahoma lost 24–17. And not only did they lose, but they trailed the whole game.

Afterward, Lincoln called a meeting with some of his top players that covered "some very specific, detail-oriented things," according to Ty Darlington. Chief among Lincoln's concerns was that their pace of play was dragging compared to what it could be— what it should be. Pace had always been one of the most important elements of the Air Raid offense, dating back to the Mumme-and-Leach days of yore, and Lincoln had certainly made the most out of a fast tempo while at East Carolina. But Oklahoma wasn't quite getting there. "We were subbing a lot," Ty said. "We weren't playing to the tempo that we wanted to early in the season, especially in that Texas game. We were taking far too long."

Lincoln also felt that he was still getting used to his new team. "For me, it's just learning our guys," he said at the time. "Trying to learn what makes them tick, what makes them go, what we're not good at and need to cover up, and what we are good at . . . As many years as I'm here, or any of us are here, it's going to always change week to week. You just have to be ready to evolve with it and continue to learn and try to get better."

He continued tinkering with how to make the most of the immense talent Oklahoma offered him, and he began getting creative with his play calling. He started mixing in plays that weren't exactly trick plays, but relied heavily on misdirection all the same—faking a handoff to a running back going one direction, drawing the entire defense that way, just to have Baker hold on to the ball and turn and fire a quick pass to a receiver waiting at the line of scrimmage in the other direction, nothing but blockers and green grass waiting ahead of him. Or he'd use a play based on a "jet motion," in which one receiver sprints across the backfield as Baker takes the snap, leaving Baker to decide whether to hand off to the guy or fake the handoff and pass to another receiver drifting into the backfield nearby.

Lincoln wasn't afraid of "gadget plays," either, incorporating more into his playbook such as a tricky play in which Baker would hand off to a halfback in motion who, instead of hitting the line of scrimmage, would fake a run only to step back and pass, usually to a receiver open down the field.

And sometimes he'd hide an eligible receiver on the offensive line, starting a play that looked like Baker rolling out, only to have one of the "blockers" break off and run the other way as Baker turned to find him, usually open.

Lincoln also made the most of how Baker was perhaps most deadly on the move, calling and developing various rollout and waggle plays that allowed him to create chaos by roaming the backfield before finding an open receiver.

And with the receivers, Lincoln stayed flexible on their routes, too, continuing to experiment with concepts that blended various "smash routes"—which sent receivers flying downfield to challenge zone coverages—with crossing routes that sent receivers over the middle, into corners, and sometimes toward the middle of the field before reversing course to sprint back toward the sidelines.

And of course, he continued to revise his option plays and run-pass options as he took advantage of his talented halfbacks.

This might have been Lincoln's most savvy move to date as an offensive coordinator. As he promised, he made the most out of Oklahoma's historically great rushing attack, and the monstrously awesome offensive linemen Stoops loved to recruit. It was, after all, Oklahoma tradition to flat-out maul opponents up front with a run game, and Lincoln did just that—but he did it his own way. He developed a "counter-trey" running scheme that could be run a few ways, the most common of which involved a quarterback keeper option that was risky in that it left the backfield somewhat exposed to pass rushers due to the four-wide-receiver spread, which left fewer blockers than there were rushers in some cases. In particular, the backside defensive end was given a virtually obstacle-free path to the backfield. However, the way the play worked, the quarterback would read the defensive end's path and simply hold on to the ball if the defensive end crashed too hard on the running back, giving the quarterback ample room to then take off down the field. Against some teams, Lincoln added a combination option wrinkle to this play, which also created a quick bubble screen for Baker to throw to a second running back if he so chose. That was particularly deadly because of offensive linemen's natural reaction to follow the path of the initial running back. With two backs coming out of the backfield on a triple option, one option of which was a bubble screen—the options were exhausting for a defense to keep up with. In this way, Lincoln still used traditional Oklahoma smashmouth running concepts but evolved them in a way that elevated the Sooners' run game to an unprecedented level.

Throughout, Lincoln talked with the players, making sure they understood not only the *what* and *when* and *how* of any given play and their assignments, but also the *why* behind it all. "At every point of adversity for the 2015 offense," Ty Darlington said, "the solution always included activities concentrated on the intangibles, such as meetings with the leaders of each position group, a full-on lesson (with handouts) on the power of unselfishness, and offensive meetings in which plays were not discussed and film was not watched."

The effect was profound. Ty went on, "He coaches the intangibles as well as anyone I've been around. Every coach will preach the importance of intangible concepts like mentality, unselfishness, and togetherness. But for most coaches, when push comes to

shove and points are not being put on the scoreboard, the invest-
ment of time and energy isn't put into those areas, it's put into on-
field skill development and execution."

Lincoln leaned on Baker, too, following his statement from the
spring: *I'm gonna push you. Just take it one day at a time.* "We had
that mindset ever since," Baker says. "And he's pushed me, like he
said."

Lincoln also learned how to manage Baker's fiery psyche. The
kid seemed brash and cocky and full of himself sometimes. When
the Sooners played Texas Tech, Baker shot some glaring looks at
Kliff Kingsbury, the coach who had dared not to choose him. He
pointed after throwing successful passes. He shook his head and
he sneered. He threw two touchdown passes and performed masterfully throughout. Oklahoma won 63–27.

But to see Baker as *just* brash and cocky meant not looking deep
enough. Beneath it all was a big heart that just wanted to win—
almost too badly sometimes. Lincoln saw that heart and he told
Baker to just be himself. That fire was what made him the leader he
was. That helped him relate to his teammates and inspire them all
to play better. Competitive fire manifests itself differently depending on the individual, but with Baker, it was right out in the open
every time he played. That worked for him, because that's who he
was. Lincoln managed that, even helped it grow, and reined it in
only when necessary—when Baker otherwise might have done
something to get himself hurt.

"I'm just learning," Baker says. "He'll coach me on the field, and
then we'll go back in the film room, and it's not like he'll chew me
out. It's like, *Okay, here's what happened, and*—he'll pull up an example . . . and then he'll teach me. He'll ask me, he'll double-check—
*Are you understanding why this happened, and why you should do
this next time?* He really leaves no questions. He makes sure there's

no doubt in your mind about what should happen, and why that's going on. He just pays attention to so much detail, and that truly is what makes him so special."

As they got more accustomed to their new roles, Lincoln steadily became more comfortable being more aggressive with Baker, taking risks with him and with the rest of his players to execute at a quintessentially frenetic Air Raid pace. "When we play fast," Ty said, "even if we're not completely sure of things that are going on—we don't get the time to see all the looks—when we play fast, we wear people out and we keep them on their heels."

Oklahoma went on a blistering run after the loss to Texas. The Sooners regularly won games by thirty and forty points, even against teams ranked in the Top 10 in the country. By the end of the season, Oklahoma was the Big 12 Conference champion, ranked No. 4, and had the seventh-best offense in the country, averaging 530 yards and forty-three points per game. They also made the College Football Playoff, where they lost to Clemson in the Orange Bowl.

Running back Samaje Perine had not, after all, been doomed, finishing with 1,349 yards and sixteen touchdowns.

Senior receiver Sterling Shepard had the best year of his career with 1,288 yards and eleven touchdowns on eighty-six receptions, giving him 233 for his career, third best all-time among Oklahoma receivers.

And then there was Baker Mayfield. Baker had finished the season with 3,700 passing yards, thirty-six touchdowns, and just seven interceptions—and was fourth overall in the Heisman Trophy voting. There was now no doubt who Oklahoma's quarterback would be going forward. Trevor Knight requested to transfer to Texas A&M, and Cody Thomas would later give up football to focus on baseball.

And for his part, Lincoln was named a finalist for the Broyles Award as the nation's top assistant coach. He was still just thirty-two years old.

"I got lucky" is all Lincoln would say. "I got lucky that Mike Leach was crazy enough to hire me when I was twenty-three years old. I got lucky that honestly the whole thing went down when he got let go at Texas Tech and got a chance to call that game and kind of get an opportunity to show what we could do. Got lucky that Shane Carden decided to come to East Carolina and Justin Hardy decided to walk on. Got lucky that Sterling Shepard stayed in school, that Samaje Perine's not selfish, that Ty Darlington is the smartest person in the room, that Bob Stoops wanted to take a chance on me and lived up to every word of everything that he promised me. I could go on and on about that for a while."

Stoops, however, gives Lincoln plenty of credit himself: "There's a lot of guys that have the speech," he says. "And they can put on the right front in front of certain people, and then you find out who they really are. You analyze them, and they're not what they appear. That can happen. Lincoln? What you see is what you get . . . There's great character and integrity there, and there's a lot of substance."

And on top of all that, Caitlin was pregnant with their second child. Stella would be born just before the next season began.

The Broyles Award ceremony luncheon to announce the winner was to be held in Little Rock, Arkansas, but it fell on the same day as Donnie Duncan's Legacy Award dinner at the Waldorf-Astoria. So Lincoln went to New York City. In light of Donnie's illness, personal achievements in football just didn't seem to matter.

Donnie wasn't doing well, and the end seemed near—but he

had done what he'd wanted to do, and he'd made it here, to be with everyone. "It's a special deal for a special guy," Lincoln said. "He's always been the guy who's done everything for everybody else. It's nice for us to all be here for him."

It was good to see Ruffin McNeill, too, who had flown in for the dinner, having been fired by East Carolina less than a month earlier. The Pirates had had a down year, going 5–7, but nobody expected Ruffin to be sent packing just like that. Some people in the college football world expressed near outrage, not to mention in Greenville itself—Ruffin was beloved in Greenville, and East Carolina was his alma mater. Ruffin had been struggling. He was adjusting to life without Lincoln, he was watching Donnie deteriorate, and he was acclimating to a new athletic director with whom he did not see eye to eye. "The biggest thing I was pushing for was—I don't mind the expectations of championship," Ruffin says, "but at least be committed." East Carolina's commitment to him did not match their expectations of him. Conflict ensued. Ruffin struggled. People around Greenville worried. And as Donnie's condition grew worse, so did Ruffin's state of mind. He skipped press conferences and gave no reason, parked on the grass in front of the athletic building instead of in the parking lot, and—he just wasn't himself.

When East Carolina abruptly fired him, it was the culmination of one hell of a rough year—but even then, Ruffin says it "just came out of left field."

Donnie Duncan's advice for Ruffin and the boat he'd sold him turned out to be spot-on. Let it be an escape, a timeout from the emotional violence that can be such an exhausting part of the college football coaching life. "That boat," Ruffin says, "saved my life."

Lincoln had decided to skip the Broyles Award luncheon so

he could be with Donnie and Ruffin and everyone else, but they talked him into flying to Arkansas for it, almost as though they knew something he didn't. A private jet was arranged, and Lincoln made it to the luncheon, where his name was called and he was officially declared the best assistant coach in college football.

He did not linger. Lincoln immediately flew back to New York and made it to the Waldorf in time for the dinner, to see Donnie accept his award. "The Broyles deal is a great thing," Lincoln said. "A really, really nice honor, but this is a once-in-a-lifetime deal for him. Given what he's meant to me, it was an easy decision to be here in New York. I wouldn't have missed it."

A few months later, in the middle of March 2016, at his home in Dallas, Donnie Duncan died in his sleep.

15

Forward

DURING THE SUMMER OF 2016, Baker Mayfield's future at Oklahoma was determined in a meeting at the Big 12 headquarters in Irving, Texas. Representatives from all the conference's programs had been debating a proposal that was being called the Baker Mayfield rule: whether to allow a walk-on who had never received a scholarship at one Big 12 school to transfer to walk on at another Big 12 school without losing a year of eligibility, as Baker had. If passed, the new rule would restore to Baker the year of eligibility he had lost in 2014 to Halo and intramural sports. Otherwise the 2016 season would be Baker's last at Oklahoma. On its face, the decision seemed obvious: do the right thing by Baker and thus set a precedent for others like him in the future, doing the right thing for student-athletes on the whole. But the proposal failed to pass after the vote locked out at 5–5. (The Big 12, indeed, has only ten teams.)

Commissioner Bob Bowlsby explained the logic behind the "no" votes: the schools didn't want to encourage teams to lure away their competitors' non-scholarship players by offering scholarships. In other words, they didn't want players whose original schools failed to deem them worthy of scholarships to go to other schools who offered them, well, scholarships. Never mind that the solution was easy: to use Baker Mayfield himself as the example, if Texas Tech had wanted to keep him, they could have offered him one of their allotted eighty-five—eighty-five!—scholarships.

Baker was hurt by the decision. He posted a long message on Twitter, pouring out his heart and talking about pain and pushing through it and how hard he'd worked to get where he was and how much he had learned along the way. "I plan on using every lesson I have learned to keep pushing myself and my team," he said. "I will be making the most out of my last season I get to suit up for Oklahoma. I can't wait to get started."

The Big 12 representatives reconvened the very next day, having made a small but significant alteration: a non-scholarship player could transfer to another Big 12 school without losing a year of eligibility if the school he was leaving did not offer him a scholarship first.

Three schools still voted against the revised proposal, but seven voted for it, and because Texas Tech had never written Baker an offer, just like that, Baker had two more years left to play at Oklahoma. "And y'all thought you were getting rid of me," he said.

Oklahoma was ranked No. 3 in the country to start the 2016 season, and within three weeks, they had fallen completely out of the Top 25. Lincoln's second season as offensive coordinator was off to an even worse start than his first.

The Sooners' season opener was a road game against No. 15 Houston, the game televised on ABC—and they lost, 33–23. After an easy win against Louisiana-Monroe, they lost to No. 3 Ohio State by three touchdowns.

"Everybody's feeling terrible at that point," Lincoln says. "And . . . we were just not playing anywhere near our capability, not even close, and we were disappointed."

Lincoln could have felt the same pressure—the same temptation to *try harder*—that he'd felt in his second year at East Carolina, devolving into giving out figurative head-butts all around, starting with himself. But he didn't. He'd learned. He'd grown. "Watching Bob helped me a lot on that," he says. "Great ability to stay positive no matter what, stay confident."

Instead, Lincoln channeled his energy into growing the good things that had been happening on the field, and showing his guys how to create more of them. He started by reviewing game film of what looked like a series of failures, but which were actually a series of possibilities that just needed the right adjustment. "We weren't just getting our ass kicked," he says. "We were so agonizingly close it was hard to watch, because it was more plays and simple things, some coaching things we put in some of the plays and play calls, just little tiny things that other people weren't causing. Self-inflicted wounds."

They were doing things that were getting them hurt. The point wasn't to dwell on the mistakes, however, and punish the players for their failures. It was to show them the causes of their failures—to show them how close they were to success. "We sat down," Baker says, "and talked to him—*let's go back to the basics.*"

"The point of it," Lincoln says, "was to show that, as bad as you feel right now—we are *this close.*"

He names the Houston game as an example. Even in a loss, the Sooners had averaged eleven yards per play in the first half. "You don't do that very often," he says.

The Ohio State game had its moments, too.

"We moved the ball very well at times against Ohio State," he says, "and had a lot of times we didn't cash in. We did some good things, but . . . we were just a fraction off."

Lincoln remembers thinking, *If we can push through this and get over the hump, then we can really do something good here. Because there were a lot of great things in those games.*

After the Ohio State loss, the Sooners bounced back by winning a close game against No. 21 Texas Christian University, 52–46.

Then came the Texas game.

The Red River Showdown.

Oklahoma was ranked again by then, back at No. 20 in the country.

And once again, Texas wasn't ranked.

Same as the previous year, Oklahoma started off slow, and Baker struggled. He threw two interceptions in the first quarter, the second of which led to a Texas field goal that gave the Longhorns a 3–0 lead, and terrible feelings were welling up again.

The way that Lincoln chose to handle this, though, would in many ways determine the course of the season. He kept in mind the lessons he had learned from Mike Leach and from his time at East Carolina. "As a coach, you have to be yourself," he says. "If that's not you, and you suddenly try to do that—I don't know. I haven't been like that, so I can't say. But I know if I went and just tried to be a hard-ass all the time, you know, every single situation, went more just the drill sergeant twenty-four-seven route, I don't think they'd respond to it, because it's just not my personality."

Lincoln told Baker not to worry about Texas and what they were doing—*just do you.*

Just do you.

"He's always saying that," Baker says. "Nothing else matters. I mean, what you put on tape and what you're doing and how you handle yourself is all that matters . . . He knows that I'm gonna be hard on myself, so he doesn't yell. He doesn't raise his voice at me. He just says, like, *C'mon, you know better than that.* So he understands that, with him saying stuff like that to me, I don't need any extra chewing or anything."

Lincoln treated Baker in a way that made Baker feel respected, and that in turn gave Baker more respect for him. "The best players have this mutual respect," Baker says. "You'll play a lot harder for somebody that you respect, and that you *want* to play hard for. You don't want to let them down. You want to take their coaching, and listen to it. Because you respect their opinion, and you think they're right, so you're going to work hard to do that."

While Lincoln, of course, could not understand all their lives from firsthand experience, he empathized as he talked with them, and, in so doing, alleviated his players' stress by making them feel seen, heard, and respected. "It's huge," Baker says. Life is hard for young athletes making the transition from high school to college sports, especially at a program like Oklahoma. "[To have] somebody relaxed, who will do anything for you," Baker goes on, "makes it a lot easier, than somebody jumping on your back and riding you and making it a miserable process. He makes it enjoyable, and he says, *Do the little things right, and everything else comes easy.* And that's true . . . He has a real conversation with you. And . . . he does so much adapting. So many old-school coaches have a certain way they were successful with, and that's the only way they'll do it. Where Coach Riley sees how someone reacts to it . . . he might push someone here or there, or take them under his wing, but he really does have a casual conversation. He understands how to . . . get the best out of somebody."

Lincoln strove to understand what it meant to be their age experiencing the things they did, leaning not on his own understanding but rather acknowledging each player's humanity. "Each guy's his own individual case," Lincoln says. "And I think that it goes back to having that individual relationship with each guy."

Lincoln's North Star in harder moments seemed to be pretty simple: he was just honest. "I think that false confidence is one of the worst things you can give to a player," Lincoln says. "There are certainly times you gotta have tough conversations, and be absolutely real with them."

And ultimately, there's the flip side of those tough conversations, of being absolutely real: it also means that when he gets absolutely real with Baker Mayfield by telling him that he has nothing to worry about, that all he has to do is *just do you*, then Baker buys into it, without doubt.

So after Baker threw his second interception in the first quarter as they were losing against a lowly Texas team, Lincoln grabbed Baker and said, "You know what, just put it behind you. Move on. We're not down by much. Don't worry about what they're doing. Just do you. Just do you."

Just do you.

They were still *this close.*

Just. Do. You.

"He knows when to come in and say the right things," Baker says. "And that's very special."

Two possessions later, Baker led a drive that ended with a rushing touchdown, and soon after that, he threw a touchdown pass to Dede Westbrook, the first of three he would throw that day. He finished the game with 390 passing yards, and Oklahoma won the game.

The way Lincoln handled Baker that day was becoming the norm for how he handled everyone and everything around there.

"After that," Baker says, "I would say we could have beaten anybody as the season went on. And that's just his coaching."

From that point on, Lincoln says, "They were able to mentally get over the hump, and go fight for that fraction—and we got it. And once we got it, we got on a roll."

The Sooners won out the rest of the season to finish 11–2, averaging 554 yards and 43.9 points per game along the way—both improvements over 2015. They ranked No. 7 in the country at the end of the season and played in the Sugar Bowl, where they beat Auburn by sixteen points.

They also led the nation in S&P+, a Moneyball-like football stat intended to be, in the words of its creator, Bill Connelly, "college football's deepest advanced analytics system." Put simply, S&P+ measures how successful a team is at gaining valuable yardage— that is, yards that put a team closer to scoring. As Connelly explains it: "All yards are not created equal. A ten-yard gain from your fifteen-yard line to your twenty-five is not the same as one from your opponents' ten-yard line to their end zone, or one from your opponent's forty to their thirty, advancing into field position."

Another simple way to put it: in 2016, Oklahoma was the best team at getting the most valuable yards on the smallest number of plays.

Lincoln was doing with his team what he'd grown up watching his father do with bales of cotton.

He was doing what all football coaches set out to do.

He was getting the most out of his players that they could possibly give him, getting more out of them than any other coach in the country, and he wasn't doing it by head-butting them into submission to his all-knowing will—he was doing it by being curious about what their minds needed from his.

Beyond the S&P+, the Sooners also became the first Big 12 team to go undefeated in conference play, in which they averaged 47.7 points per game.

Not one, but two Oklahoma running backs finished the year with more than a thousand total yards.

Wide receiver Dede Westbrook had fifteen hundred receiving yards and seventeen touchdowns, was named a finalist for the Heisman Trophy, and won the Biletnikoff Award as the nation's top wide receiver.

And then there was Baker Mayfield.

He threw for four thousand yards and forty touchdowns, rushed for six more touchdowns—and was also a finalist for the Heisman Trophy.

This is why Bob Stoops brought Lincoln in.

In two years, Oklahoma's offense had gone from aimless and struggling to a juggernaut, the most dominant in all of college football. The Sooners seemed unstoppable.

For about a month, anyway.

And then Baker went to a wedding in Arkansas.

He was in Fayetteville in early February to celebrate a friend's nuptials, and after one festivity led to another, next thing you know, it was 2:30 a.m., and Baker was drunk on a sidewalk with soy sauce spilled on his hoodie. While visiting a food truck, he either stepped in to break up a fight, or started a fight (depending on who you believe), and the police got involved. As an officer coaxed Baker over to take his statement, the boy stumbled down some concrete steps and started yelling, cursing, and generally "causing a scene," the officer later wrote in his report. When the officer told Baker to come talk to him, Baker pulled his hoodie up over his head and started to walk away.

The cops told him to stop, but instead, Baker took off running.

A cop took him down with a quick and inescapable tackle,

the momentum of which carried them both into a brick wall. Baker's head smacked the brick as he went down. "I'm done!" he cried. "I'm done! Oh my God!"

He was arrested and charged with public intoxication, disorderly conduct, fleeing, and resisting arrest.

Upon learning who he was, one of the cops joked, "I thought he'd be faster."

Bob Stoops and the university took an official stance of being "disappointed" and declined to say much else or decide on any sort of discipline until the legal case was all worked out.

Baker issued a long and earnest apology on social media, in which he bemoaned the way his behavior reflected poorly on the university and the team and his coaches. "The biggest mistake of my life," he called it. He went on to say he was suffering from "guilt, shame, and embarrassment" that he "wouldn't wish on anybody." Sooner fans more or less accepted this, but critics called it image and crisis management, and the Twitterverse and blogosphere unloaded on the kid, with calls for Baker's suspension alongside all manner of requisite braying about the awfulness of it all.

In the meantime, Lincoln's phone was ringing, a lot.

It wasn't so long ago that he had been unceremoniously dumped from Texas Tech, and now he was one of the most sought-after coaches in football. The University of Houston, in particular, made a strong run at him, its head coach, Tom Herman, having just left for the University of Texas. Hunter Yurachek, Houston's athletic director, said, "When Tom left for Texas, Lincoln's agent was one of the first people I called."

Oklahoma athletic director Joe Castiglione was so concerned about this development that he visited Lincoln at home the weekend before his interview with Houston. And as Lincoln traveled to Houston, Castiglione commiserated with Bob Stoops and university president David Boren. At some point, the idea was floated that Stoops should name Lincoln as his head-coach-in-waiting. But Stoops wasn't sure how that sat with him as a leader—that's not what he'd want for his team. "I'm either the boss or not," Stoops said. "You can't sort of be the boss."

"At some point," Castiglione remembered thinking, "he's going to take a head coaching job. We knew he would be successful. And at whatever point Coach Stoops decided to retire, we knew he'd be the one we want to hire to replace Coach Stoops."

Meanwhile, Lincoln was busy crushing his interview in Houston. Yurachek and seven other administrators and boosters asked Lincoln dozens of questions about just about anything you can imagine—budgets, compliance, types of players he liked to recruit, the style of offense he wanted to run. And Lincoln answered with clarity and authority—and without using notes, a rarity in such interviews. "He blew us away as a committee," Yurachek said. "He was so unbelievably polished and well spoken about every aspect of being a head coach. He was wise beyond his years."

Soon after the interview, Lincoln was on the phone with Castiglione, Boren, and Stoops, and they were having a conversation not unlike the conversations Lincoln used to have with Donnie Duncan, talking about how his choices could affect his family and his future, and which decision would make the most out of his unique gifts. "We were in close contact throughout the entire process," Castiglione said. "All three of us were talking . . . and Bob was especially helpful in talking about his past experiences."

Ultimately, Oklahoma offered Lincoln a new three-year contract at $1.3 million a year to stay on as offensive coordinator. "We weren't going to let him walk right out the door," Castiglione said.

And then, just a few weeks later, Bob Stoops called Lincoln Riley into his office. He had some news.

It was his new office, the one that had been tailor-made for the legendary coach.

Lincoln sat down across from Stoops on one of the leather couches, and they had an unexpected conversation—one that would shock the college football world. Stoops later said that ever since the difficult 2013 season, he had been having thoughts that were growing harder to escape: *Do I really want to do this anymore? Maybe I've run my course here. Maybe I need to do something else.*

The man had won more games than any other coach at Oklahoma.

He won a national championship in just his second season.

He won ten conference championships.

He won 80 percent of his games in eighteen seasons.

He coached not one but two Heisman Trophy winners.

He was still young, too, just fifty-six years old.

He was nothing if not a legend in Norman.

"I feel like I've been absolutely the luckiest, most fortunate guy in the world and incredibly blessed to have experienced what we have over the last eighteen and a half years," he said.

But he felt it was time to step away.

For himself and, just as importantly, for the program.

Stoops had been thinking about it for a while.

"I loved it," Stoops says. "I had a ball. But there's more to life than just this, and I've been getting anxious to see what else comes my way."

Stoops's father, Ron, was a high school coach, and he'd died of a heart attack *during a game* in the late 1980s.

Steve Spurrier, a fellow legendary coach and good friend of Stoops, put it this way: "He didn't want to go from the sidelines to the graveyard."

As Stoops would later reflect, "The more I thought about it, the more I thought, *This is an opportunity here with a really good football team.* The players had the maturity and leadership, with Baker and so many older guys. They could handle it without a lot of disruption. The coach staff was strong. We'd had back-to-back top-five finishes. And in my mind, I was thinking, *If this is what I want to do, this is the right time to do it.* Because we also had Lincoln."

That was the kicker. "If it had been anybody but Lincoln," Stoops said, "I might have reversed course and returned for 2017 and perhaps beyond . . . I felt I just didn't want to miss the right opportunity to be able to step away and hand this baton off to Lincoln Riley and to help this all just keep going in a great direction."

He was going to miss it, in some ways. But he says he just wasn't as hungry as the job required you to be: "Bottom line," he says, "is after eighteen and a half years of doing this, it'll fill you up."

Lincoln, on the other hand—he was hungry.

After he was hired, one of the first calls Lincoln made was to Ruffin McNeill.

Ruffin had landed a job at Virginia as defensive line coach and assistant head coach, but then Lincoln called and said he wanted Ruffin to coach his defensive line and be his assistant head coach.

"He can get along with anybody," Lincoln says. "So I knew staff chemistry was gonna be great. He's a great D-line coach and defensive mind . . . and a guy I can bounce ideas off of as a head coach, a guy I know is in my and our corner. He's got a great wife who's gonna get along great with other wives. The energy he brings is unmatched. It was just easy. Easy, easy decision."

Ruffin responded the same way that Lincoln had responded to him years earlier: "I'll be there tomorrow."

It had been only a year and a half since East Carolina had abruptly fired Ruffin, taking his already-rocky world and turning it upside down. He laughs about it now. "God doesn't go, 'Oops, my bad,'" he says. "He doesn't make mistakes."

He'd been grateful for the Virginia job, but this, with Lincoln? He says, "It saved my life."

Ruffin, who normally wears outfits like cargo shorts and hoodies, arrived in Norman wearing a formal suit and tie, same as Lincoln had worn when Ruffin first hired him at East Carolina years ago. They both laughed. And they couldn't help but think of Donnie Duncan.

"Up in heaven," Lincoln said, "if he's able to see Ruffin and me here at Oklahoma, he's smiling."

Lincoln Riley grew up in the tiny West Texas town of Muleshoe. As the quarterback for Muleshoe High School, he led his team to new heights but also suffered an injury that changed the trajectory of his life. (Bryan Terry/ *The Oklahoman*)

Mike Leach was the forward-thinking and somewhat rebellious head coach at Texas Tech who launched the Air Raid concept into the national consciousness—and who convinced Lincoln that he could be a great college coach, too. (ZUMA/Alamy Stock Photo)

Lincoln became Leach's personal assistant at just nineteen years old and quickly rose through the ranks to become the receivers coach by age twenty-three. (ZUMA/Alamy Stock Photo)

Donnie Duncan (right), seen here talking with some colleagues at the Big 12 championship game in 2000, was instrumental in creating the Big 12 Conference—and he became one of Lincoln's mentors and closest friends. (Tom Gilbert/*Tulsa World*)

Texas Tech defensive coordinator Ruffin McNeill celebrates with his players after defeating Michigan State in the Alamo Bowl on January 2, 2010. Ruffin took over as interim head coach when Mike Leach was suspended the week prior to the game. Lincoln served as Tech's interim offensive coordinator for the bowl game. (Karl Anderson/Icon Sportswire)

Later in 2010, Ruffin McNeill was named the head coach at East Carolina University, his alma mater. (AP Images/Chris Seward)

Lincoln was Ruffin's first hire at East Carolina, making him at twenty-six the youngest offensive coordinator in Division I football. (ZUMA/Alamy Stock Photo)

East Carolina University's "real" pirate—portrayed by local actor Steve Whetzel—leads the football Pirates onto the field before every game. (© Charles Harris)

Dwayne Harris was a star senior wide receiver at East Carolina when Lincoln arrived and was skeptical of the wunderkind offensive coordinator. In time, however, he came to see Lincoln as "a football genius," and began to appreciate how much Lincoln cared about him as a human being. (Courtesy of Gray Media Group, Inc., [WITN])

Quarterback Shane Carden was an overlooked prospect from Texas who became one of the most dazzling quarterbacks in college football at East Carolina, where he broke just about every school passing record. (Cal Sport Media/Alamy Stock Photo)

Likewise, Justin Hardy was virtually unrecruited as a high school receiver in North Carolina before Lincoln and Ruffin discovered him. He electrified college football and wrecked all kinds of receiving records. He still plays in the NFL today. (AP Images/Don Petersen)

Donnie Duncan (left) received the National Football Foundation Legacy Award at the Waldorf-Astoria in New York City in December 2015, shortly before cancer took his life. He is seen here with former Oklahoma head coach Barry Switzer. (National Football Foundation)

After Bob Stoops made the stunning decision to retire in the spring of 2017, the University of Oklahoma named Lincoln Riley as the Sooners' next head coach. Stoops handed his successor a football during Lincoln's introductory press conference. (AP Images/Sue Ogrocki)

Lincoln inherited the massive and gorgeous brand-new office that had been built for Bob Stoops. (Steve Sisney/ *The Oklahoman*)

Lincoln's first hire as Oklahoma's head coach was his former boss Ruffin McNeill, who had been let go by East Carolina. Ruffin and Lincoln have said that they wouldn't be where they are today without each other. (Steve Sisney/*The Oklahoman*)

Lincoln, always one to "get in the mix," worked hard with Sooners quarterback Baker Mayfield to help him become the exceptional player they both believed he could be. (AP Images/Sue Ogrocki)

Ty Darlington, Oklahoma's star center, was one of the Sooners' on-field leaders. He overcame his initial doubts about the spread offense and developed deep appreciation and respect for Lincoln as a coach. (Joe Buettener/*OU Daily*)

Lincoln celebrates winning the Big 12 championship in December 2017, in his first season as Oklahoma's head coach. (Cal Sport Media/Alamy Stock Photo)

A few weeks later, Lincoln led the Sooners to the College Football Playoff. Here he gives his players some love before the national semifinal game at the Rose Bowl on January 1, 2018. (Caitlyn Epes/*OU Daily*)

After a long and dramatic saga, Baker Mayfield won the 2017 Heisman Trophy. He went on to become the No. 1 overall selection in that year's NFL draft. (AP Images/Craig Ruttle)

Although Kyler Murray's story wasn't quite as drama filled as Baker's, his performance on the field was also impressive, and he won the 2018 Heisman Trophy, making Oklahoma the first school to ever have back-to-back Heisman-winning quarterbacks. He was also the No. 1 selection in that year's NFL draft. (UPI/Alamy Stock Photo)

Caitlin Riley has been by Lincoln's side since they began dating during Lincoln's freshman year at Texas Tech. They have two daughters, Sloan (standing at right) and Stella. (AP Images/Matthew Pearce/Icon Sportswire)

16

Challenge

HISTORICALLY, ROUGH TIMES AWAIT coaches who take over from legends. And in some ways—at least from the sports narrative standpoint—there was almost no way for Lincoln to win. "All coaches get measured against their predecessor," noted the sportswriter Stewart Mandel in a piece analyzing the "13 Kings of College Football." Included on that list were Alabama's Bear Bryant, Ohio State's Woody Hayes, Florida's Steve Spurrier, Florida State's Bobby Bowden, Notre Dame's Knute Rockne, and Penn State's Joe Paterno, among others. The successors of those thirteen all-time greats lasted just five seasons on average, compared to their predecessors' twenty. The average all-time great coach won 75 percent of his games, while the successors won an average of 65 percent. Ten of the thirteen successors either were fired, resigned under pressure, or left for a job at a smaller school.

When Knute Rockne died in a plane crash in 1931 and Heartley Anderson took over for him at Notre Dame, a *Chicago Tribune* reporter wrote, "His position was regarded as the hardest any college football coach had ever undertaken." Anderson lasted only three seasons before retiring, having gone 16–9–2 in those three years.

Mandel put it frankly: "Riley is attempting to succeed the all-time winningest coach at one of the sport's most prestigious programs. Stoops won nearly 80 percent of his games, a national championship, and 10 conference titles. No pressure, Lincoln. Just go do that—if not more."

He would always be measured against the man he was replacing. How do you match that kind of success? How do you deal with that kind of pressure? Especially at thirty-three years of age?

But Lincoln didn't see himself as a character in a sports drama, or as a young man building his legacy in the shadow of such an illustrious predecessor. Such narratives did not weigh on him. Nor did the expectations placed on him by anyone in the outside world, be they writer or critic or fan. Nobody would have higher expectations than he already had for himself. He didn't think about failure. "I just see it so much more from the other side," Lincoln says, "of the great opportunity to win games, to compete for championships."

He felt the pressure of his new responsibilities, sure, but he was focused on other things. Better things. The sort of pressure that most people seem to imagine simply does not occur to Lincoln. "Doesn't occur to many coaches," Stoops says. "Nobody coaches that way. Nobody that I've been around, anyway."

They don't even necessarily feel it as pressure. It's enough to make you wonder if the concept of pressure isn't as real as we think. Pressure is not a force of nature like gravity. It is created only by an awareness that it should exist, an awareness created by human beings in the first place. Often, the more we want something, the more tightly we attempt to hold it in our grasp—the more pressure we then unconsciously place on the thing we want—and the more likely we are to accidentally squeeze too tight and break the thing we love.

To someone like Lincoln, pressure was what he felt when he first set foot on Oklahoma's campus. A sense of responsibility, a respect for history, a desire to build upon it—an indication of the fullness of life that lay ahead. "I just see it as a climb," he says. "Something to go attack. Something to obtain."

The focus was on something else: "Do the things necessary here to win every game we play."

It's a focus on what good can be achieved, not on what bad may occur.

What many see as dangerous pressure, he sees as opportunity. It's a perspective shift.

He loved what lay ahead, challenges and all, and love has a way of casting out fear.

Helping matters, of course, was the fact that Lincoln had himself a very good team. And to lead that team and to make the most of his ever-creative offensive mind, Lincoln had a very, very good quarterback.

But that good quarterback also offered Lincoln his greatest challenge.

Baker Mayfield seemed poised to get even better and contend once again for the Heisman Trophy, but he was also a wild card. Barely a week after Lincoln became Oklahoma's head coach, his star quarterback was sitting in a courtroom in Fayetteville, Arkansas, agreeing to a plea deal. The most serious charge—resisting arrest—was to be dropped, and in exchange Baker pled guilty to the rest and paid a few hundred dollars' worth of fines and another few hundred more in restitution.

And so, back in Norman, the task of determining Baker's discipline became one of Lincoln's first duties. Same as when he had to decide at Lake Lyndon B. Johnson whether to grow up, when he had to decide at East Carolina what kind of coach he really was, and when he had to decide what opportunities to take after finding success there, now he had to decide what kind of head coach he wanted to be. And his decisions would be seen on the national level, put under the national microscope that is sports fandom.

Baker's remorse seemed real. This was the university Baker had adored as a kid, after all, and he had become its star quarterback. Now he had embarrassed that university. Baker couldn't bring himself to face his teammates for days. He waffled between despair and anger at himself.

The hardest part for many people who make mistakes, especially today, is moving on from them. It can feel impossible, especially when you're constantly reminded of your failures. The Internet is absurd in its relentless memory of everyone's worst moments, and in its insistence that something a person did months or years ago reflects who he is now. We're beyond the age of private mistakes.

The way the public responded to Baker was the equivalent of Lincoln's old crazy coach's rousing pre-practice speech and head-butt and spilling of blood. Memorable but not necessarily helpful, and possibly damaging to all parties involved.

There are a few ways to move on from mistakes like these. Some are toxic. One of the more common ways we see is when people more or less act as if the mistake had never been made at all. Ignore it and act as if it never happened. This damages everyone involved. So, too, does its toxic inverse: never letting the offending party forget what he did, regardless of the remorse he feels and the behavior he changes.

Lincoln wanted to move forward in a way that would help Baker and help the team, and he didn't feel that more public humiliation was the way to go. Oh, he and Baker had some tough private conversations. "I think you already have to have that relationship built up with them before," Lincoln says. "To be able to have that real conversation with them in that moment, there's got to be some trust built up. That's part of it. And I think you gotta have just a true interest in the person . . . Balance what's best for them with what's best for the program, too. And hopefully find some common ground there."

What those conversations were, they have chosen to keep private. "That's the whole beauty of it," Ruffin says. "It was in private, one on one . . . It was not in front of an audience. That's what is most effective."

For a young man Baker's age, the brain has developed enough to feel every ounce of every emotion, but not quite enough to fully grasp the weight of the consequences of the behavior those emotions can compel. Lincoln opted to exercise patience with Baker. Football is all about concepts, and Lincoln understood that a player's psychology matters as much as his physical ability. And it matters in a way that stretches beyond "mental toughness," a term that has always been tragically misunderstood. Lincoln might recall with fondness his freshman football coach's head-butting, but there's a wide gap between that being a favorite memory and that being the way he thinks football players ought to be handled now.

Players' psychology has always mattered, of course, but there have never been more direct threats to their psychological well-being than there are today. Lincoln knew firsthand what it means to make mistakes, to do things that hurt you. He also knew just how much it can mean to get a break when you're still a boy learning how to become a man.

"Lincoln believes in an ethos of family," Ruffin says. "In your family, if someone does great, the reaction is going to be that . . . of pride. But if someone has a setback in your family, if you truly mean the word *family*, you'll work with that person."

Baker knew what he'd done had been stupid. The temptation existed for Baker to shrink, to make himself smaller, to immerse himself in the criticism, to simultaneously take it to heart and become defensive in the face of it. If he did that, he would neither truly acknowledge what happened nor learn from it. Holding on to the pain of his mistakes wouldn't help anyone at that point. Lincoln gave Baker one piece of advice that had shaped his own life: "You gotta be yourself."

Just do you.

Lincoln reminded Baker that no matter what others want to say about him, the good things he did were as much if not more a part of him than even the worst things. He reminded Baker of the effect he had on the kids at the local children's hospital when he would, just as impulsively, swing by unannounced, with no cameras around, just to see if he could make them smile. And the way that he did things, even on the football field, that the rest of the world never seemed to see because the cameras never seemed to be on him at those moments—like the way he'd jump around in the Oklahoma student section, getting fired up with them, thanking them for being there for him and his team.

Lincoln told Baker, "Ninety-nine percent of who you are is awesome. We don't need you to go change the whole person. You're a good person. You made one bad mistake. Let's learn from it. Let's figure out how you can make it a positive. Let's grow from it. Let's move on."

Same as Lincoln had responded when Baker threw interceptions to start a losing first half against Texas, he chose to respond to Baker's guilty plea to his crimes: with calm grace and assurance that yes, Baker had made some bad mistakes, but those mistakes were not the sum total of Baker's parts.

And he had plenty of help reassuring Baker of that. Baker got a call from Barry Switzer, who said, "Baker, I'm not calling to chew you out. I just want you to know that the same thing happened to me in 1958. All I want to know is, have there been any improvements to the Fayetteville jail? Because it was a hellhole back then."

Lincoln and the university agreed to impose discipline that included Baker completing a university alcohol education course and a few dozen hours of community service. Baker would not be suspended. That would teach him nothing more than he'd already learned, and it would help no one. Baker took food to the elderly in the community by volunteering with Meals on Wheels, and he reveled in the fact that most of the senior citizens he visited had no idea who he was. He also volunteered with the local police department, and helped kids who did know who he was learn how to ride bikes safely.

This wouldn't be the last incident for which Lincoln would have to discipline him. But Lincoln saw a boy learning to be a man, and same as Ruffin had let him learn how to be his own kind of coach at East Carolina, Lincoln was letting Baker become his own kind of man.

In the weeks leading up to Lincoln's first season as the Sooners' new head coach, the vibe at the team's practices was one of fun, and adrenaline, and the pursuit of excellence. It was at once lighthearted and fully committed, which is what it should be for college athletes working hard to be very good at the game of football. This is not life or death. This is play. And they knew how to play. When Lincoln walked onto the field, his offense was already getting loose. Baker was already going through some light passing drills in his sandals and socks. Hip-hop music thumped loudly. Players joked around one moment while taking their drills dead seriously the next. Sometimes Lincoln was serious—yelling, critiquing, instructing—but there were far more moments when he was laughing, smiling, bouncing around.

He and Ruffin were working together well. They had switched roles—Ruffin had once been Lincoln's boss, but now Lincoln was Ruffin's boss—and they had done it without friction.

"It was really easy," Ruffin says. "No hiccups."

He even began calling Lincoln "boss."

"I have no ego," Ruffin says. "Just swallow it. Ego is zero calories."

And Lincoln remained unconcerned with any notion of pressure, with the challenge of staying ahead of opposing defenses trying to figure him out, with any of the things you might think he'd be concerned with. Instead, he was concerned with how he would maintain his relationships with his players now that he had so many larger demands on his time. He still found moments to talk to individual players, but he sought to foster an authentic relationship with them by doing what he'd learned to do best: listen to them. He wanted what was best for them and wanted to give them that in ways that were best for the program on the whole. But with less time to have one-on-one conversations, he'd have to find a new way of doing that. He'd have to adapt. Be creative, same as with any of his on-the-field schemes and concepts.

In his new position as head coach, he had to make time not only for the offense but for the defense as well. "In the hallways, in the locker room, in the coaches' office," says senior defensive back Steven Parker. "Just steady talk. He's wondering what's on everybody's mind, and what's going on in everybody's life—and he actually wants to know. And he just talks to you . . . It comes through as really genuine, because we have lots of people who act like they do—but you can tell he's genuine. You can just have an everyday conversation with him. It's not always just a coach to player, or player to coach. It's like, man to man. And for us to be talking man to man, to a coach—that he's our football coach, but we can talk to him as if he's one of us—that's pretty cool."

Lincoln made his defensive players comfortable enough that they could go to him before or during a practice, say they thought they needed to run more of a certain formation, and Lincoln would go to the defensive coordinator and put in the request.

In team meetings he spoke to the players, and then he would give the players their turn to speak, listening to their concerns, suggestions, and requests. Sometimes, he called meetings for the sole purpose of making sure the players were getting what they needed. These meetings were built around a simple question: What can I do for you?

"Basically," Steven says, "[Lincoln was] asking us, *What can I do to improve the team? What do you guys want that's not getting done?* He listens to us. For a coach to actually sit down and listen to his players is very encouraging."

It was about more than just football, too. "Like, *Hey, Coach, we need to clean up the locker room better.* So he'll assign us players to clean up better. We want better food, so he'll talk to people to get us better food. Just little things like that."

This wasn't something they were used to.

"Yeah," Steven says. "That's very uncommon . . . He flat-out asks, *What can I do better for you guys?* Never seen that before from anyone else. But from him, all the time."

"It's a lot of things," says Dimitri Flowers, a senior fullback. "The joking that we do on the field, not even talking about off-the-field stuff . . . He gets tense when he needs to, and he gets strict, and discipline, and all that stuff is key with him. But at the same time, we have some fun."

To have fun, Lincoln would invite the whole team to the house, all 115 players on the roster. "It's like a herd of animals coming in and out of the house," Baker Mayfield once said.

Caitlin had no complaints. "I love to be involved in the middle of it, get to know the boys as people and learn about their families and what they love," she said.

"For kids who come a long way from home," Baker said, "it's important to see Coach Riley and his wife really hold together the family and the unity."

One of Lincoln's favorite ways to have fun was to jokingly subvert coaching stereotypes. During one team meeting Lincoln said they were going to have a demonstration of what not to do at practice. He had a slideshow presentation up on the screen, and went through a few standard concerns, and then he came to the last slide. Lincoln spoke harshly, letting the players know that This Was Very Serious, saying, "Guys, this is nothing I'll stand for on my team. If I see it again, you're done."

Lincoln played a video: A large player was moving downfield carrying the ball as a smaller player attempted to tackle him. Despite heroic efforts, including an unsuccessful attempt to plant his feet and throw the bigger ball carrier down to the ground, the smaller player was dragged along, flailing and helpless, and the entire room was laughing, and some of the players would later agree that it was one of the funniest things they'd ever seen.

17

Proven

LINCOLN'S TENURE AS HEAD coach at the University of Oklahoma began on a warm and sunny afternoon in Norman. The Sooners started the 2017 season ranked No. 7 in the country and were hosting unranked University of Texas, El Paso. Chief among Lincoln's goals heading into this game was to get the season off to a strong start. The Sooners had begun their seasons sluggishly in recent years, and none worse than in 2016, when they lost the season opener and then lost to Ohio State two weeks after that. So that was the goal: not just win, but win in a way befitting the team's talents and ability. "Which has been . . . a point of emphasis for this group," Lincoln said. "We really take it personal, the way we've played early in the year the last few years."

In front of a full stadium of some eighty-six thousand fans, Baker Mayfield completed his first sixteen passes and only threw one incomplete pass the whole game, and Oklahoma put up 419 yards of total offense in the first half alone. The Sooners won the game by forty-nine points. It helped that Baker had some excellent receivers to throw to, such as Jeff Badet, a transfer from Kentucky who made a stunning catch in the second quarter. After a defender almost intercepted it and Jeff battled him for the bobbled ball, Jeff secured the catch on his way to the ground for a fifty-one-yard gain.

Baker's perfectionistic tendencies were as acute as ever following the game, when he criticized himself not only for the single incompletion, but also for a pass in the first half that was caught only because the receiver jumped for it. "We've got a long way to go," Baker said.

Lincoln was less pessimistic. After all, Baker finished nineteen of twenty with three touchdown passes and 329 total passing yards, and that without even playing the second half. The offense on the whole finished with 676 yards and fifty-six points. "I'm really proud," Lincoln said after the game, which he described as "fun."

Their real test would come the next week, against No. 2–ranked Ohio State.

The Buckeyes, coached by one of the best college football coaches ever in Urban Meyer, had thumped the Sooners the season before by a score of 45–24, and that was in Norman. This time, the Sooners were going to Columbus, to play in the iconic Ohio Stadium—"the Horseshoe," or "the Shoe." It was a brisk evening game under partly cloudy skies, and no fewer than 109,000 people filled the stadium, the most to have attended an Oklahoma game in years. *College GameDay* made the game its focus for the week. There could not have been more attention, relative to the world of college football, than there was on Lincoln Riley, Baker Mayfield, and the Sooners that week. The outlook was not in their favor, with Vegas oddsmakers slotting them as a seven-and-a-half-point underdog. "Takes a special team to deal with this environment on the road," a television announcer said prior to the game.

It was a riveting matchup the likes of which rarely happened so early in the season. Oklahoma had 873 total wins in its history next to Ohio State's 887, and each school had won a slew of national championships, Oklahoma seven and Ohio State six. Oklahoma had won forty-four conference titles, Ohio State thirty-six. Oklahoma had produced five Heisman winners to Ohio State's seven.

It was a poetic matchup, too, for Lincoln, facing a living coaching legend in Urban Meyer. Meyer had been thirty-seven years old when he got his first head coaching job, and Lincoln reminded Meyer of himself in some regards. Young, forward-thinking, ambitious, fearless. Before Ohio State, Meyer had tremendous success as the head coach at Florida for five years, where he won two national championships and concocted a slew of creative plays to make a national sensation out of quarterback Tim Tebow.

The teams' collective personalities were on display from the outset. Ohio State was buttoned-up, literally, its players entering the stadium wearing shirts and ties, while Baker Mayfield got off the Oklahoma bus and walked into the Shoe wearing a T-shirt under a jacket with music blasting in big headphones.

As for the game itself, it started slowly, with both teams playing well but not finding the end zone for the entirety of the first half. The score at halftime was 3–3. In the third quarter, Ohio State scored a touchdown on its opening drive, but Lincoln had been feeling out Ohio State's defense and was poised to begin exploiting its weak parts, particularly if Baker was in good form. And Baker was feeling himself—that much was for sure. Witnesses later recalled that some Buckeye fans behind the Oklahoma bench, by then in a state of total inebriation, were yelling in what can safely be described as a hostile and profane manner, with Baker their primary target. After Ohio State's touchdown, Baker returned fire. "Get ready," he told them, followed by a profanity-laden promise that Oklahoma would now score a touchdown of its own.

That very drive, Baker led the Sooners down the field with an array of fine passes and finished with a thirty-six-yard touchdown pass.

He returned to the sideline and went straight for a bench, upon which he stood to face his drunken antagonists, and reportedly said, "You like that one? I've got three or four more of those coming up. Get ready."

Baker predicted the rest of the game correctly, and he produced an astonishing performance. He finished the game with 386 passing yards and three touchdowns, and the Sooners went on to win, 31–16. Baker was impassioned as ever throughout, but also calm and methodical and above all, accurate, particularly when he was on the run, evading Ohio State's fearsome pass rushers. "His decision making and his accuracy in that game were outstanding," Urban Meyer says. "That's when I became a huge fan." So compelling was Baker's performance that it reverberated throughout the Internet, to the point that Siri, the iPhone's AI assistant, would answer the question "Who owns Ohio Stadium?" with "Baker Mayfield."

Lincoln had called the game masterfully and had even mixed in some trick plays. "His creativity is tremendous," Meyer says. Lincoln balanced Baker's overwhelming ability with a stable of respectable running backs who were more than capable of throwing defenses off with an explosive run attack at any moment. "His ability to adapt, along with creativity, is what separates him from the rest," Meyer says.

Lincoln was able to unleash that creativity in no small part because of Baker, and Baker was so good because of Lincoln's creativity. It was a beautiful synthesis of coach and player. Lincoln could use plays that exploited Baker's unique gifts of mobility, accuracy, and decision making. That, as much as anything, is what Lincoln loved about Baker as a quarterback: how quickly he could process information on the fly. "You can put in a new concept and with a couple days of practice he's ready to go," Lincoln said. "And probably his best trait is his mentality—the competitiveness, the toughness. He's one of those guys that when it's all on the line and you're in a big-time game and atmosphere, you want him on your sideline."

Baker also possessed superb touch and arm strength that enabled him to make passes that might have otherwise been impossible, delivering precise deep throws over double coverage and finding narrow windows among receivers in the middle of the field.

And what really opened up Lincoln's play calling was Baker's ability to move and to throw while on the move.

Despite what the Fayetteville police department might have had to say about Baker, the young man was, if not traditionally "fast," definitely evasive. Ohio State had a remarkable defensive line that included multiple future NFL players, and although Oklahoma's offensive line was one of the more impressive in college football, the Buckeye defensive front was able to get into the backfield with regularity. Baker, however, was able to avoid them, which enabled Lincoln to mix in several run-pass options because of the threat Baker posed on his feet. Multiple times, Baker took the snap, faked a handoff to a halfback, stepped between two oncoming Ohio State rushers, ran away from another, and delivered a bullet some ten or fifteen yards downfield for a significant gain.

Lincoln also identified weak spots in the Ohio State defense in the second half, calling plays that drew experienced linebackers and cornerbacks in various directions and leaving their younger, less experienced safeties to cover receivers that were either too fast or too open for the safeties to do much about until it was too late. When Ohio State's defense compensated, Lincoln called plays that exploited the slower linebackers over the middle. One particularly impressive play saw Baker fake a handoff that drew the linebackers forward and allowed halfback Dimitri Flowers to curl out of the backfield into an open midfield. Baker stepped out of the way of oncoming pass rushers and delivered a strike to Dimitri at the 30-yard line. Dimitri ran it the rest of the way for a touchdown without any defender laying a finger on him.

Lincoln and Baker also picked apart Ohio State's coverage of Oklahoma's "trips" concepts (three receivers on one side of the field). Early in the game, Ohio State's defense more or less covered the three receivers with just three of their own men. Lincoln called plays that exploited this, and Baker made precise passes, and they wore the defense out until adjustments were made. And then Lincoln just called new plays, allowing Baker to move around in the backfield in order to find open receivers elsewhere. By the end of the game, nine different Oklahoma receivers had caught at least one pass.

The Ohio State game elevated Oklahoma to No. 2 in the country and moved Baker to the top of the Heisman leaderboard, vaulting him over USC quarterback and future first-round NFL draft pick Sam Darnold and placing him close behind the sensational young Louisville quarterback Lamar Jackson.

What was certain was that Baker was a talent to behold, and also that he would remain a force of nature for good and for bad that Lincoln would have to manage carefully. For instance, with emotion overflowing after time expired and the victory was theirs, Baker grabbed a massive Oklahoma flag and trotted to the center of the field with it amid all his celebrating teammates, waved it back and forth, and then raised it above his head in order to thrust it down into the ground, planting it in the center of Ohio State's midfield O. The field, being artificial turf, rejected the flag, which fell over. Later, people would criticize Baker for this, calling it classless, and Baker would issue an apology that he would later say he did not mean.

This was just the first of several incidents throughout the season in which Baker would do something thrilling but controversial, his emotional way of being all at once constantly galvanizing and threatening the good of the team.

Against Baylor two weeks later, Baker started the game by telling the Baylor team, "You forgot who Daddy is! I'm gonna have to spank you today!" The chippy talk didn't concern Lincoln. "Guys barking back and forth before the game," he said, "that happens every single game with every single player on the field. I could care less about that."

What Lincoln did care about was how Baker and the rest of the team performed come game time, and whether the barking back and forth helped or hurt the team. And against Baylor, Baker ended up having a down game against a winless team that the Sooners ought to have dispatched easily. Instead, the game became an ugly slog that the Sooners escaped with a 49–41 win. Baker's numbers were fine—thirteen for nineteen, 283 yards, three touchdowns—but his ego hurt the team in ways that left Lincoln displeased. During one drive in the third quarter when the Sooners were trailing 31–28, Baker was mouthing off again at Baylor players, and one referee had enough of it, flagging Baker for unsportsmanlike conduct. The fifteen-yard loss could have been devastating for the Sooners, but Baker redeemed himself on the next play, a forty-eight-yard touchdown pass to Jeff Badet. Lincoln himself was criticized for not seeming to care enough about Baker's behavior in the moment—he remained surprisingly calm and unmoved—but later he said, "I wasn't happy with him."

Baker's fire, his barking back and forth, the way that motivated him and his teammates—all of that was fine, but only to a point, especially if he was drawing penalties that hurt the team. "Regardless of what kind of player that you are, nobody is valuable enough to have those," Lincoln said. "He has to know where he is. His energy and mentality brings a lot to our team, but he can't cross the line. He knows that. He has to do better than that."

Lincoln's decision not to chew Baker out in the moment, however, was a conscious one. He knew that people might take it as his letting Baker's behavior go. "For me," he said, "it's not about what it looks like on TV, or if everybody loves it in the stands when the coach is ripping a guy just to rip him. My whole deal is, 'What's going to help us on the next play?' I'll get him later. Trust me. But what's going to help us on the next play? Is having me tear him up right there going to help him, help the team?"

Lincoln sacrificed his image for the sake of the team, knowing what Baker did and did not need in that moment. "My ego's not too big for that," he said.

That kind of levelheaded leadership was just what Baker needed. "I'm an emotional player," Baker says. "I play with high intensity . . . He's always told me, *Find the middle. Never get too high. Never get too low.*"

And Lincoln lived by that himself. "You see how he handles us through the good and the bad," Baker said. "He doesn't get too high or too low. He sets a standard, and anything that dips below that, he'll let us know if it needs to be picked up and anything that gets too high, he levels it out."

This approach is more important than ever in the age of social media, when countless fans—and armchair critics—can reach a kid simply by typing a message on Twitter. Lincoln couldn't understand that, exactly, from firsthand experience, but he connected with it by talking with his players and remaining in touch with his empathy. He had experienced some of the stress they had, but not all of it, especially not a kid like Baker, and the attention—the vitriol—to which fans subjected him. Especially on social media. "You had fifty, sixty, seventy thousand people watching you thirty years ago," Lincoln says. "Now, you've got millions of people watching you across the world. Any person in the world can pick up Twitter—can pick up their cell phone and immediately connect with them—negatively or positively. Almost every game now is televised. It's such a bigger stage, and they deal with so many more distractions, good and bad."

Baker says, "It's not that he has the same mindset, but he understands it. And . . . he just gets it. And so he can talk to us about it. And no, he can't put himself in our shoes exactly, and he's said that. He's said those exact words. But he can also understand it. And he can tell us and he can coach us on how to handle it too. He always says, *Don't listen to the outside opinion*."

"Like with the Texas and Tennessee games," Baker says. "He just said, *Don't worry about it, don't worry about what they're doing*. You could say the same things about the Internet and anything social media–wise. *Forget about what they're doing. You just do you*."

Just do you.

But find the middle.

And that was something that Baker was still having to learn. Idiotic disrespect from fans on the Internet was one thing. Maintaining grace in the face of disrespect on the field was another. And Baker still had to learn to prevent his passion from burning him alive. Late in the season, before a game against Kansas, as the team captains met at midfield prior to the pregame coin toss, the Jayhawk captains refused to shake Baker's hand. Baker was irritated, to say the least. He nodded and clapped his hands at them and laughed at them, and then proceeded to spend the game taunting them. Kansas continued to play provocateur, with defensive players hitting Baker well after he'd thrown a pass in what seemed to be intentional late hits. In reply, Baker led one touchdown drive after another, offering Jayhawk players and fans a stream of advice such as "Stick to basketball." Then, in the third quarter, as Oklahoma took a 27–3 lead, Baker shouted at the Kansas sideline and grabbed his crotch. Many were instantly offended by the crude gesture.

Lincoln had to make a hard decision after that. After the game, he wanted to defend Baker because he hadn't seen the footage yet, and he was angry about the late hits Baker had been taking throughout the game. Upon reviewing the incident later, however, Lincoln recognized that Baker needed to learn another hard lesson: regardless of what's been done, if you allow someone to provoke you to anger, it is you, and not the other person, who will pay the consequences for how you choose to express that anger.

Lincoln removed Baker as the starting quarterback for senior day and stripped him of his captaincy. It was a punishment that many in the football world scoffed at and called meaningless, but it was also a decision that made Lincoln emotional. He cried over it. "That," Ruffin says, "was a tough decision."

Lincoln said later, "I don't know that I'll ever have a player that's as special to me as he is." And that's why he did it. He wanted Baker to succeed, but to do that, Baker still had a lot to learn about how not to do things that hurt you. The only way to learn, as Lincoln learned in high school when he chased the linebacker, was to lose something important to you.

Baker had spent his whole life dreaming of glory at Oklahoma.

And on a day meant to glorify seniors, the senior who'd perhaps earned it most of all was sitting on the bench when the game began.

Other than a surprising loss to unranked Iowa State a couple of weeks after the Baylor game, the Sooners won every game during the regular season and claimed the Big 12 Conference championship title. They won the ever-important annual Red River Showdown against Texas, in the Cotton Bowl in Dallas, by a score of 29–24. They beat No. 11 Oklahoma State 62–52. They beat No. 8 TCU the week after that by a score of 38–20. And in the Big 12 championship game, they crushed TCU again, 41–17.

Oklahoma finished the season ranked No. 3 in the country. And once again, the Sooners made the College Football Playoff, where they would face Georgia on New Year's Day in the one place Lincoln once considered his dream place to play or coach: the Rose Bowl.

It was a slugfest in which the teams would combine for nearly one hundred points. Baker threw for 287 yards and two touchdowns, and Lincoln masterfully incorporated the rushing game to keep the Bulldogs as off balance as he could, resulting in 200 yards rushing for halfback Rodney Anderson, who scored two touchdowns as well. Lincoln also mixed in some of his signature trick plays, such as a sublime one pulled off at the end of the first half from the 2-yard line. Baker pitched to a running back, who sprinted to the left only to hand off to a wide receiver sprinting in the opposite direction—and then, as the defense swarmed toward the receiver, he pulled up short and flipped a quick pass over everyone's heads and into the end zone, where Baker was standing all alone in the corner for the touchdown reception. That gave the Sooners a 31–14 lead going into halftime, but they were unable to maintain it: the Bulldogs surged to a comeback, and regulation ended with the score tied at 45. And then, in the overtime, Oklahoma gave up a quick touchdown, and the game was Georgia's.

That ended the Sooners' season with a loss, but Lincoln's first season as a head coach was nonetheless a success. He had led his team to college football's biggest stage—and not only that, he had guided Baker Mayfield to success unimaginable when the boy had first arrived. "I don't know if we have ever had a player with his charisma, enthusiasm, and ability," said Barry Switzer. "It's all there in one package." He joked that Baker did deserve criticism for one thing: "The only mistake he made was not outrunning the Fayetteville police."

The best coaches and players alike desire team accomplishments and championships above all, but there was no small satisfaction in how Baker's season ended: he finished with 4,600 passing yards and 43 touchdowns, and he ultimately surpassed even Lamar Jackson to claim the Heisman Trophy. When he accepted the award and started his speech, he began to cry as he thanked Lincoln. "You've been a great mentor to me," he said. "Been through a lot together. So appreciate you."

As Baker prepared for the NFL draft over the next couple months, he and Lincoln remained in close contact. Meanwhile, Oklahoma knew what they had with Lincoln, and they did something about it: they offered him a five-year contract worth $25 million.

After Baker had spent some time training in Los Angeles, he and Lincoln went to an Oklahoma basketball game together in

February and caught up. Baker showed up wearing a long, flowing cardigan. "What are you wearing there?" Lincoln asked in his country drawl. "What do you call that?"

"It's a cardigan," Baker said.

"LA's wearing on you a little bit," Lincoln replied, deadpan.

Baker carried on as Lincoln smirked playfully, listening to his protégé talk about visiting the actor Mark Wahlberg at his home and then complain about having to fly all over the country to various banquets for awards.

"Where are you going from here?" Lincoln asked.

"Down to Fort Worth for Davey O'Brien," Baker said, meaning the award for best college quarterback.

"Oh," Lincoln said. "And then back to LA?"

"Yeah," Baker said, adding with a tone of youthful disdain, "All these people, with these banquets, they don't realize the timing of it."

Lincoln just said, "Yeah."

"Terrible," Baker went on.

Lincoln let that hang in the air for a beat, then smirked and said, "Tough winning all those awards, isn't it?"

A beat passed, then Baker dropped his face into his palm as though realizing how childish he'd just sounded, and he and Lincoln both laughed.

Find the middle.

Never get too high.

Never get too low.

"For us," Baker says, "it's been a steady incline. And that's what's been special. He's never let it get too low for me, but he's also kept me grounded."

Lincoln was by Baker's side at the pro day held at Oklahoma's facilities, where Baker performed well. Lincoln continued to encourage him with the same advice that had always seemed to work: *Just be yourself.* And Baker was. He didn't shy away from questions that general managers and scouts asked him about his various exploits, from the Kansas crotch grab to the Fayetteville arrest. In a way, they became some of the best things ever to happen to him—by accepting responsibility, and acknowledging the ways he had been wrong and the things he had learned from them, he showed maturity. If nothing else, he showed growth. Cleveland Browns general manager John Dorsey, who had the first pick in the NFL draft that year, visited Baker in Norman and took him to dinner at a restaurant called Red Rock. While sitting at their table by a window, Dorsey looked outside and said, "Here's what we're gonna do: open up restaurants right here, all lined up, and they're all gonna be food trucks." And Baker laughed about it with him.

The day of the draft, Lincoln joined Baker and his parents and extended family, along with a large number of friends, at the Mayfield residence outside Austin. When Dorsey called to tell Baker that the Browns were taking him with the number one pick, Baker got choked up, and after the announcement was made on television, in the middle of all the celebrating going on, Lincoln grabbed Baker, and the two former walk-ons shared a big hug for a long moment, laughing in ways that also sounded like crying.

"Great job, man," Lincoln said. "So very proud of you."

Epilogue

HUNGER

LINCOLN often visits a marina on a lake about a half hour northwest of Dallas. The marina is kind of hidden, the type of place you only find if you're looking for it. It's a getaway for the area's rich and famous, although it's open to the public, too. There's members-only parking, but also a seafood restaurant and bar on the water, open to all. The restaurant overlooks the docks, and the docks lead out to a small cove through which boats can make their way to a vast lake. It's reminiscent, in a way, of Lake Lyndon B. Johnson, where Lincoln decided it was time to grow up.

Lincoln takes to the water whenever he can. Sometimes, that's here, outside Dallas. Other times, Vermejo Park in New Mexico. But he still always finds his way back to the water. No matter how good life gets as a football coach, you always need a way to get away from it all.

And life has been good for Lincoln since that first season.

For starters, Baker Mayfield helped turn the Cleveland Browns around. Before he arrived, they'd lost every game for two years straight. In 2018, Baker wasn't named the starter, but he won the locker room. After a few games, he got a chance to play and he played well, throwing for some touchdowns and making some plays and electrifying his teammates by doing what Lincoln had always told him to do: just be himself. For reasons that were never clear, Browns coach Hue Jackson remained unwilling to name Baker his starter, but soon that didn't matter, because Jackson got fired, the new coach named Baker the starter, and the Browns started winning football games.

Meanwhile, Lincoln's second season as Oklahoma's head coach was going as well as his first. He had a sharp new quarterback to work with, a junior named Kyler Murray who'd transferred the season before from Texas A&M. When Kyler was looking to transfer, Bob Stoops was still the head coach, and Kyler was just one of three options Bob and Lincoln were considering for a scholarship. The other two were more prototypically impressive quarterbacks, bigger and taller pocket passers with good brains and good arms. At five foot ten, Kyler was short for a quarterback, even shorter than Baker, but he reminded them of Russell Wilson, down to also playing baseball—only he might have been even more athletic and explosive than Wilson overall. Their other two options were excellent, but as Lincoln studied Kyler, he told Bob, "Kyler could win a Heisman here."

Turned out that Lincoln was exactly right.

With Kyler leading the offense, the Sooners went 12–2 overall, finished the season ranked No. 4 in the country, and once again went to the College Football Playoff, though this time they lost to No. 1 Alabama in the semifinal by a score of 45–34. Kyler finished the season with 4,300 yards and forty-two touchdowns with just seven interceptions, rushed for another 1,000 yards and twelve touchdowns, and, just as Lincoln predicted, won the Heisman Trophy.

That made Kyler and Baker the first two quarterbacks from any school in college football history to win Heisman Trophies in back-to-back seasons.

And, just like Baker, Kyler was selected No. 1 overall in the NFL draft. He was drafted by none other than Kliff Kingsbury, the quarterback at Texas Tech back when Lincoln first walked on there, who was now the head coach of the Arizona Cardinals.

In January 2019, Oklahoma offered Lincoln yet another new contract: six years for $32.5 million, with bonus incentives built in for every year he stays. "We want him at the University of Oklahoma for a long time," the university's president, James Gallogly, said. "He is a great coach and role model for our student-athletes. His record of success speaks for itself. I am proud to work with him and anxious to support him as he takes our program into the future."

For the 2019 season, Lincoln landed another star transfer quarterback: Jalen Hurts, who had taken Alabama to the national championship two seasons prior. He'd lost his starting spot, he sought a transfer, he and Lincoln connected, and the rest was history.

Unlike with Baker and Kyler, Lincoln didn't have years to teach Jalen his offense and work with him to get him adjusted to it. They had only a few months. That didn't matter. Lincoln's third season went virtually as well as the first two. The Sooners again went 12–2, and again made the College Football Playoff before losing in the semifinals. Jalen became one of the most dynamic dual-threat quarterbacks Oklahoma had ever seen. He didn't put up quite the same passing numbers as Baker and Kyler, but he still threw for 3,800 yards and thirty-two touchdowns. He was, however, as fearsome a running back as he was a passer, a power-running threat who put up 1,298 total rushing yards—a school record for a quarterback—and twenty additional rushing touchdowns, both of which led the team.

In his first three years as the Sooners' head coach, Lincoln has won thirty-six games, more than any other Oklahoma coach has ever won in his first three seasons. He's gone 27–3 in Big 12 Conference play, and he's won the conference championship all three years. He shared the conference Coach of the Year award in 2018. All three of his quarterbacks have been Heisman winners or finalists. Two of them went on to become No. 1 overall NFL draft picks, and in 2020 Jalen Hurts was selected in the second round by the Philadelphia Eagles with the fifty-third pick of the draft. And the Sooners made the College Football Playoff all three seasons.

Lincoln is now considered possibly the greatest contemporary offensive mind in all of football, and that includes the NFL. He's also proving to be a savvy head coach. For years, Oklahoma's glaring weakness was its defense. Before the 2019 season, Lincoln made the difficult decision to fire his defensive coordinator, Bob Stoops's brother Mike. In his place, Lincoln hired Alex Grinch, who promptly made the Sooners' defense respectable: they finished the 2019 season ranked No. 26 in the country in total defense, and No. 1 in the Big 12. "That was a gutsy move," Urban Meyer says. "And it worked out."

Even the earliest concerns that players and fans had about Lincoln have been assuaged. Despite his reputation as an Air Raid savant, he also uses the run, now more than ever. In 2019, the Sooners averaged just over forty-one carries a game, in line with their two-decades-long average of thirty-five to forty carries per game. They averaged more than 250 yards of rushing per game, making it their seventh straight season averaging 200 or more yards per game. "I always felt like to win championships," Lincoln said recently, "you had to be able to run the ball."

One of the most impressive qualities of Lincoln's success isn't just that it has happened, but that it has happened so consistently. "They get out of the blocks and they kill it," Mike Leach says of the Sooners. "It'd be easy to get a big head and lose perspective and not do it again. Well, they did it again. I think that's impressive. And . . . I know that sounds easy, but if it was that easy, everybody would do it. And they don't."

It has been so impressive that there was a swell of rumors following the 2019 season that Lincoln might get hired by the Dallas Cowboys. Lincoln already had a relationship with Cowboys owner Jerry Jones after having recruited Jones's grandson to Oklahoma. And as the Cowboys moved on from their coach Jason Garrett, the rumors continued to build until the job was ultimately given to Mike McCarthy. Lincoln said he's not looking to coach in the NFL anytime soon. He told a reporter in early 2019, "Right now, it wouldn't surprise me at all if I am a college lifer." And a year later, as he was talking with another reporter, his feelings didn't seem to have changed. "I do not have a long-term goal of coaching in the NFL," he said. "It's not a bucket list thing for me. It's not something where I'm like, 'I've got to do that before I retire.' I want to just live in the now. Enjoy the now. I want to enjoy the place I'm at now and work hard at the place I'm at now and appreciate that. Just try to make each year as good as we can."

One of the most interesting things about Lincoln's story isn't just the surreal nature of its Hollywood narrative, although it is surreal indeed—boy who grew up in the middle of nowhere in West Texas and dreamed of being a quarterback fails, learns hard lessons, becomes a wunderkind of a coach who then helps a boy dreaming of being a great quarterback win the Heisman Trophy and become the No. 1 NFL draft pick. And it's not just that Lincoln has achieved remarkable success at a young age, or even that he's achieved that success because he seems to be some kind of football wizard. The most interesting thing about Lincoln and his success has been the evolution of his nature as a human being along the way. He grew up brilliant, seeing the world differently than most around him, and as he became a man, he came to embrace that fact about himself. And like many brilliant young people who recognize that they are different from most around him, Lincoln went through a phase he recalls as "arrogant." He talked over coaches in meetings, he debated reporters who criticized him, he grabbed those reporters' shirts to celebrate big wins in almost aggressive joy. And then he grew. He grew, in Ruffin McNeill's words, from smart to wise. "He is continuing to seek knowledge," Ruffin says. "What I love about him is he's always . . . searching for knowledge. It's never ending. I'm talking about never, ever ending. From any source possible. Knowledge. Knowledge."

He seeks knowledge from the best to do what he does, befriending some of the greatest coaches in the game, such as Bill Belichick of the New England Patriots. "He's really tight with Coach Belichick," Ruffin says.

This continuous seeking of knowledge has led to continuous growth.

And at the core of that growth has been deepening his connection with the people on whom he depends the most. Taking the time not only to talk to his coaches and players, not only to hold extra meetings and invite them to gatherings at his home, but also to spend the energy required in order to make them feel seen and heard—to make them feel like not only great football people, but also worthy human beings. And to do that, he has continued to evolve. That requires a certain softness of heart and spirit—a vulnerability—that traditional sports culture has deemed weak but that wisdom is revealing to be nothing less than ultimate strength. A man most firmly establishes himself as a leader when he first shows those he leads that he can bend for them. Lincoln seems to have done this every passing year.

And yet by its very nature, coaching a college football team can make a young man get lost in his ambition, which has a dark side. "I worry about guys like that," Urban Meyer says. "Guys that are so young, so successful."

Meyer knows a thing or two about chasing success and the ways it can hurt you without your realizing it. "You become a product of your own success," he says. Which, for him, meant working obsessively long hours, getting little sleep, constantly taking to the road to find the next great player, and generally forsaking those he loves, including himself. "There's only one true goal: win the national championship," Meyer says. And he said that to win the national championship, the goal can't be "anything other than undefeated."

This can become unhealthy. It can reach a point where, Meyer says, "The only thing that is acceptable is perfection. And that's not a good thing."

It can wear a coach down, the chase for perfection. It's a new potential version of chasing the linebacker. There's a fine line between chasing perfection and being consumed by it, and many a coach has sprinted past that line and not realized it until they were figuratively running off the edge of a cliff. Urban Meyer thought he had a handle on everything, too, even as he was chasing Ambien with beer to sleep, until he collapsed, mentally, figuratively, and literally, found by his wife on the floor in their home late one night, unresponsive.

Coaches know that perfection isn't technically possible—even in the rare undefeated season, you can always find something to improve on—but coaches also seem to accept this only in the abstract. "At some point," Meyer says, "it might be injuries, or whatever, they won't make it, and you gotta be able to handle that."

Mike Leach agrees. "There's not way better days ahead," he says. "I mean, he might win the whole thing. They've been in the playoffs the last several years. But there's potentially some down days ahead. And there is for everybody. There is for every program. Because you know the thing was on top when he got there. I hate to say it. It might get a little better. But it's damn sure gonna get a little worse. There's gonna be a point it gets a little worse."

Lincoln also hasn't yet dealt with serious adversity at Oklahoma. His worst season as a coach came that second year at East Carolina, and that was in relative anonymity, in an island of a town with a team that didn't matter on the national level. "He's still young," Urban says. "He hasn't had one of those bad years yet."

Lincoln got a small taste of hard times in the 2019 playoff semifinal, when the Sooners got walloped by No. 1 LSU, giving up forty-nine points and a slew of passing records in the first half alone. By the fourth quarter it seemed that both teams were just running out the clock.

Afterward, Lincoln did what he always does, which is find a different angle on things, find a good perspective. True, the Sooners had lost three straight College Football Playoff games, but that meant they'd also reached three straight College Football Playoffs, and they'd reached the CFP four times in the past five years. "Just putting yourself here four times in five years is—I mean, that's so hard to do, man," he said. "I think we've made some great improvements with the program. I'm excited about where we're heading defensively. I think we've just scratched the surface about how good we can get on that side. This program has championship DNA. We kind of find a way, and we'll be back."

He makes it sound easy, and it is anything but. Baker Mayfield once thought he'd become a coach one day, until he saw what it took. "I used to think I wanted to coach and I would be a great coach," he said not long ago. "But after watching some of the hours those guys put in, and they have families, and it takes them away from that so much, it is hard to watch. I respect them so much for that."

In many ways, Lincoln would not be where he is without Caitlin, and a fitting picture of that was the way she stood by his side, literally, at weekly media-day luncheons during his first season as Oklahoma's head coach. "I've always felt it's important to be by his side in the good and the bad, so I want to be there every week no matter what," Caitlin said. "Honestly, it's a good ten-minute walk [from his office] that we get to see each other and visit alone. It's some time we get to catch up during the day."

"I think she really understands everything that he goes through," said Oklahoma defensive tackle Orlando Brown. "For the most part, I think the reason he's able to be so calm and be there for us is because of her and all the pressure she takes off of him."

Even when things are going well and a coach and his family are happy and healthy, there's always a sense of lack on the family side of things. This is not lost on Lincoln. "It really is a hard life for them," he said of his wife and daughters. "It's lonely a lot, and all that goes along with it, especially if something doesn't go well."

For a man who says he loves his family as much as Lincoln does, this requires no small sacrifice. "I only get to be a dad once," he once said. "My girls only get to be little once. I only get to be a husband once. I don't want to take those things for granted."

They grab every moment they can together. Caitlin will bring the girls to practice, and they'll have "practice picnics." She will bring the girls to his office. And when he is home, he does the dad thing with his girls. He watches *Paw Patrol* and Mickey Mouse. He plays tea party. He swims with them in the pool, and when they say it's time for makeovers, he's ready for all the lipstick and glitter.

Even so, one has to wonder if it's ever enough. "It's hard to spend time with them as often as you like," Mike Leach says. "They and you both get cheated out of some of the time you spend with them. There's no way around that. There's guys that talk a good game, but it's indisputable that they lose some time."

As with all concepts in football, there's a give and a take, a push and a pull, a sacrifice and a payoff. "They do get to be involved with something that's pretty cool, that's kind of a big deal, that's pretty exciting," Leach says. "And they get to include other people with it. The trouble is you don't fully get to enjoy the fact that they're enjoying it as much as you would like, because they're having a blast, but the thing is, you're working the whole time. You know? So, yeah, it's a little incomplete."

The key to sustained success, both with the team and with one's personal life, is as easy to forget as it is simple: "Keep your priorities," Urban Meyer says, "and have mechanisms in place to handle the non-perfection."

One of Lincoln's favorite ways to do this is to take to the water, sometimes with friends and members of his coaching staff, sometimes with his family. Same as when he was a boy, out on the water he feels that he returns to himself. Out on the water, when it's just him and Caitlin and Sloan and Stella, it's not about, as Sloan loves to say, "how high up we are," how far Lincoln has come from Muleshoe, how brilliant he is or is not, how much he can or cannot do in football. Out on the water, it's just about them, the people they love, the purpose of everything. Out there, with his family, he's still the same guy he's always been. The boat's a little nicer, but he still feels that shoulder he hurt as a kid.

That's why, too, Lincoln said he didn't want the Dallas job. And if you're a man with ambition, a man who desires to fulfill his potential, it's hard not to be tempted by it. For a kid from Muleshoe, few things feel bigger than a football game at Oklahoma. Maybe the game at Ohio State. Maybe the Rose Bowl. But there is no electric charge like the one you feel on the sidelines during a Dallas Cowboys football game at AT&T Stadium. It does not simply feel like a football game. It feels like experiencing another universe. It is, in a word, consuming—it feels, in its own, different way, very much like the vast night skies in West Texas.

"I don't ever want to be the guy that says, *I'm never going to do this. I'm never going to leave*," Lincoln said recently. "Then if it happens at some point, people could look back and say, *He wasn't truthful with me*. That's the part I can't live with. I never know what the future is going to bring. I never know how college football is going to evolve. You never know if things at any job get out of your control and change. The way college football is going right now, the situation and setup we have here at Oklahoma, it's hard to imagine there being something out there better for me and my family."

Still, Ruffin says that he can see Lincoln in the NFL one day. "I wouldn't put it past him," he says. "But I know he's having a good time here at Oklahoma." Ruffin calls Oklahoma "a one percent school," one of the best there is. And then there's this: "He impacts kids from up close," Ruffin says. "I think that's the difference . . . Everybody has a mission. Right now he's impacting a lot of young people. He's paying it forward."

Remember what Ruffin said made Lincoln so good: If something's hurting, having the answer. In the summer of 2020, Lincoln became a voice of caution as others in football wanted to rush back to campus in the midst of the COVID-19 pandemic. "We're constantly learning more and more about this virus," he had said in March, "and why we would not [take] our time is beyond me." As other teams, such as Clemson, Ohio State, and Texas returned to their facilities in June, Lincoln and Oklahoma opted to bring the players and staff back later in the summer, choosing safety over practice time.

Meanwhile, Lincoln did not keep silent as Black Lives Matter protests rose up around the world in May, with millions taking to the streets to march against police brutality and systemic racism after a white Minneapolis police officer killed a black man named George Floyd. On May 31, six days after George Floyd's death, Lincoln wrote on Twitter, "I was raised in a home that taught me that no human, regardless of race, religion, or any other factor, should ever be treated differently. We have a long ways to go as a society. I am committed to being a part of the change." Two days later, on what became known worldwide as #BlackoutTuesday, he posted a blank black square captioned "#BlackLivesMatter."

He may have been the first white college football coach to use that sentence in such explicit support of the movement. "All lives can't matter," Lincoln said, "until the black lives do, too. And on an equal playing field." For better and worse, none of us are who we are on our own. "Having been on football teams, been in those locker rooms," he said, "I've seen how awesome it can be when everybody takes an approach of, We're all on the same playing field, we're all equal, and how beautiful that is."

When Lincoln was asked if he would join his players should they protest, he said, "As long as it's done tastefully, it's well-thought-out, it's done peacefully, there is certainly nothing off the table in that realm for me."

Whatever the future is going to bring, whether Lincoln is still in Norman or off to the NFL, Oklahoma feels like home for him right now. He says he just wants to keep building what he's building here, and keep helping guys do what he couldn't do, and be a dad.

After Lincoln's first season as head coach, Gil Brandt, the long-time Dallas Cowboys executive, said, "Lincoln Riley can do anything in the world that he wants to do. He's as good as any college coach there is in America. He could be president of the United States and be good. He could be an NFL coach and be really good. The guy is an unusual talent."

It all sounds like the same sorts of things people used to say about Lincoln when he was a kid growing up in Muleshoe. And same as always, Lincoln avoids talk of that nature, and he avoids anything that could make people think he actually believes it. He appreciates people's admiration for the success he's had so far, but he doesn't seem to enjoy thinking about it all that much. He prefers to think about what he wants to do next. He remains hungry. He preaches that hunger now, too. Only it's not just hunger.

He has begun to coach according to this ethos, a mantra the team has begun to carry: "Not satisfied. Starving."

Not just hungry.

Starving.

He preaches it in team meetings. *Starving.* He talks about it in interviews. *Starving.* He inspires his players to do the same, to post workout videos after wins with the hashtag "#starving." They said it all the time. *Starving. Starving. Starving.* Winning won't fill them up. Nothing will fill them up. They were starving and it seems they will suffer from this starvation until they have won every game, gone undefeated, claimed the national championship. Until then, they *starve*. Never mind the meteoric rise, the three straight conference championships, the three playoff appearances.

Talking with Mike Leach recently, Lincoln was bothered by the fact that people think so much of him already, that some people think he should even have a book written about him. He said he feels like he hasn't really done anything yet.

A Note on Sources

I first met Lincoln Riley in the summer of 2017, about a month after he was named the head coach at Oklahoma, when *Bleacher Report* sent me to write a profile of him. I spent roughly a week in Norman, talking with Lincoln and his coaches and players, as well as members of the community, and generally getting to know the town. I also spent a lot of time on the phone with players and staff at East Carolina University and Texas Tech, as well as people from Lincoln's childhood. Some of what is written in this book first appeared in that article.

When I told Lincoln in the spring of 2019 that I was writing this book, he expressed reservations and said he would have to think about whether or not he wanted to be involved. He said he had no problem with my doing the book and did not want to get in the way of it, but he wasn't sure he was comfortable actively participating in a biography project when he was so young. He worried about how people would perceive it—that if he did participate, then people would get the impression that he somehow thought that he already had everything all figured out.

As he thought it over, I moved forward.

First off, it was just pure fun, from a football-story standpoint.

And on a deeper level, I was fascinated by the human elements at play, particularly the lessons that naturally emerged from Lincoln's story—lessons about being a dreamer, being a thinker, being a coach, being a man.

I gathered much of the material for this book while reporting my article in 2017. At that time, I spoke with, among others, Lincoln Riley, Mike Leach, Baker Mayfield, Ruffin McNeill, Caitlin Riley, Bob Stoops, other members of the Oklahoma coaching staff, other Oklahoma players, and some members of the East Carolina team he coached prior to Oklahoma, including Dwayne Harris and Zay Jones. I also spoke with Garrett Riley, Lincoln's younger brother, and David Wood, Lincoln's old high school coach.

In the summer and fall of 2019, I made additional reporting trips to Muleshoe, Lubbock, and Norman, and I also conducted research and interviews in Greenville, where I currently live. In all these places I spoke with many new people, enough to feel that I had gained a true grasp of Lincoln's story.

The prologue draws mostly from my time in Norman with Lincoln and the team in 2017. Through the first few chapters that cover Lincoln's childhood up until he goes to Texas Tech, I got most of my information from my reporting in Muleshoe. On that trip I flew into Austin and then drove up and down the length of West Texas. I'd never been there before and wanted to make sure I knew what it felt like. This was partly because I have a somewhat obsessive research process, but also because Lincoln made a similar drive himself while wrestling with the end of his football career in college. In Muleshoe I was given a thorough tour of the town by Alice Liles. I ate at several local establishments and talked for a while with various members of the community, all of them lovely. I drove out to a few of the other small towns where Lincoln played football as a kid, including Dimmitt, where he met his wife, and Friona, where he graffitied a water tower. David Wood invited me out to his ranch for a day and I spoke at length with him and his delightful wife, Jody. Ralph Mason spoke with me at length by phone. Matt McDonald showed me around the grounds of the cotton compress that Mike Riley, Lincoln's father, used to own. I also spent a day going through the archives of the *Muleshoe Journal* in a dusty and disorganized room lined in huge and beautiful leather volumes that reminded me of the work I did in college for the *Kenly News*. I loved going through those old papers. Every town has lore that makes its roots unique and beautiful, and the same is true of Muleshoe.

For the next part of the story, which unfolds at Texas Tech in Lubbock, I received a tour of the stadium and its grounds from a helpful member of the Red Raiders' football media relations staff. I spent two days going through decades of *Lubbock Avalanche-Journal* microform archives in the George & Helen Mahon Public Library near campus. I also spoke with Mike Leach again by phone for several hours, which would prove helpful not only for this section but for the rest of the book as well. He referred me often to his book *Swing Your Sword*, which I read multiple times. I read hundreds of pages of depositions and legal documents via LexisNexis and the *New York Times* website. I spoke with a number of people in town, too, and the most helpful was without a doubt the local sports reporter Don Williams, who gave me an excellent tour of Lubbock and helped me a great deal as I sought to understand the town and Lincoln's time there.

After Lubbock, there was Greenville, North Carolina, home to East Carolina University. I grew up in Greenville. I was a graduate student at East Carolina when Lincoln was the Pirates' offensive coordinator. I've stayed in town for family reasons. So I know Greenville well. I've been to more Pirate football games than I can count, including the game in which they trounced North Carolina by a score of 70–41. The university's media relations staff was very helpful, as was local sports editor Nathan Summers, who has covered Pirate football since before Lincoln arrived. Ruffin McNeill also took some time to talk with me on the phone.

Then there was Norman. I took multiple trips there and spent a lot of time in various sports bars and restaurants around town, just talking with people. I also wandered the area around the stadium on a game day to speak with tailgaters. While I was in town, Jason Kersey, a local reporter who has covered Oklahoma football for the better part of a decade, generously spent time talking with me—and introduced me to the Mont and its dangerously excellent drink, the Swirl. Again, Mike Leach and Ruffin McNeill were helpful. I spoke with Urban Meyer, among others, to better understand Lincoln's place in the history of the game and the challenges he may face as he moves forward in his career. And Bob Stoops's book *No Excuses* imparted a wealth of inside information.

As for Lincoln, he ultimately decided that he did not want to be involved with a book project right now. As a result, the University of Oklahoma respectfully declined to participate, along with many other people close to Lincoln. I am grateful to the dozens of them who spoke with me on condition of anonymity. They helped confirm a slew of details and generally helped me feel more comfortable with the story I set out to tell here.

I also feel deeply grateful to the many journalists whose work helped me flesh out this story. Some I've already mentioned: Don Williams at the *Lubbock Avalanche-Journal*, Nathan Summers at Greenville's *Daily Reflector*, Jason Kersey for the *Oklahoman* and, later, the *Athletic*. In addition to Mike Leach's and Bob Stoops's books, among others, I also read *Tales from the Oklahoma Sideline* by Jay Upchurch. And I have several hundred if not more than a thousand articles downloaded from various newspapers, websites, and magazines. Some of these writers are identified in the story, such as Chris B. Brown, whose *Smart Football* blog and book *The Essential Smart Football* helped me better understand the Air Raid offense and its history. Ditto for articles by Michael Lewis in the *New York Times Magazine* and Kevin Van Valkenburg in *ESPN The Magazine*.

Others whose work I relied on include, in no specific order: Ryan Aber, Jenni Carlson, Joe Mussatto, Brooke Pryor, and Berry Tramel at the *Oklahoman*; Eric Bailey, Bill Haisten, and Cody Stavenhagen at the *Tulsa World*; Barry Horn at the *Dallas Morning News*; Marc Tracy at the *New York Times*; Jake Trotter and Dave Wilson at ESPN; Tyler Palmateer at the *Norman Transcript*; Shaker Samman and Michael Weinreb at the *Ringer*; Dennis Dodd at cbssports.com; Viv Bernstein and Greg Couch at *Bleacher Report*; Jimmy Burch at the *Fort Worth Star-Telegram*; Howie Beardsley at the *Grand Rapids Press*; Dave Fairbank at the Virginia *Daily Press*; Brian Haines at the *Charlotte Observer*; Luke DeCock and Chris Kudialis at the *News and Observer*; Joedy McReary at the Associated Press; Brad Crawford, Josh Graham, Joey Helmer, and Stephen Igoe at 247sports.com; Bill Bender and John E. Hoover at the *Sporting News*; Steve Doerschuck and George Schroeder at *USA Today*; Sean Labar at herosports.com; Ty Darlington at thefootballbraniacs.com and tydarlington.wordpress.com; Mike Houck and John Rohde at soonersports.com; Tony Zarrella at cleveland19.com; Bill Connelly and Morgan Moriarty at SBNation; Jerry Ratcliffe at the *Daily Progress*; Dede Westbrook at the *Players' Tribune*; Thomas Fleming at pistolsfiring.com; Ian Boyd at footballstudyhall.com; Bruce Feldman, Robert Klemko, Michael Shapiro, and Andy Staples at *Sports Illustrated*; Clay Skipper at *GQ*; George Stoia and Mason Young at oudaily.com; Joseph Duarte at the *Houston Chronicle*; Stewart Mandel at foxsports.com; Chris Foster at the *Los Angeles*

Times; Jack Shields at crimsonandcreammachine.com; Cedric Golden at the *Austin American-Statesman*; Emily Giambalyo at the *Washington Post*; and Peter King at nbcsports.com.

I also gleaned helpful information from the archives of Toby Rowland's *Sooner Sports* radio show, the archives of the *Freddie and Fitz* ESPN radio show, Fox Sports's *All the Way Up* documentary about Baker Mayfield, the *Behind Baker* documentary, a couple of Joel Klatt interviews for Fox Sports, various game broadcasts, and, last but certainly not least, the social media accounts of many people in this story.

Acknowledgments

To echo Lincoln Riley, I feel lucky for getting to work with great people without whom I could never have finished this book. Among them are:

Ben Osborne, Matt Sullivan, Bill Eichenberger, and everyone else at *Bleacher Report* for first giving me the opportunity to write about Lincoln.

Eric Lupfer, my agent, for first pushing me to write this book.

Paul Golob, my editor at Henry Holt and Company, for believing in this uncertain young writer in times of doubt, and for giving me excellent and much-needed advice: "The only thing truly fatal to a book is not writing it."

Natalia Ruiz, for being a great assistant to Paul and for your thoughtful feedback throughout this process.

The rest of the team at Holt, with whom I feel so grateful to work.

My sons—I love you two more than anything else in the world.

Katie, for loving our sons.

Mom and Dad, for being fantastic grandparents.

Albert and Susie, for the same.

Jonathan Abrams, Lars Anderson, Howard Beck, Mirin Fader,

Ben Osborne, Matt Sullivan, and more, for being there for me and believing in me during a challenging year.

Brandon Hassell, for reminding me who I am while encouraging me to explore what I really want.

All my younger siblings and siblings-in-law—Kramer, Kara, Lyndell, Logan, Heidi, and Jeremy—for your love of sports and stories, and for being amazing aunts and uncles.

Dan Chartier, for helping keep my mind on track.

Rick Stewart and Glenn Stout, for continuing to be great mentors and friends.

Carol, you unexpected gift, for everything.

And so many writers whom I may not know personally, but whose work has inspired me for years. I could not possibly name you all, but as I wrote this book I read Margaret Atwood, Buzz Bissinger, Joseph Campbell, Ta-Nehisi Coates, Paulo Coelho, Blake Crouch, Ted Dekker, Joan Didion, Kate Fagan, Tim Ferriss, Gillian Flynn, Richard Ford, Neil Gaiman, Robert Greene, John Grisham, Heather Havrilesky, Jemele Hill, Joe Hill, Ryan Holiday, Chris Jones, Austin Kleon, Anne Lamott, Jenny Lawson, Michael Lewis, Mark Manson, John McPhee, J. R. Moehringer, Toni Morrison, Delia Owens, Jeff Pearlman, Joe Posnanski, Stephen Pressfield, Shea Serrano, Jia Tolentino, Hunter S. Thompson, Wright Thompson—and many, many more.

Stories are what make us who we are, both individually and as a species, and I'm grateful to be part of the group that devote our lives to telling them.

Index

Notre Dame University, Fighting Irish,
57, 149–50, 213
Number Sense Contest, 24

O'Brien, Davey, 236
O'Hagan, Gary, 53
Ohio State University, Buckeyes, 201,
202, 203, 213, 224–30, 250
Oklahoma State University, Cowboys,
19, 234
Orange Bowl
1998 (Florida vs. Syracuse), 162
2015–16 (Oklahoma vs. Clemson), 196
2018–19 (Oklahoma vs. Alabama),
240

Palo Duro High, 29–31
Parker, Steven, 221–22
Paterno, Joe, 213
Penn State University, Nittany Lions,
213
Pepperdine University, Waves, 54
Perine, Samaje, 163, 175, 196–97
Philadelphia Eagles, 242
Pincock, Steve, 103–4
Potts, Tyler, 111
Power 5 conferences, 153

Quanah High, 19

Ramirez, Danny, 34, 35, 38, 40, 41
Red River Showdown (Oklahoma vs.
Texas)
2015, 191–92
2016, 203–4
2017, 234
Rice University, Owls, 128
Riley, Caitlin Buckley (wife), 6, 127
children and family life, 148, 197
Lincoln's career and, 247–49
on Lincoln's difficult year at East
Carolina, 133–34, 136
marries Lincoln, 79–80
Oklahoma job offer and, 165–66
opens home to players, 183, 222

Riley, Claude (grandfather), 15, 36
Riley, Garrett (brother), 15, 43–44
as Mules starting QB, 90
at Tech as walk-on QB in 2008, 96
as Texas 3A Player of the Year, 91
Riley, Lincoln, 33
Adam James controversy and, 94–95,
100–107
advised to coach, not play, at Tech,
66–67
Air Raid adapted by, at East Carolina,
145–46
Air Raid adapted by, at Oklahoma,
173–75, 183–84, 192–94, 242–43
Alamo Bowl and, after Leach firing,
105–12
anger and, 31–32, 40, 76–77, 99,
132–37, 145, 233
birth of daughter Sloan and, 148
birth of daughter Stella and, 197
Black Lives Matter and, 250–51
brother Garrett and, 43–44, 90–91
Broyles Award and, 197–99
childhood and youth in Muleshoe, 2,
10–12, 15–16
Coach of the Year award and, 242
communication skills of, 33–34
concepts grasped by, 7, 29–30
COVID-19 and, 250
creativity of, 227–28
decides to attend Texas Tech, 44–48
Duncan mentors, 107–10, 124, 146,
150–51, 170–72, 212
Duncan's illness and death and,
186–87, 199
Duncan's Legacy Award and, 186–87,
197–98
Dwayne Harris on, 127–28, 136
early work for father, 15
East Carolina 2010 season and,
124–29
East Carolina 2011 season and,
129–40
East Carolina 2012 season and,
142–47
East Carolina 2013 season and,
148–49
East Carolina 2014 season and,
154–58, 160

About the Author

BRANDON SNEED IS THE author of *Head in the Game: The Mental Engineering of the World's Greatest Athletes*. He has written for *Bleacher Report*, ESPN, *GQ*, and *Outside*, among other publications. His work has been recognized multiple times in *Best American Sports Writing*, and he was a finalist for the Livingston Award. He lives in Greenville, North Carolina.